PAUL TOURNIER'S Christian faith is an adventure, exciting, difficult, and exacting, but full of poetry, of new discoveries, of fresh turns and sudden surprises.

THE ADVENTURE OF LIVING

"**THANK GOD FOR PAUL TOURNIER** and a Christian life that is a daily adventure."—*The Banner*

"**ANOTHER EXCITING ADVENTURE.** Invigorating but never difficult reading."—*Mennonite Book Reviews*

"**TRANSMITS A JOYOUS APPROACH TO LIFE.** Refreshing in his view of God's relationship to the whole person."—*Christian Life*

"**THE GOOD NEWS OF THE GREAT PHYSICIAN** comes through strongly and clearly."—*This Day*

"**ENCOURAGES THE READER TO DISCOVER** his potential creativity and greatness not in what he does but in doing it with God."

—*Journal of Pastoral Care*

"**AN EXCELLENT GUIDE AND TONIC** for those who have lost either their direction or their zest."—*Faith At Work*

"**PUTS EXCITEMENT BACK INTO LIFE** with pertinent comments on conversion, work, marriage, failure and success, old age."—*Christian Herald*

HARPER JUBILEE BOOKS

THE ADVENTURE OF LIVING

BY

PAUL TOURNIER

Translated by EDWIN HUDSON

Harper & Row, *Publishers*

New York, Hagerstown, San Francisco, London

First Harper & Row paperback edition published in 1976.

ISBN: 0-06-068291-4

Library of Congress Catalog Card Number: 65-20459

76 77 78 79 80 81 10 9 8 7 6 5 4 3 2 1

Contents

Part I

THE ADVENTURE

CHAPTER 1

An Instinct Peculiar to Man

I AM WRITING these lines in Palma de Majorca. From my balcony I can see the elegant curve of the roadstead, its waters calm and glistening. Opposite is the big mole, where several ships are moored under the precise, busy swinging of the cranes that are unloading them, and the big white ship, which later on we shall watch, in our evening ritual, as it maneuvers its way out of the harbor toward Barcelona. To the left is the town, dominated by the imposing square mass of its cathedral, looking for all the world as if it wanted to gather its scattered chicks under its wings.

A little farther along I can see the tower of the monastery of St. Francis. It was from here that the Franciscans set out on their great epic of evangelization along the Pacific coast to San Francisco, which they founded in 1776. In California last year we followed in their footsteps, along the "royal way," and visited one of the settlements which mark the stages of their journey: a tiny island of charm and silence surrounded by the bustling activity of America, three old bells on a wall, and innumerable pigeons, so tame that they let one go right up to them.

What a tremendous adventure it was, the peaceful and victorious advance of the Friars Minor along that far-off coast! Today, as our plane takes us in a few hours across the Atlantic and the American continent, we recline in comfort, protected against every danger by the security services, which function with clockwork precision and have all the prodigious inventions of modern technology at their disposal. We think of Christopher Columbus and the whole host of navigators who for centuries braved the perils of the sea and its murderous storms as they set out into the unknown to discover new routes and new lands.

This island of Palma, which was one of their ports of call from the remotest times, and this very sea before my eyes still symbolize the spirit of adventure that exalts humanity century after century. And now a Caravelle, its powerful jets roaring, passes just above the roadstead and the town, on its way to touch down neatly in the new airport—still under construction like every other airport in the world, unable to keep pace with the development of new types of aircraft.

This adventure of aviation has taken place entirely within my own lifetime. I went as a child to Viry, in Haute-Savoie, to watch its earliest exploits. I lay flat so as to be able to see properly whether the wheels of the flying machine were really leaving the ground. What excitement to see one of the machines in the air and making a turn round the church steeple! And now I can buy up-to-date toys for my grandchildren—rockets, cosmonauts' outfits, exact-scale models of the big toys of the scientists who are in the forefront of human adventure.

I have seen the whole adventure of radio, too. Shortly after I was married I built my first wireless set, in the days when the amateur made with his own hands almost all the components he needed: Coils were made by winding wire round a twist of paper or a cardboard tube, resistances by making pencil marks on a piece of ebonite, and condensers by building up sheets of silver paper alternately with sheets of insulation. Every week I awaited with eager impatience the appearance of the wireless magazine, which would bring me some new layout for an improved receiver—a superhet! And every week we amateurs would take our sets to pieces and put them together again differently. They did not always work, but what a thrill it was to hear the Eiffel Tower! Now in my armchair in front of my television set, which I would not dare to tamper with myself, I watch pictures from America, transmitted via Telstar.

So all human enterprises start amid the exciting fever of discovery, with its countless difficulties and its improvisations. Gradually they become more organized, and the very fact of their progress brings standardization. They become commonplace, a matter of mere routine. They work then with impeccable smoothness, much better than in the days of the earliest prototypes. But the joy of adventure has gone out of them; it must find other channels to spring to life again.

This is the subject of the present book. I should like to depict as I see it the great impulse toward adventure which is peculiar to man, and which can scarcely ever last, which must be constantly renewed if it is to avoid the tedium of organization. I even think that the urge to adventure must be considered an instinct, since it has the universality and the indomitable power characteristic of instinct, and because its satisfaction affords the specific joy which always accompanies the satisfaction of instinct. The instinct of adventure may be cloaked, smothered, and repressed, but it never disappears from the human personality. The timidest pen-pushing clerk will disclose under psychoanalysis, and particularly in the analysis of his dreams, a secret nostalgia for the adventure which he has sacrificed to security. Without really understanding why, he will have a predilection for the most frightening of adventure films, mentally identifying himself with the hero so as to procure vicariously the joys he deprives himself of in real life.

It seems to me that this instinct of adventure is one of the most obvious explanations for the characteristic behavior of man, one of the great driving forces behind his actions, as important as the instinct of self-preservation, which has so often been described as the mainspring of civilization and its technical progress. What I am undertaking, therefore, is a study of the significance of human work.

It is striking how every adventure follows the same pattern, develops along the same curve. There is first an abrupt ascent, explosive, all-powerful, and irresistible, casting its spell on men. And soon comes a long descent, in which the adventure is exhausted as it is consolidated, in which those who have experienced it try to preserve the treasure of truth and excitement that has thrilled them, but without believing in it any longer with the same boldness or feeling the same joy. This alternation of brief phases of growth with long phases of organization corresponds with the nature of life itself, as I described it in *The Meaning of Persons*—life which has scarcely sprung from its mysterious sources when it becomes crystallized in the automatisms which are the only manifestations of it that are accessible to our analysis, and which are at once its fruit and its tomb. Adventure ceases as soon as normalcy begins.

The first appearance of adventure is often so sudden that it gives the impression of being the result of spontaneous generation, as was for so long believed of life itself. And like life also it is propagated by contagion. When you come into contact with a man who is deeply committed to adventure you become possessed yourself by the demon of adventure; and once it takes hold, it does not easily let go.

Think of all the great adventures of history, of Alexander the Great, of the French Revolution, of Gandhi and all the rest. The historians strive laboriously to throw light on the mechanisms involved, each interpreting them in accordance with his own outlook: the idealists, in terms of the movement of ideas; the realists, in terms of economic needs. All their explanations are true, but there is always something missing, something elusive and imponderable, something in man himself: his tremendous need for adventure, which is always ready to break out.

This explains something which it is often hard to understand, namely, that serious, cultured, and thoughtful men, even apparently circumspect and moderate-minded men, should be capable of throwing themselves suddenly into an extremely doubtful political adventure. At last, they think, something new, to break the deadly monotony and impotence of a society that is overorganized and fossilized! As soon as a man thus throws himself into adventure, the satisfaction of his latent instinct arouses in him such a feeling of exaltation, rejuvenation, and renewal that he is persuaded that the cause to which he is giving himself is a good one. Even though he had doubts about it he would no longer be able to disengage himself from it—he is the prisoner of the formidable determinism of adventure.

With adventure more than with most things, it is the first step that is the most difficult. One is struck by the contrast between the extreme difficulty a man has in taking this first step over the bounds of habits of thought and accepted conventions, in committing himself, burning his boats, and the inner dynamism of adventure which thereafter takes such a hold on him as to blot out all power of critical reflection. This is always the way with the automatisms of life. He is the pioneer of the new current of life as soon as it is set going.

You can see the same thing at work in the difficulty you have in tearing yourself away from the mere reading of a detective novel, despite the good resolutions you have made about going to bed early. You want to know how it ends. People say it is curiosity. There is more to it than that: An adventure has begun; a problem has been raised and must be solved; you identify yourself with the detective in the story; his adventure is yours now; with him—before him, if possible—you want to solve the mystery.

For my part, I much prefer real-life problems to fictitious ones, perhaps because so many of them are brought to me—and such difficult ones! But also because I have a cast of mind that is fascinated by problems of technique. I am particularly susceptible to the fascination exercised by the sort of technical problem that will not let one rest until one has found a solution for it. When I was in training I held a resident medical studentship under Professor Bernard Wiki, in his therapeutical laboratory. I owe him a great debt, for he had a high sense of scientific doubt. But we also shared a keen interest in mathematics. I once found in some periodical a subtle, difficult, and fascinating problem, and for three days we remained shut up in our studies trying to work it out, even taking our pages of equations home in the evenings. Our good lab assistant shook his head as he fed the guinea pigs. He reckoned we were a little mad—and he was not wrong. But that sort of madness I value highly. For there is no true scientist without it; and no true artist either.

The demon of adventure is the great motive force behind scientific research. Science is much less of an intellectual pursuit than is generally thought, and much more of a passion! Consider the excitement of a scientist when an unexpected development in an experiment goes against the accepted theories and so sets him a new technical problem. He at once conceives a series of experiments to be carried out to elucidate the mystery and control his first results. He outlines one bold hypothesis after another. The adventure is on. He will forget his wife and children and miss an appointment with the Minister of extreme importance for his university career. He is no longer a professor; he has been transformed by the miracle of adventure into a research worker once more.

If this is true of the great discoveries of science, it is also true of the least little technical problem which comes up in the workshop, when the mechanic must find a cunning means of assembly that will allow a certain regulating screw to remain always accessible. On my birthday last year, in Grand Forks, North Dakota, Professor Charles Hatfield, professor of mathematics in the University of North Dakota, offered me a puzzle he had invented, one of those little brainteasers in which you have to remove a loop of string from a tangle of bent and twisted wire. He could not have given me greater pleasure—the pleasure of research, with its dash of exasperation and humiliation when one attempt after another comes to nothing, which only heightens the eventual satisfaction of success.

Those who want to lay down limits to scientific research in order to ward off the danger of the atomic bomb are, it seems to me, singularly naïve. The forward march of science will not be halted; it derives its power from a strong instinct within man himself. Now and again it happens that rock climbers, cavers, or other enthusiasts undertake rash enterprises, which turn out badly. Rescue teams have to set out to find them, often at the peril of their own lives. There follow letters to the press, protesting against imprudence of this sort, which exposes the rescuers to possible death. Such protestations, however, are quite fruitless. The lure of adventure is not amenable to reason.

Consider this big businessman: Already overworked, he comes back in the evening to his office; he can scarcely fit in a holiday, and when he does he keeps in touch with his associates and gives them instructions. Now he is opening yet another branch, absorbing a competing firm and tackling the great problems of integrating it into his own organization. It is not that he wants to earn more money—he does not even enjoy what he has already. It is that he has fallen under the law of adventure, a law which requires that an enterprise once embarked upon must be pursued, developed, and then organized until it exhausts itself in its own organization.

For other prople, who also are not lacking in money, the amassing of more and more of it may take the place of the real adventure which is absent from their life. And all they can buy with their money acts also as a substitute for adventure: cars, shows, pretty dresses, and organized tours. There is not an impresario in the world who does not strive to exploit this hunger by providing prefabricated adventures for those who are bored and blasé. But an adventure that is bought is not quite the same as a personal adventure of one's own.

Nevertheless I think we often fail to do justice to people who are caught up in this frantic scramble for money and all that it can procure. We see in it nothing but selfishness, greed, and lust for pleasure. Of course I know that men are selfish, but all men are equally so—those who look for cultural and spiritual satisfaction quite as much as those who go after material goods. In both types much more is involved than the mere desire for pleasure described by the Freudians. There is a need for fulfillment that is part of the stuff of life itself, a need for personal adventure which is peculiar to man, a thirst for the absolute, which in the last analysis is an expression of man's hunger and thirst after God.

9

A most important observation must, however, be made at this point, and that is that a distinction is to be made between *quality adventure* and *quantity adventure*. Whether or not he is aware of it, man lives in the world of values. The inner urge toward an ultimate which is always driving him on is an aspiration toward the realization of experiences of value, of quality. But because he fails in this, he is always tempted to make up in quantity what he has not achieved in quality. For example, if you particularly want to make a gift that will mean something special to the person to whom you are going to offer it, you try to think of something original and personal; but if you cannot find the sort of thing you want, you fall back on a very expensive present. Similarly, if you do not land the job that would make your career an exciting adventure, you fall back on trying to get one that carries a high salary.

But when adventure is shifted in this way from quality toward quantity, it enters a tragic vicious circle. Quantity always leaves something more to be desired—an even more expensive present, or an even higher salary. Money is the thing above all that is reckoned by quantity, and those who make it the material of their adventure find themselves experiencing the dissatisfactions of this kind of vicious circle. It is in vain that they buy themselves a more luxurious car each year. They are never completely satisfied.

Nevertheless, in capitalist countries financial success, for those who succeed as for those who do not, is still, if not a truly satisfying adventure, at least a symbol of adventure. Americans are known for the importance they attach to money, the simplicity with which they say what everything they buy costs them, and their tendency to evaluate a man according to his income. One often hears Europeans criticizing them for this. It could be that in America a man's salary more accurately reflects his value (one might say his adventure value), what he contributes that is new and valuable.

But it seems to me there is a deeper cause, bound up with the heroic origin of America: It arose under the impulsion of the emigrants, who had to face risks and carve out a new life for themselves. They had not, like many Europeans, a ready-made situation into which to fit themselves—no name, no hereditary fortune, no university degrees, and none of the requisite diplomas. The American pioneers had to face adventure at first hand, and the financial stake was the symbol of it.

That the need for adventure lies behind the passion for gambling hardly needs mention. There are few moral ills more difficult to cure in a man. As I write, I am put in mind of some of the most painful failures of my career as a doctor. The real blame lies with those who cynically exploit this passion. In Switzerland a solemn prohibition of games of chance is written into our Federal Constitution. But the state itself runs lotteries, on the ground that it is the only means available to it of procuring the funds necessary for projects of public welfare, aimed particularly at helping those who have been ruined by gambling.

A habit that is quite as difficult to cure as gambling is that of drug-taking, in all its various forms. This too can be regarded as an expression of the instinct for adventure. The subject is fascinated by the marvelous illusion of adventure which the drug provides. In Santa Monica, California, I visited a wonderful community of former drug addicts, who by means of mutual help succeed much better than any psychiatric clinic in rescuing other addicts.

But this is just because the fraternal community, inspired by an unusually dedicated man, is itself a great adventure, because it enlists newcomers in the adventure of rescue, thus substituting a finer adventure for the degrading one into which they have fallen. One small detail: on the walls there were slogans, in the American fashion; my knowledge of English did not permit me to understand them all, but there was one that I have never forgotten: "We are not in a position to solve our own problems, but we are ready and willing to help you to solve yours."

There are of course other *quantity adventures* aside from those of money, gambling, or dope. There is, for example, that of frenzied activity. It is obvious that for many people these days the whirl of activities with which they fill their lives is a compensation for a profound dissatisfaction in regard to the quality of life they are living; and that the quality of their lives in fact deteriorates even further in the course of this restless activity. As a result they are always trying to catch up. They get more and more worried at not having sufficient time—and have less and less time to spare. They are acutely conscious of time slipping inexorably away. I shall always remember a man who came to see me for persistent insomnia. It did not take him long to see that he was not sleeping because in reality he was afraid of wasting time alseep. Count Dürckheim tells of another man who came to him and said, "I wonder if by any chance I am ill, because I caught myself with nothing to do for several minutes!"

The adventure of power is another quantity adventure. This is what condemns all dictators—in the cultural, artistic, and economic spheres as well as the political—to harden in an attitude of intransigence, to silence every voice raised against them, and inexorably to climb the path that leads up to the Tarpeian Rock.

More subtle is the fact that the satisfaction peculiar to adventure may be experienced even in misfortune—in sickness, for example. For many people an illness, especially if it is not too serious but is difficult to cure and taxes the resources of the cleverest doctors, is the great adventure of their lives. Something is happening to them which is not happening to others. This is not to say that their illness is imaginary. There are no imaginary illnesses. Nor do I deny that they really suffer, and I am not insinuating that they are getting pleasure out of suffering. Nevertheless, without always admitting it to themselves, without being conscious of it, they cling to their illness as to something which distinguishes them, and of which healing would deprive them, and this is not conducive to healing.

I remember the time our younger son broke his leg while skiing, at the age of fourteen. My wife and I were naturally very upset. But he said to us: "You know, I'm quite glad, because I've had a personal experience at last. My life was so normal and sheltered! Something's happened to me at last!" Alas! Since then he has had plenty of adventures of a more serious kind and on one occasion escaped death by a miracle. But, thank God, he has kept his spirit of adventure. Like our elder son also, he has preserved an inexhaustible capacity for enthusiasm. Woe betide those who no longer feel thrilled at anything, who have stopped looking for adventure!

Another memory comes into my mind. It touches a still more disturbing aspect of the blind instinct for adventure which is at work in man. It is of a remark made by Pastor Ochsenbein, who has recorded the astonishing adventures of his work as chaplain to prisoners condemned to life sentences.[1] He had been invited to give a lecture in Geneva, to rouse public opinion in favor of the setting up of an organization to assist discharged prisoners. On the previous evening, in a fashionable salon, a few of the leading personalities in various committees of social service had been invited to meet Pastor Ochsenbein so as to have an opportunity of questioning him in private. A lady who was present asked him, in an aristocratically genteel voice, "Can you tell us what it is that drives these poor criminals to do the things they do?" The reply came like a shot, and sounded odd in such surroundings: "It is the same force that drives you, madam, to distinguish yourself by your good works." He did not, I think, say that it was the need for adventure, but that was what his reply really meant.

Looked at in its best light, adultery may be seen to be for many men the only means of satisfying their craving for adventure. It is no coincidence that the very word "adventure" is used of the sudden blaze of passionate love that turns a man's ordered existence upside down. Falling in love with a capricious woman who makes him do mad things is his way of escaping from the hopeless monotony of a convention-bound life and rediscovering the intoxication of adventure. It is, so to speak, an adventure within the reach of everyone. The woman may be an "adventuress," and this will particularly outrage the virtuous and injured wife, who will never suspect that she is partly responsible because of her too matter-of-fact, unadventurous attitude. The mistress, for her part, can fairly boast that

[1] Henri Ochsenbein, *Les Compagnons de la Vie*, Oberlin, Strasbourg, 1946.

she has miraculously made her lover thirty years younger, transformed his life, and introduced him to a joy in living that he has never before experienced. But the wife may rightly retort that she would have been happy if her husband had brought a little adventure into her monotonous life, too, and complain that he has never indulged her whims as he does those of his mistress.

CHAPTER 2

Adventures Fictitious
and Real

OUR ACTUAL LIVES rarely suffice to assuage our thirst for adventure. Fortunately we can all supply the want by using our imaginations. The dullest and most humdrum life can be enlivened by imagined pleasures. The child very soon feels the awakening within himself of a need for adventure, but he comes up against the restrictive severity of his parents' protective caution. Unable to escape from the prison of his well-regulated life without being severely rebuked, he becomes interested in fairy stories, in which everything is possible and permitted; later on he turns to adventure stories. Then he invents his own, perhaps even coming to believe that he has actually experienced them himself. He builds his own little private world in which all his desires are fulfilled. What wonderful hours I spent telling myself childish stories of this sort, in which I played a leading part, at the time when I was a shy little orphan, lacking in self-confidence and feeling that no one could ever be interested in me. Some children get revenge for the wickedness of their parents by inventing new ones who are important and wealthy. They pretend that they are their *real* parents, from whom they have been stolen.

A very close bond of confidence has to be established between my patient and me before he can bring himself to tell me all the fine dreams that have been the constant delectation of his childhood. They are a sort of hidden treasure which would lose its precious fascination if it were to become generally known. And there is also a certain simple, primitive, childlike pride involved in these fantasies, a pride which social life soon teaches us to conceal. But in this respect, as in many others, we always remain children; and on the threshold of old age, though loaded with real adventures, I am not cured—I am glad to say—of my childlike romance.

Those who are lacking in imagination of their own can always use that of other people. There is no shortage of novels to read, and many readers show themselves to be not very demanding provided their search is rewarded by something that fulfills their longing for adventure. They find it difficult to be honest about how much time they spend reading whatever comes to hand. Certain notable novels, of course,— *Robinson Crusoe*, the tales of Jules Verne, and many others— owe some part of their tremendous success to the adventures into which they draw their readers. But besides novels there are all the serial stories in newspapers, the cheap story magazines, and the patchwork of five-minute adventures in miniature represented by the digests and potted books so much in vogue today. And then there are the fashion journals, with whose extravagantly made-up cover girls any woman can identify herself.

Popular festivities, such as carnivals, provide a necessary safety valve to give vent to our longing for adventure. For a few days people are allowed to be noisy and even coarse, to tease the stuffed shirts with impunity and flout convention, to let themselves go. All this evokes a sensation of engaging in a liberating adventure which makes a pleasant contrast with the boredom of ordinary life. One can, indeed, wear a mask and, thus disguised, identify oneself in this way with some comical and brazen character and feel free, like a real adventurer.

The same mechanism of identification makes it possible in the cinema, through the radio or television, or at a circus to procure cheaply the feeling of taking part in an adventure. This is the case too with "sportsmen" who come back from a football match proudly proclaiming, "We won!" although they personally have done nothing but applaud the winners. Likewise there are many people who in an election, when the party they favor—even though they are not members of it—wins two more seats in Parliament, will excitedly exclaim, "We are the winners!" And perhaps they did not even turn out to vote.

But of course it is wrong to mention only that caricature of sport or politics which is indulged in by armchair sportsmen and politicians with their fireside arguments. Real sport, with the rigorous training it entails, its calcualted risks and well-merited truimphs, is a high adventure in which a man attains fulfillment. Similarly a political struggle to which a man dedicates himself with conviction and courage, forgetful of himself in an effort to bring about just reforms for the benefit of society, is an authentic adventure. This in fact explains the popular prestige enjoyed by great sportsmen and political leaders, and it is why so many less active people identify themselves with them.

We ought not to smile at the idea of identification. It is a normal phenomenon to which every one of us is subject, a powerful social force, and also a valuable outlet without which the instinct for adventure would do more serious damage, driving men and nations to undertake courses of action that might be a danger to themselves and to others. Everybody cannot be a cosmonaut—today at any rate; and when everybody can be it will no longer be an adventure. But everyone can participate in spirit in what is a thrilling episode in the great human adventure. This is legitimate and beneficial. National solidarity, of course, promotes identification, so that a Russian identifies himself more completely with a Soviet cosmonaut, and a citizen of the U.S.A. with an American. Hence the powerful attraction of the Olympic Games and the big international matches, when whole nations get as excited as if each individual were involved in a personal adventure. The ancients understood this quite well, and when he re-established the Olympic Games Baron de Coubertin provided modern nations with a means of uniting through their need for adventure, a need which might well drive them into conflict with one another. He ought to have been given the Nobel Prize for Peace.

Many parents identify themselves with their children and realize in them, or dream of realizing in them, the adventure which they themselves have missed. One father had had in his youth a devouring passion for electronics, an interest which he continued to cultivate in some secret garret. He knew more about the subject than many a qualified engineer. But his faint-hearted parents had compelled him to become a bank clerk. A career as a bank clerk offered, they felt, material security, and in it of course he made little progress, since his adventure lay elsewhere. In his turn he became as authoritarian in his attitude to his own son as his parents had been to him and forced the boy to become an engineer. The son had equally little success as an engineer, since he would have liked to live the adventure of music.

A mother had read a lot of novels in her youth and had had dreams of a brilliant marriage. She has never been able to forgive herself for a strange shyness that overcame her on the one occasion when, it seemed to her, a brief encounter gave her the chance she was looking for. She finally decided to marry a parsimonious petty government clerk. For her own daughter, however, she builds grand schemes for a marvelous match—but the girl persists in going out with a boy whom the mother considers far her inferior.

But for all parents, and especially for those who respect the personalities of their children, the development of the latter is an incomparable adventure. For the child everything is an adventure: his progressive discovery of the world, of ugly and dirty things as well as of beautiful ones, the puddle in which he can paddle with his new shoes, a flower opening at the window, his mother's smile, the first snow of winter, and the Christmas celebrations. But what an adventure for the parents as well! It is more conscious, and more moving perhaps. Parents keep notes in a pretty album of when the baby cut his first tooth, said his first real word, walked for the first time, spoke his first amusing remarks. What an adventure it is for a father to take his child into the fields and woods and awaken the love of nature in him! And for the grandparents it is an even more affecting adventure!

Every present he receives is an adventure for the child. His father wants to show him how the toy works, but he jumps up and down impatiently: "I want to do it by myself!" It is his own adventure, and he must not be deprived of it. One can already see much of his future from his reactions to the difficulties of this adventure. One child soon gives up and holds out the recalcitrant toy to his mother. Another keeps on trying all the more stubbornly the more difficult it is. Many a parent may watch him then with a certain envy, thinking of the times when he himself has capitualted, and say to himself, "Long may he keep that determination, and his love for adventure!" How dull, therefore, are the lives of children who are spoiled, so that they lose all ambition and become weary of everything!

What an adventure it is for parents when their child starts school; when, deprived of their protection, he receives his first blows from unfriendly associates, when he wins some modest championship, when he goes to his first dance and takes with him some girl they do not know, when he graduates or wins a doctorate!

A child's games are all wonderful adventures, especially those he invents for himself. One may see the whole outline of his future already traced out, as in the case of Marshal Lyautey, who while still a small child used to construct new countries in the sand. A child's games are a better indication than his schoolwork of what he will do when he is grown up. The child who can play well will also do well in his career; the true meaning of man's work, that is, is the realization of his need for adventure. But listen to the parent with his "Do your homework first; you can go and play afterwards." Such a remark suggests a false association of ideas—that it is work that is boring, and that what is interesting must be more or less wicked.

In ancient times pedagogy had more to say than it has now to the great thirst for adventure that motivates the child. There were the great epics of the *Iliad* and the *Odyssey*, the beautiful legends of mythology, and later on Plato's myths— all were the basis of teaching from earliest childhood. The pupils learned the poets' lines by heart. Here is what makes for the formation of a cultured mind, greedy for learning, much more than encyclopedias and the memorization of dates.

There are even well-intentioned people who wish to rid the teaching of history of everything that is too warlike. But for the child these are not cruel wars! They are fine adventures and stories of heroism. We were taught about William Tell as if he were a living person—and indeed in our hearts he did live. His story stirred our patriotic fervor, even though the events in it took place more than five centuries before the entry of my little Genevan homeland into the Swiss Confederation. Patriotism very largely derives from this sort of identification of the individual with the collective adventure which we call the history of a nation.

Happily, education, particularly that of the very young, has made great progress in recent years. The pioneers of the new movement in education, who in Switzerland have been connected with the Rousseau Institute—people such as Claparède, Pierre Bovet, Adolphe Ferrière, Jean Piaget, and many more— lived lives that were in fact a great adventure. What they have called the Active School is nothing but a return to the spirit of adventure in education. The school makes use of the pupil's pleasure in personal activity, rather than reducing him to the passive role of a well-behaved and rather inattentive listener. The method depends, of course, more upon the personality of the teacher than upon the organization of the school. Some teachers in every grade have learned how to turn each lesson into an exciting adventure. But such teachers are rare. Despite everything, it is still outside the confines of the school, at the knee of a grandmother who is always ready to tell a fairy tale, in the cheap comics (sometimes of very mediocre quality), or in science fiction magazines, that children of today must seek the food they need for their adventure-starved curiosity.

It is impossible to overdo the cultivation of a liking for adventure in children. Baden-Powell understood this fact well when he made the lure of adventure the chief educative motive in the Scout movement. But an observation should be made at this point: Some people remain Scouts all their lives. They take pleasure in wearing the juvenile uniform complete with its mysterious decorations. It is not difficult to see that they also retain an infantile personality; in some way they have become fixed at a stage of youthful adventure. They have not accepted the law of adventure, which is that it must die in order to be born again. It is in fact through the continual dying of even our most exciting adventures that we reach maturity. In this way we are made available for other adventures, adventures which will be less infantile and naïve, more adult and fruitful.

Many people are never able to come to terms with the death to which every adventure is inevitably subject. We see them everywhere in search of some stimulant, some new and life-giving current that will relight the torch of their passion. Their lives are a succession of wild enthusiasms for one idea after another, no matter what. But the very versatility of their advocacy largely detracts from its effectiveness. Rather are they a liability to the various causes they claim to serve, since in reality these are only being used as a means of satisfying their own need to be active.

Nevertheless, is it not to some extent true of all of us that in our feverish activity we are seeking what Pascal called a "diversion," to take our minds off our haunting fear of the vanity of life? "Vanity of vanities! All is vanity," said the Preacher. Men are born, they live, and suffer, and die; then come others, to be followed by others yet again. Every morning at the same time they catch the same bus, to go to the same place of employment, where they will be doing the same work until they retire. Then they will be thanked; they will be told that they will never be forgotten; and their places will be taken by others, whose lives will be exactly similar.

Men work, sleep, enjoy themselves, eat, make love, and then

it all starts over again, and so on indefinitely. There will always be more men, more machines, more books, more things to learn, without mankind's ever being able—even in interstellar space—to get outside the narrow limits of its own nature. No new idea is thought up without there being someone to point out that such-and-such pre-Socratic philosopher or a certain medieval monk had already thought of it before, and that the possible objections to it are already known, as well as the objections to the objections. What and where is life?

The young people who rebel against their parents, who do not want to work because their parents have done nothing but that, who dress differently, who wear different hair styles, who use different words and adopt different ideas, who go to the Café de Flore, to the cellars of St. Germain-des-Prés, to Saint-Tropez or elsewhere—we must understand that what they are doing is seeking life. People call it a fashion. It is much more than that. It is the instinctive craving for adventure, the search for that feeling of really living which only adventure affords. It is a hunger for an adventure that will be personal to oneself—a hunger, that is, to be oneself and not a copy of someone else, to become a person.

Even philosophy itself is not exempt from this law. Really new ideas are rare, and their vogue is ephemeral, however great a stir they make at first. As soon as they make their first appearance, whether it be boldly or timidly, they open a new prospect of adventure to philosophy. They catch on like wildfire, until they exhaust themselves in banality. Such was Descartes's famous "night of illumination." Georges Gusdorf once told me the story of a certain young philosopher who was walking gloomily along the Boulevard Saint-Germain when he met a friend. "I am ill," he told him. "I have just given my publisher a manuscript and it is worthless. What I've said in it that's new is not interesting, and what I've said that is interesting is not new." That young philosopher was Henri Bergson, and the book was his essay on the immediate data of consciousness!

But the adventure had begun, almost without the author's realizing it. It was to shape the whole course of his work and the thought of many other philosophers after him. I had an echo of it, indirectly, when I was at college. Sad and strange to relate, we young students in the Department of Humanities at Geneva were not taught philosophy; at least what we got—a little formal logic and a few lessons on the "faculties of the mind"—had little to do with either philosophy or adventure. But we had a French teacher named Grandjean who had just written a book on Bergson, entitled *A Revolution in Philosophy*.[1]

You can imagine the prestige enjoyed among us by a teacher who had written a book—and on such a subject, too! So a revolution was taking place in our own day, in philosophy! By means of artful questions we endeavored to divert our teacher from his meticulous exposition of the French syllabus into digressions on the famous revolution. We avidly read *Creative Evolution*, which was not one of our set books. We were all followers of Bergson, without understanding very much of what was new in his teaching, since we knew practically nothing of what had been thought before him.

Many other "revolutions" have come and gone since then. In their turn younger men than I have discovered Heidegger, Sartre, Gusdorf, and Ricoeur. Their ideas are doubtless important, but the joyous thrill which their converts experience as they read them does not come only from the interest of their ideas. It derives also from the fact that in reading them they are taking part in a quite new adventure.

Even in religious matters, the joy believers have in propagating their faith does not stem only from their conviction that they possess and are speading the truth. It derives also very largely from the specific feeling of exaltation which we all feel when we are engaged in an adventure. I am of course not referring here to the learned theologians who meditate in the tranquillity of their studies upon the mysteries of their faith and seek to express them as accurately as they can. I am speaking of the great mass of members of every church, right down to the tiniest chapel. They do not generally have the spiritual

[1] Frank Grandjean, *Une Révolution dans la Philosophie. La Doctrine de Henri Bergson*, Geneva and Paris, 1913.

or intellectual maturity to formulate a really personal doctrine for themselves. But they have been won over by a particular belief, and they devote themselves to its propagation with admirable ardor. What a tremendous adventure! To feel oneself the repository of a divine truth that is unrecognized by unbelievers, and even by the other churches! Is it not the supreme adventure, to be one of the little flock of the elect?

This is where the strength of every sect lies, what makes it a powerful evangelizing force, a sort of dynamic wing of the church, despite the opposition of the official church which fears and combats it. For theologians see only arguments about doctrine—which I am careful not to meddle in: it is not my domain. Theologians smell out heresies and refute doctrinal errors, and without any doubt it is right that they should do so.

There is, however, another aspect of the matter—and this is within my competence—which I must point out. It is that any sincere conversion draws the convert into a great spiritual adventure. He has had an experience; he has received something; he proclaims the fact. His dynamic energy is effective in making new proselytes; he begets spiritual children; the adventure is on. This is very often what happens in the case of converts from one of the great Christian churches to another. The doctor cannot help noting the psychological factors which generally play some part in such conversions, independently of the conscious doctrinal debate—whose reality, of course, is not for this reason to be denied.

A Protestant, for example, has been brought up in a strictly puritan family. He has suffered grievously from the tyrannical attitude of his father, who, to make matters worse, always invoked his religion in support of his authority. The father was constantly talking about God and his demands in the sphere of morality, but without seeing that he was making his wife and children miserable. A time comes when the son rejects his father's authority, and with it the austere teachings which the latter had tried to inculcate in him.

Nevertheless the son retains a certain religious nostalgia. Despite all his mistakes the father has awakened in him a thirst for spiritual things which remains unassuaged. The reading of a Catholic book, a chance conversation in a train with a priest of infectious piety, or a religious ceremony full of beauty and mystery suddenly reveals to him an aspect of religion quite different from what he was taught in his childhood—that religion is reconciliation with God, who accepts him just as he is, that it is the grace dispensed by the Church, the Eucharist of which the Catholic Church is the repository. The clouded, rebellious life of the young convert is transformed; he enters upon a wonderful adventure—the adventure of God's grace.

An exactly similar experience—I mean, of course, from the psychological point of view—may befall another man, who has been brought up in an agnostic family, or one, nominally Christian, whose Christianity is no more than a hereditary attachment to one of the great historic churches. One day he meets an evangelist whose wonderfully dedicated life exerts a powerful attraction upon him. The evangelist explains to him that the failure of the churches is due to their unfaithfulness: they have compromised on this point or that of biblical teaching—they have, for example, given up baptism of adults by total immersion, or altered the day of rest from Saturday to Sunday, or abandoned some article in the Creed. What one must do is choose, resolve to accept all God's commands, commit oneself utterly, if one is to experience the power of the Holy Spirit. After much inner struggle, our man decides to accept, and the "Yes!" he says to God is inseparable in his mind from his incorporation in the congregation or the church of the evangelist who has converted him. He finds at once that it brings him great blessings. The adventure with God is on.

What I should like to stress here is that there is a certain community of spirit among all the converts in the world, whatever the church or sect to which they belong. By the very fact that they have all passed through an analogous experience of revolution in their spiritual lives, they have—and always have—a revolutionary spirit, whereas other believers, those who believe because that is how they have been brought up, have a conformist spirit. All converts have changed from a routine of religion to an adventure of religion. I myself have a

keen sense of this kinship of the spirit. I often have as patients
people who are active members of a different church from my
own, or of denominations whose teachings I do not agree with.
I find no difficulty in discussing with them all the problems of
their spiritual life or their ministry. I am quite willing to talk
to them about my own difficulties, and I always recognize
that though we may differ on certain points of doctrine, we
are surprisingly close to each other in the practical domain of
our disobedience or obedience to God's call.

The more ardent they are in their convictions, even if these
are not exactly the same as my own, the stronger do I feel the
fraternal bond between us to be: we belong to the same family
of the converted. Naturally, the same thing applies to all those
who, without ever having changed their church or creed, have
moved either suddenly or gradually from a static and conventional Christianity to a living, personal faith—those who have
passed, might I say, from nominal Christianity into a Christian
adventure.

When my wife and I came into contact with the Oxford
Group Movement and were thereby shown how abstract and
theoretical, how little incarnate in our real life, our faith was,
my wife paid a visit to an old friend. "I cannot understand,"
this friend said, "what more you want, when you have been
brought up in a Christian family, by grandparents and parents
whose faith has always been an example to admire."

"Faith," my wife replied, "is not hereditary."

Our experience at that time, and on many occasions since,
has established a kinship between us and all those other men
and women who have become adventurers of faith like us,
whatever the community they belong to. Whether they have
been converted in the J.O.C.[2] or in the Pentecostal Church, by
Christian Scientists or Seventh-Day Adventists, as followers of
Barth or as liberal Christians, they of course hold to their
doctrines as a result of the dogmatic arguments by which they
have been convinced, but they also stand by them because
they are indissolubly linked with the spiritual adventure which
illuminates and gives value to their lives. Do not attempt to

[2] Jeunesse Ouvrière Catholique (Young Catholic Workers).

contradict them. The only ones you will shake are the weak, those who follow other people's adventures, without really making them their own. The rest are immovable. They are defending a doctrine, but they are also defending their treasure, their adventure, and you would be acting wickedly and destructively in seeking to sow the seed of doubt in their hearts.

CHAPTER 3

For Better, for Worse

I THINK this analysis can be taken farther. For instance, it may be observed that a conversion to atheism may present the same psychological characteristics as a conversion to faith. When a person rejects the traditional beliefs in which he has been brought up, we must look for the explanation in the circumstances of his personal life, in the conflicts that have set him against his parents or against society, in the frustrations or injustices to which he has been subjected and which have set up in him this attitude of rebellion against a social order identified in his mind with religion. But at the same time he has an opportunity of transforming his quite negative attitude of revolt into a constructive adventure. His feeling that he is working for the liberation of mankind from the prejudice imprisoning it, that he is fighting to make the world less hypocritical, is a source of excitement to him. It is clear, then, that subjective experience must never be taken as proof of the authenticity of any doctrine.

The same may be said of all political creeds, of whatever color—whether communist, liberal, individualist, or fascist. The moment a man believes in any of them with sufficient ardor to commit himself without reserve, he experiences a feeling of fulfillment which makes him doubly sure that his cause is just. This is perhaps particularly noticeable in the case of Marxism, with its claim to possession of a scientific method of shaping society and transforming mankind by overthrowing institutions. I have seen many people adopt its doctrines because they have seen it as a great and wonderful adventure. They have taken over its vocabulary, its dialectic, its ideology, because unless one does so one cannot really take part in the adventure. They have something to say to the world, a goal to achieve, an answer for our times, and all this gives a meaning to their lives. It also explains why one may find the same people belonging successively to various political movements very different in doctrine but still having some psychological kinship.

The phenomenon is, of course, of much more general occurrence. It is not limited to religion or politics. The devotees of homeopathy, psychoanalysis, or the medicine of the person, as well as those of technology and the conquest of interstellar space, jazz enthusiasts as well as naturists, theosophists and pacifists—all defend their ideas in order to defend their adventure, for adventure is precisely this devotion to an idea, the struggle to win, to convert others.

Naturally this is not to say that all ideas are equally worthy, or that the aim of an adventure is a matter of indifference. I do not say, "The adventure matters little, provided there is one." By no means! On the contrary, there is no adventure if there is no conviction that one is fighting for the truth, for the right, for a valid cause. What I do say is that there is in the human heart an instinct for adventure, a sort of blind force which brings its dynamism into play in every crusade, whether it be bad or good. I say blessed is he who can dedicate himself wholeheartedly to an aim that he feels worthy of his devotion. Even if he is mistaken, he is undergoing a wonderful and profoundly human experience, since he is fulfilling an instinctive aspiration.

In the same way, the sex instinct brings its dynamism and its specific pleasure into every love affair: to a happy marriage as well as to the most degrading liaison. Here again people feel that their happiness derives from the fact of their having chosen an ideal partner, when really it comes from the satisfaction of an instinctive urge. The comparison is often made in this connection with a car, which moves only under the power of its engine, but which may be propelled by the engine in any direction—along the road or into the ditch—unless there is a conscious driver at the wheel.

It is a passion, just like that of love, which takes hold of a man as soon as he commits himself to taking part in a real adventure. For the unmarried person to turn his life into a great adventure is the best substitute for sex. The same terms are used both of sex and of adventure—we talk of wander*lust*, of a *love* of adventure, of being bitten by the bug of the one or the other. Just as it is said that love is blind, so it may be said that adventure is blind. The instinct of adventure is the source both of humanity's greatest triumphs and of its worst catastrophes. And just as two cars may come into collision, both being propelled by the same energy in their internal-combustion engines, so also the instinct of adventure may throw into direct conflict peoples, social classes, and alliances. The role it plays in wars and revolutions is obvious.

Consider the enthusiasm that takes hold of a whole nation as it enters upon a war. It is sometimes cause for surprise how lightly such an undertaking is begun. This attitude derives, I believe, from the sense of relief experienced by the nation as it feels itself suddenly freed from the stranglehold of determinism. Human beings always experience a subconscious anguish at being imprisoned in a state of immobility in a political impasse. It is a kind of claustrophobia.

People feel in a vague sort of way that all social organization tends by nature and through increasing complication to become crystallized. They feel it in the tiny details of public life when they come up against unjust privileges and vested interests. It is not only the injustice that worries them, but the immutability of these things. And they feel it in the great problems of international life that rear themselves up and stubbornly remain, intricate and seemingly insoluble.

Then when national leaders dare to draw the sword to cut

these Gordian knots they seem to be setting about the liberation, not only of their nation, but of the whole of humanity,
from the fate that has befallen it. The proof is in the fact that
whenever a nation goes to war it is always in the conviction
that it is facing a sacrifice, not for itself, but in order to build a
new and better world, to usher in an era of greater liberty and
justice.

It is this that lies behind the miracle of unanimity in a nation
at such a time; there is zeal in a joyful common effort, such
as peace could never bring about. At last the rigid structure of
the *status quo* is cracking, and in its disintegration every man
sees the possibility of the renewal that he has hoped for—not
only the attainment of the aims of war properly so-called, but
a new social setup, new possibilities of life, a new beginning
that would have been inconceivable without the upheaval of
war.

Look for a moment at my own country, Switzerland, spared
the experience of war for the last century and a half, save for a
brief civil war in 1847. The whole organization of political and
social life seems to be so carefully regulated, down to the last
detail, that it leads to immobility, if not to impotence. All
the political forces are so nicely balanced that no change can
be made, despite the fact that nobody is content. The country
has become, in the words of one of my German colleagues, a
"little museum of the defunct bourgeois world," whereas profound changes have taken place in all the neighboring nations.

Consider too the enormous difficulty encountered by re-
turned colonials in readapting themselves to their new life in
the home country. They feel that there is not enough room to
live here, that in Europe people are treading on each other's
toes. Of course, in their colonies they enjoyed privileges to
which they had unfortunately become accustomed. But there
is more to it than that: In Asia, in Africa, in newly emerging
countries, their lives were an adventure, while here they must
be fitted into a routine.

Some time ago, at the height of the O.A.S.[1] terrorist campaign, a young fellow citizen of mine, Olivier Juilliard, a stu-

[1] Organisation de l'Armée Secrète (Secret Army Organization).

31

dent at Geneva University, published an article in a French
weekly that caused a considerable stir among us.[2] He described the deadly boredom which he said abounded in our
country, where young people are chafing at inaction but do
not know to what great cause to devote themselves. He went
on to tell the French that he even envied them their O.A.S.
Obviously at my age I no longer use such extreme terms. But I
understand only too well the state of mind of the rising generation that that article expressed. Paul Ricoeur has also described this boredom that lays hold on civilized and secure
societies.[3]

There has never been any lack of good people to reply to
Juilliard that if young people want to attach themselves to a
cause there is plenty of opportunity for them to do so, beginning with the International Red Cross—a great Genevan adventure. But for the young people of today the Red Cross is an
old lady of a hundred, very honorable and highly respected,
but no longer surrounded with the halo of novelty. Nevertheless it was under her aegis, in 1920, that I experienced the
youthful adventure that has had the greatest influence on my
whole life, when I worked on the repatriation of prisoners of
war and on children's famine relief.

And what a lot of other youthful adventures I enthusiastically threw myself into! At the same time I was central president of the Zofingen Students' Association. Shortly before, I
had collaborated with a friend in writing and staging a play. A
professor of law had entrusted to me an important piece of
documentary research on the functioning of direct democracy
in Switzerland, having found no student in his own faculty
willing to undertake the task. The documentation was required by an English author, Lord Bryce. I at once threw
myself heart and soul into the work and found it an absorbing subject. That was when I discovered the little half-canton
—Rhodes Intérieures, in Appenzell—where, on every occasion

[2] Olivier Juilliard, "Vive la France!" *Express*, Paris, December 21,
1962.
[3] Paul Ricoeur, *Histoire et Vérité*, Aubier, Paris, 1955.

except one, the people had consistently voted "No" on any Federal project submitted to them.

I also took out several patents on calculating machines, the only prototypes of which that ever existed were those I constructed myself, cutting the little toothed gear-wheels in my room between deliveries in the maternity ward. Then I founded the General Society of Students, a Preventorium, an International Secretariat for Youth Movements concerned in child welfare work. I organized big collections in aid of famine-stricken children in Russia and elsewhere.

One of my professors at that time was a strict disciplinarian who did not look with a favorable eye on students who cut his lectures. I thought it right, therefore, to send him a letter explaining that the reason I was not going was that his whole course of lectures was printed in a book which I could study at home, and thus gain time for other activities quite as important, I thought, to my training for a medical career. In his reply he warned me against playing Don Quixote and dissipating my efforts in tilting at every windmill. For the examination, of course, I worked hard, and my professor showed himself to be severe but just.

Soon I joined the Consistory of my church. I was its youngest member and the mouthpiece of a group of young people who wanted to reform its organization and spirit. There followed some quite lively and occasionally painful controversies. Of course, in all these activities I was working for causes which seemed to me to be worthy of my devotion, and which I do not disown even today. But I was also working for myself, for the satisfaction of my need for adventure, for the pleasure it gave me, and also, without knowing it at the time, to compensate for the feelings of inferiority that were poisoning my mind.

But all that one adventure may build can be destroyed by another, and all that one can destroy may be rebuilt by another. Think of the saga of the colonial conquests of the last century and the beginning of this one. What an outlet for the need for adventure of a Western world smothered in its bourgeois conformity! During the same period the growth of missions in pagan lands, as they were then considered, had its roots in the same desire for exotic adventure. The "little black boy" for whom we gave our halfpennies at Sunday School was an accurate symbol of the conquering power of faith which the comfortably ensconced middle-class church had markedly lost.

And think now of the great adventure of decolonialization which is unfolding before our eyes with an invincibly contagious power; it not only exalts the energy of those who are its leaders in the new countries but is also purging our churches of their prejudices—to a point where they are looking for their own renewal to a reversal in the direction of the missionary process! It is to the emergence of the Negro races into civilization that we can look for a new impulse in the whole of human society, art, and culture, for they are at the dynamic opening phase of their adventure. I have just seen a newspaper account of an interview with the Negro pastor Alex Bradford, director of a fascinating religious singing and dancing show that was performed yesterday in Geneva, "Black Nativity." "Your churches are iceboxes . . . ," he says. "I think that your society prevents free expression. You are formalists. . . . You've had everything written down for years. We are still improvising."[4]

Think too of the great adventure of the Reformation, which once threw up heroic martyrs, as in the early years of Christianity, in its attempt to renovate the whole Church, though unhappily it succeeded only in dividing it. And think what has become of the churches born out of the Reformation: venerable institutions, full of tradition. Iceboxes? Pastor Bradford's remark is perhaps a little exaggerated. The Negroes are like adolescents who have reached the age of emancipation and freely hurl hard words at their parents, words containing nevertheless a certain amount of truth. Think too of the ecumenical adventure which is only just beginning, and which will perhaps succeed both in bringing the various churches

[4] "Interview with Pastor Alex Bradford," *La Suisse*, Geneva, March 28, 1963.

closer together and in quickening the faith of each.

All the waves, however, that break over the human race follow the same curve of which we have been speaking. Camus has shown this clearly in connection with revolt.[5] Revolt is a good example of an instinctive adventure which grows like a whirlwind until it becomes a revolution, sweeping aside everything that stands in its path and incarnating for the moment all that is noblest in man, his eternal refusal to allow himself to be trampled upon. But sooner or later it reaches the stage of instituting a new established order which in its turn has to defend itself against fresh revolts, until the day comes when it will succumb before them.

The history of art richly illustrates this law. What a magical renewal is set in motion as soon as a few painters, instead of going on slavishly copying the old masters, resolutely set out along untrodden roads! It is tremendously contagious. Take, for example, the School of Paris and the way it has developed since the end of the last century. This very contagiousness gives rise to a school, which is nothing other than a collective adventure. Not that the painters are copying each other, as in the obscure preceding centuries. Rather, each stimulates the other to rediscover his own originality, and the excitement of adventure. But make haste, painters, to join in this creative current! It will soon be dried up. You may indeed imitate the new masters—Cézanne, Picasso, or Klee—but it will not be an adventure any more.

It is easy to see such creative explosions in history—the age of classical Greece, or of Louis XIV, with their incredible riches—because a wind of adventure had arisen. But it can never last. The new style is very soon codified in an obligatory creed which stifles all fresh creativity. There comes a period of decline in every adventure; everyone comes to a time when he has eaten his fill.

Some people resign themselves to going over their adventures in their hearts or recounting their memories to everyone they meet. I remember a story told of the "Brigadiers de la

[5] Albert Camus, *The Rebel*, translated by Anthony Bower, Hamish Hamilton, London, 1953.

Drôme," the small group of French pastors who drew me into the vigorous wake of their adventure of faith about the year 1925. During a mission to a remote French village they were lodging with a good man who proudly announced, "You know, I have had a religious experience as well!" Then, turning to his wife, he said, "Just go and fetch it from behind the big trunk in the attic, and show it to these gentlemen." Alas, when the wife brought it, there was nothing left but tattered remnants. The religious experience had been eaten by the rats.

All movements are subject to this inexorable law of silting up. Without doubt one of the causes is to be found in a well-known phenomenon, namely, that the thing one possesses always seems less attractive than the thing one has desired. The excitement of desire has lent magic coloring to the coveted object, but almost as soon as it has been obtained it loses its brilliance. The adventure lay in the desire and the hope, not in possession. "Strife alone pleases us and not the victory," Pascal said. "We never seek things in themselves, but only the search for things."[6] There are people who suffer tragically as a result of this fact. I had one patient who was very conscious that it was a serious defect in her character. Ardent and idealistic, she experienced overwhelming desires, but as soon as she obtained what she had desired so keenly, it lost its attraction for her.

But there is, I think, a much more profound cause behind this law of the progressive extinction of all adventures. During the first phase, that of its ascending, dynamic growth, an adventure provokes little opposition. It attracts the support, more intuitive than rational, of those who feel that it contains a truth worthy of their devotion. Other people scarcely understand it; they do not take it seriously; they do not believe it will be successful and do not combat it because as yet they do not fear it. It is when it reaches its peak, when it is gathering strength, that resistance to it takes shape.

Even if the resistance is not strong enough to block the road to success, the adventure is compelled to organize itself, to

[6] *The Thoughts of Pascal,* translated by C. Kegan Paul, George Bell, London, 1905, pp. 40 and 41.

36

justify and defend itself in order to maintain the positions it has won. Already at this stage it has ceased to be an adventure; it has become a debate, a discussion, an argument—very judicious, perhaps, but its face has changed. The intuitive and prophetic factor which was dominant at the start, and the source of its magical power, gives way to reasoned argument and systematic organization. The critics get to work, explaining and defining the adventure and putting it into formulas and dogmas. Then come the historians with their magnifying glasses, locating it in the perfectly natural evolution of things and discovering its precursors and its successors. It is measured and classified. The idea may go on living, forming part of the heritage of mankind. Students write theses about it, but no one gets worked up about it any more. The adventure is over.

So all movements begin in a fever of improvisation. Convinced pioneers bend themselves to the task with infectious zeal and put out a tremendous effort of work for no payment at all. They brave all the skepticism and mockery of others, as did the Salvation Army, for example, in the beginning. A movement will begin in some old disused attic with packing cases for chairs and tables, and a typewriter that jumps a space after every *e*. But what an atmosphere—it is like a conspiracy!

Then when success comes things have to be organized. There are considerable sums of money to be administered; order is essential. Offices must be rented; the day will come when a magnificent office block will be built. There will be a president, vice-presidents, a whole committee of influential personages, a secretary-general, chartered accountants, and smart shorthand-typists. But it will no longer be an adventure. It will be an organization—accepted, respected, and honored. Like all such societies it will have its contributors and will call on them for subscriptions. They will pay without joy, and out of a sense of duty, as little as they decently can. And meanwhile new enterprises will be launched, perhaps some "chain of happiness," hastily set up in the emotion of the moment on the occasion of a disaster, which will collect incredible sums of money in a few days of enthusiastic activity.

In the same way, churches, religious orders, and all religious movements and sects, which have been constituted under the powerful impulsion of the Holy Spirit, tend, because of their very growth and success, gradually to become big organizations. Their leaders are often worried at this point; they are snowed under with administration and feel guilty at having scarcely any time left for the exercise of a truly spiritual ministry. They had been answering an apostolic vocation in accepting the task laid on them, and they have the painful impression that to some extent, and against their wishes, they are being turned into civil servants.

The phenomenon is not confined to churches and charitable organizations. It happens with movements of all kinds—literary, artistic, scientific, and political. Consider the enthusiastic new literary reviews of the work of "young writers" which we see from time to time, and the theater groups that aim to rejuvenate dramatic art. They last hardly any time at all: either they disappear or they are rapidly absorbed into the tradition. There they lose their drive, without really imparting it to the society that swallows them up. Their adherents are then prompted to exhort each other to "revive the flame!" They recall the stories of the heroic pioneering days. But it is an artificial effort, no longer a spontaneous tide.

I have seen many people in this situation, who will even go so far as to lie to themselves rather than admit that they are disappointed. They seemed to be looking forward to the future, but in reality their eyes were fixed on the past, remained fascinated by the past. It is dangerous to have one's golden age behind one. It is the opposite of adventure. Life is a one-way street. The past is never brought back. Of course, we may feel ourselves called faithfully to pursue an undertaking once it has begun, in order to preserve alive the treasures handed down from the past. A pious duty or a useful task may be accomplished in this way. But to describe as an adventure what is no more than a normal service is to some extent to deceive oneself. A "reheated" adventure, however sincerely carried on, is no longer an adventure, in the sense that it has lost its vital impulse. In the case of a religious movement this situation may take on tragic dimensions; it may give rise to a vague sense of guilt.

Take, for example, the case of a man who once was roused by the powerful inspiration of the Holy Spirit. Now he strives, by disciplining himself, to retain the old spontaneous ardor. But he fails. He reproaches himself for his lukewarmness, for the ineffectiveness, not only of his actions, but also of his prayers and resolutions. He reproaches himself for not having been able to preserve the "heavenly gift," as the apostle urges. But in spiritual matters nothing is preserved, nothing can be saved up. This man is mistaking a psychological problem for a religious one. He refuses to recognize the law of adventure, which is that it dies as it achieves its object. The first requirement of religion is that we accept the laws of life. The spiritual life consists only in a series of new births. There must be new flowerings, new prophets, new adventures—always new adventures—if the heart of man, albeit in fits and starts, is to go on beating.

CHAPTER 4

Taking the Plunge

CLEARLY, a most important problem with which we now have to deal is that of the renewal of adventure, its periodical revivification, since it is always burning itself out—and that sooner than we think. If I can borrow an illustration from electronics, we have to pass from damped waves to undamped ones. Even the Church carries on only because of the constant appearance of new prophets—a St. Jerome, a St. Francis, a Luther, a St. Ignatius, a Wesley.

Its leaders are always hoping for a renewal of fervor, but can only conceive of it as taking the direction in which the Church is already traveling. But when it comes it usually takes the form of a new departure, and one which is at first disconcerting to them, because it runs quite counter to the view they have of the Church in the light of the past. They feel that the new movement of the Spirit is betraying and destroying more than it is preserving and accomplishing. And so the official Church always resists these far-reaching spiritual adventures and only afterwards perceives that it has been saved by those whom it has persecuted.

The Holy Spirit is always calling us to look forward, not back. This fact was well expressed by the presidents of the World Council of Churches in their Whitsun message, 1963:

"Nostalgia is a temptation for our Churches (one into which they often fall), nostalgia for the first century of our era, or for the twelfth or the sixteenth, or even for the first fifty years of the ecumenical movement!"[1] Of course we want to rediscover the close fraternal fellowship which reigned in the primitive Church, but it must necessarily take on a new shape in the different world of today. Certain communities claim that they achieve this atmosphere of pioneering adventure more successfully than do the official churches, and such is often the case, since for these communities the effort to get back to the primitive sources is a real present adventure. But of course it is a new adventure, and never an exact reproduction of the primitive Church. History never repeats itself. We shall only be deluding ourselves if we hope to experience what others have experienced in a different age. The real adventure for us is our own day and age.

Every age is an adventure. Every life is an adventure. Every adventure has its own individuality, which cannot be mixed with any other. I have known several couples who have had the great sorrow of losing a child. An instinctive reaction of rebellion against death has made them to some extent identify the lost child with one of their remaining children, or with a new child born after the tragedy, as if the second child could in some way prolong the adventure of the first beyond his death. It is a sort of make-believe; it depersonalizes the child, who is thus forced to play a role in life not his own, and deprives him of his right to live his life as a strictly personal adventure.

As time rolls on, adventure succeeds adventure, but they always remain distinct the one from the other. This fact may be observed in every sphere of life. There is the eternal conflict between the heirs of yesterday's adventure and the adventurers of today who push them aside and are in reality more faithful to yesterday's adventure because they have rediscovered its innovating spirit. It is no use for the Old Guard to denounce the incompetence of the newcomers, pointing out

[1] "Message de Pentecôte des Présidents du Conseil Oecuménique des Eglises," *La Suisse*, Geneva, June 2, 1953.

that they do not understand the problems they are dealing with. That is precisely what makes it an adventure for them! Many of man's triumphs have been in origin the work of amateurs—precisely because there were not yet any scholars in that particular new branch of knowledge. The scholars come along afterwards, analyzing, explaining, codifying, and perfecting the details of the doctrine and techniques involved, and teaching them. And that reminds one of G. B. Shaw's quite unjust remark: "He who can, does. He who cannot, teaches."

But pioneers are amateurs who do not know how to set about their task and must put their trust in a hunch. St. Peter is a fisherman who finds himself suddenly promoted to the leadership of the Church; Calvin is a lawyer who becomes the founder of reformed theology; Pasteur is a chemist who opens to medicine wider horizons than any doctor of his day; Pascal is a mathematician who—like many other mathematicians—enriches philosophy; and Leonardo da Vinci, an amateur in the most varied domains, well characterizes that prodigious era of explosive adventure, the Renaissance.

I think this is why I have always had a keen preference for amateur work. I am an amateur in my workshop and derive the keenest joy from working there in wood and metal. But I am also an amateur psychotherapist, amateur philosopher, amateur theologian, amateur lecturer, and amateur writer. For me, to write a book is not to teach or to create a work of literature, it is to have an adventure in company with my readers both known and unknown. It gives me that same enjoyment that is inherent in all adventure.

Of course I know that the word "amateur" can bear a quite different meaning. We say that a man is working amateurishly if he is not taking his work seriously. My readers will certainly understand and I need hardly say that this is not the sense in which I am using the term. On the contrary, I associate the word "amateur" with the idea of adventure, and the idea of adventure with that of commitment. The amateur is one who chooses his activity according to his taste, who commits himself totally to it and pursues it because he likes it and not from a sense of duty, even if he makes it his daily work.

A real new adventure in my life had its beginning a few days ago when I wrote the first few pages of this book on this balcony overlooking the roadstead of Palma. Now my pen is already running more easily. I am caught up in the adventure that has begun. Before taking the plunge I was turning over in my mind all sorts of ideas on the subject of this conception of life that I have. My brain was seething with thoughts about the various lines I could take. Was it worth making a book out of it? And what form ought it to take? Might it not seem pretty poor stuff? Or perhaps too paradoxical? Would such a book help people to commit themselves to engage more boldly in their adventure? Or would it discourage them, turn them away from the simple and faithful performance of the daily task traced out for them?

But basically the question was one of committing myself. I myself was hesitating to take the responsibility for my own thoughts by setting them down in so many words. Now the die is cast. I am no longer free to stop. The evolution of my thoughts presses me on. My wife says I have started muttering in my sleep. How great is the contrast between the long, hard perplexity of the period of gestation and the momentum of the process of birth which carries me along with it once it is set in motion.

There are people who find taking the plunge much the easier part; what they find hard is to persevere. They often confess as much to me. They readily undertake all kinds of things but have great trouble in bringing them to a conclusion. They have to take themselves in hand, summon up all their will power, and drag themselves along willy-nilly, instead of being swept along by one of the forces of nature. It seems to me that this is because in fact they have a different view of life and work from mine; they look upon them as a duty and not as an adventure.

They work, while I play. Life for me is like a great game of chess. A game of chess is an adventure, in fact, with the risk of losing and the hope of winning. But the chess player has always the hope that if he loses this game he will get his own back and win the next. Life, on the other hand, is a game played only once. Everyone has an intuitive sense of the tremendous gamble of life: that every move, every choice, every personal decision, every initiative we take, every adventure to which we commit ourselves is going to determine the rest of the game and will have its repercussion on the outcome.

The more conscious the player is of what is at stake, the more he hesitates to make his move. Even in chess championships a clock limits the time allowed to each player to think about his move. The same applies to life. The more one is aware of life as an adventure, the more conscious he is of what is at stake, and the risk of every move, so the more he hesitates to make a move. This was the case with me a few days ago as I sat on this balcony with my blank paper in front of me, in a state of perplexity. This is the case with every book I write, with every consultation I give. I hesitate anxiously, assessing the risk, and am secretly ashamed of my hesitation, which I look upon as culpable timidity. And when this sense of guilt becomes intolerable I take the plunge, saying to myself, "Oh well! I must say what I have got to say, and accept the consequences."

At once the game is on. Having made the first move, one is led on to another. One page written calls for another. The adventure has begun, and I cannot withdraw from it. It becomes compelling. It forces me to be bold where previously I was in doubt. I have burned my boats and cannot turn back; I have crossed the Rubicon. I am well aware that the enthusiasm which is carrying me forward now is a sort of protection against the return of my doubts. Before, while I was hesitating as if paralyzed, I was in two minds, like the two sides of a pair of scales, balanced between the forces that were pushing me toward the adventure and those that were holding me back. The latter—my fears, the objections which I make to myself—have not in fact disappeared. I have merely repressed them, and I must brace myself, and rush into action in order to counteract them and stop them from calling everything in question again.

We were noticing just now how as soon as an adventure is set in motion it tends to harden, to become more intransigent, to organize itself in order to overcome the resistances that rise up against it. But the resistances against which I must necessarily strive are not only external but internal as well. I have to protect myself against my own doubts. Every man of action thus has inevitably to fight on two fronts, one external and quite conscious and the other internal, scarcely if at all conscious; and he shows himself all the more bellicose externally, the more he is dogged by his own inner enemy, by his resistances and his doubts.

Proof lies in the dramatic crises which we may sometimes witness. After a lifetime of fruitful and brilliant service a man suddenly feels himself assailed by disturbing doubts. Everyone is congratulating him on what he has accomplished, and suddenly the whole thing seems to him to be pointless. He has thrown himself into one adventure after another, but what does it all mean? What is left that has any value? Does not everything drop back inexorably into the unspeakable monotony of the universal wheel of time? Has he not been deceiving himself, has he not himself invented, in order to hide the emptiness of his existence, the goals toward which he felt himself being called? All the skepticism he has for so long repressed, in the heat of battle, comes back once more to the surface and refuses to be thrust out of his mind.

But the intellectual, who tries hard to be sincere and objective, the man with the sort of mind that sees both sides of every problem, who analyzes his own feelings and never permits his passions to obscure his judgment, especially the level-headed person, who refuses to commit himself until he is quite sure it is worth while—such a man represses his instinct for adventure and remains paralyzed in an endless perplexity. Now, I am both of these men, turn and turn about—first the one who hesitates until he wonders if he will ever be able to act at all, and then the one who commits himself because he is unable to resist the urge to be committed. Are not the decisive moments of our lives those in which we make a choice? It is the mysterious moment at which an adventure begins that seems to me to be the most fascinating problem of the present study.

I say "mysterious" because it is impossible to analyze it,

because the subject himself has no clear idea of it. Why do so many adventures come to naught before they have got going? Which of us cannot remember in his own case a large number of projects which have set his heart beating faster but in the end have never seen the light of day? How many people have some manuscript locked up in a drawer at home? Many have been kind enough to give them to me to read, and I have found them remarkable. I should like to encourage these clandestine authors to publish their works. But it is their adventure and not mine. It is not my job to decide for them about eventual publication, and so to deprive them of one of the fundamental prerogatives of the person, namely, personal commitment.

But as soon as a man makes up his mind to take the plunge into adventure, he is aware of a new strength he did not think he had, which rescues him from all his perplexities. That is the problem: It is perplexity which bars the road to adventure; but it is adventure which sweeps perplexity aside! Similar vicious circles are to be found in every domain of biology: One must have hens in order to gather eggs; and one must have eggs in order to obtain hens. No biological problem can be resolved by static analysis alone; rather, it must be worked on in the context of the dynamic movement of life.

I always remember one of my patients, an intelligent, sensitive, and artistic man, whom I treated over a long period. Our discussions were fascinating. The percipience of his observations on himself and his memories, their psychological analysis, and that of his dreams, captivated me. But I felt that I was getting more out of them than he was, since no change followed in his way of life. And then suddenly, with my encouragement but without my pressing him, he wrote, almost at one sitting, a play which was a resounding success. From then on he had no further need of me! This did not mean that he had no more psychological problems. It meant that in the current of life that had been set going by adventure they were becoming fruitful instead of being sterile and paralyzing.

All the problems in a person's life are linked together, like children holding hands and dancing in a ring. The analysis of one leads on to another, and so on. Liberation from one requires liberation first from another, and so on. One can spend a long time going round and round from problem to problem. But if the circle can be broken at some point, it becomes a game of follow-my-leader, with a chain reaction taking place among all the problems which up to now have been blocking each other, so that one solution leads to another. This breaking of the ring is the leap into adventure.

So there is an astonishing contrast between the heavy perplexity that inhibits before the adventure has begun and the excitement that grips us the moment it begins. I experience this afresh with every book I write. I hesitate for a long time, in a sort of paralysis. I formulate laborious plans, making them as logical as possible, but none satisfies me. And suddenly, moved by a quite different force—not of the intellect, but of life—I put them aside and begin to write, and I feel that nothing now can stop me.

Naturally my first book was much more of an adventure. Would I dare to have it published? It is always most difficult to judge one's own works; I am always struck by this difficulty. At one moment they seem all white and the next all black: their merit appears quite certain at one moment and a matter of the gravest doubt a moment later. The same is true if you ask a person if he is happy. He may unhesitatingly answer that he is, and go through all his reasons for being happy; then later he may begin wondering whether he is not putting up a pretense of happiness in order to console himself for not being happy.

The same thing applies to any work of art. Each picture is a new adventure for the artist. The more keenly he realizes this the more he hesitates to begin, and the harder he finds it to judge himself. One painter tells me about his long periods of vacillation. He feels guilty because his output is so small; yet weeks pass before he can bring himself to take up his brushes again. Is he being lazy? Then he thinks of one of his fellow artists, who, he tells me, works hard and produces an ever-increasing flow of canvases. But they are basically all alike. He changes his subjects but not his style or his technique. He remains outside the great evolving movement of modern painting. "At bottom," says my friend, "with all his activity he is a lazy man. He is too idle to try and understand modern painting and assimilate it, and make his own original contribution to it."

Moreover, the public hardly encourages him to do so. What the public wants of a painter is that he go on churning out the sort of pictures it expects of him, and likes because it is used to them. Such a painter thinks he is engaged in a fine creative activity but in fact he is creating nothing; he is only copying himself. If he turns to new paths, everyone will cry out, but he will find himself once more launched into adventure and once more vacillating between contradictory judgments about the value of his own work.

Perhaps he will run to his friends for advice. This was what I did with my first book. I submitted the manuscript to six of my friends, and they took the trouble to spend a whole day all together, in Berne, discussing it with me. None of them encouraged me to have it published, apart from one who suggested that I send the first chapter as an article to some medical magazine to see if it aroused any interest. Do not depend too much on others to assume responsibility for your adventure. After all, it is yours and not theirs. A true adventure always has an eminently personal character and demands a quite personal decision. Besides, other people's advice is conditioned to a considerable extent by your own attitude: If you are borne up by a solid conviction, many people will give their approval. But if you are doubtful, not many will encourage you to go ahead.

In order to help me my friends put forward all their criticisms of what I had written, one of them having done a considerable amount of careful work on it. But I was paralyzed! Although I recognized that most of their criticisms were valid and that my work could not stand in its original form, I felt that I could not make the modifications they suggested, because then it would have been no longer my own work, my own adventure. In perplexities of this sort one tries to take oneself to task, but it does not do much good. I recall the naiveté with which I told myself that I simply must get the book published in one form or another so as to leave something behind if I should happen to die. My readers will surely smile at this, but I can assure them that such thoughts are less rare than they imagine. The instinct of adventure is closely linked with a certain instinct of death haunting the mind of every human being and prompting him to make some personal mark which will survive him.

That was insufficient, however, to get me out of my difficulty. My wife was becoming more and more worried about me. After some months had gone by she decided to go and see a friend of hers, in order to seek in prayer with her to know what she could do to help me. What she could do was in fact just what she did in making that visit. It showed me that there was, after all, someone who believed in my adventure enough not to give in because I had encountered a setback, someone who did not accept that my adventure must be stillborn. Without doubt God used this encouragement on the part of my wife to show me the way forward. Many wives who sincerely want their husbands to do something useful are themselves standing in the way, either because they are too impassive, or lacking in faith, or, on the contrary, because they are too free with advice and exhortation, or even because they drag their husbands into the sort of social whirl that is scarcely conducive to creative thought.

Moreover, that first book was itself the result of a bolder decision which I had taken three years earlier, after much more serious hesitation—the decision to change the orientation of my life's work toward the study of the role played by the spiritual and moral life in health, disease, and healing. That, too, my friends had also strongly advised against, and it was my wife's confidence which had given me the courage to step forward into the unknown. From then on it had been not *my* adventure but *ours*. Happy are those marriages in which both husband and wife live the same adventure together. It is astonishing how it strengthens the bonds uniting them.

And so it was that three years later I was putting down on paper some of the experiences I had had since then. With my manuscript tucked under my arm, I set out to offer it to three publishers. It is at this point that the adventure begins to be real. As long as one is alone, writing, in one's study, it is only a dream. Adventure must be incarnate. Adventure always means facing up to the world and its judgments. The third publisher I visited, Mlle. A. Delachaux, at once declared herself disposed to take my manuscript, and she confirmed her decision soon afterwards. For her too it was an adventure, after two other publishers had turned it down. So I have remained faithful to her, and the original edition in French of this work was the ninth of my books she has published.

We come again, then, to that important aspect of the problem of adventure: the quite special bonds forged between those who are engaged in the same adventure. Think of the emotion with which old army comrades meet each other again, particularly if they have shared a campaign or captivity together. They recall their memories of the times when they experienced the same fears, the same hopes, the same hardships, and the same joys.

Think of a reunion of former pupils of a college or school, whose all-important early years were spent side by side. Out come the old nicknames, even though they may not have seen each other for many a long year. Looking back over a score or two of years, one is astounded at the variation in the destinies of people who began at the same starting point. It has needed only a few of those decisive turning points we were considering just now—those points at which a difficult decision had to be made—for those lives to take each a quite different direction and shape. So a single point on a railway line will send one train toward Paris and another toward Rome. And yet these old comrades remain astonishingly interdependent because they once lived together through the same adventure of learning.

Think also of the intimate relationship that is established between a hunter and his dog through their experiencing together the same adventure of the hunt. Or of the intimacy of rider and horse in the adventure of the fields and woods, or in that of a riding competition. Master and pupil also experience a common adventure, and when the pupil takes his examination the master will also be put to the test, because by the success of his pupil people will judge the value of his teaching. The criminal and the judge seem far removed from one another, each on his own side of the bars of the accused's box, yet they too are engaged in the same adventure. While the accused is judged by his judge, the latter is judged by public opinion, and maybe he will owe it to some notorious criminal that his own name goes down in the annals of history.

But surely the bond I ought to be talking about here—I have so often experienced its effects—is that which attaches the doctor to his patient. The struggle for healing, with its daily hazards, its progress and its setbacks, its hopes and fears, is for both a common and a single adventure binding them together forever. The forms it may take are immensely diverse. There is the "dramatic suspense" of surgery; there is the long toil of psychoanalysis; there is the patient collaboration aimed at the rehabilitation of a handicapped person; there is the hard struggle to avoid the danger of blindness or deafness; in acute diseases there is the anxiety and urgency with which one tries to solve the problems presented by diagnosis, so as to be able to fight the disease effectively; in chronic illnesses there is the long series of visits, with their increasing familiarity and intimacy, in which fidelity reveals its riches.

There is also the profound and moving bond that is established between the patient and his doctor when the latter realizes that from the human point of view the game is lost. He is careful not to express his anxiety in brutal terms. But usually the patient feels it, guesses at it vaguely, being careful for his part not to put a direct question. He knows his doctor much better than one supposes. He notices his slightest gestures and silences, the signs of a greater tenderness, a mere intonation in his voice, even the joke that is made in order to cover up something else, which deceives neither of them. The day comes when the doctor too feels, because of some almost imperceptible little sign, that the patient has realized the gravity of the threat hanging over him. The failure which they now have to face together will be the painful adventure of their common failure.

CHAPTER 5

The Meaning of Work

AS WE HAVE SEEN, those who have shared a common adventure —particularly if it has involved rich personal and spiritual relationships—remain permanently bound one to another. There is a certain spiritual kinship between them. I am made aware of this now when I meet, in different countries, those who have been influenced, as I was thirty years ago, by the Oxford Group Movement. Even if I do not know them, I soon sense that we belong to the same spiritual family.

Joining the movement was a great adventure for my wife and me. Through it God influenced our lives in a way that has had a lasting effect. The movement later changed its character, when it became Moral Rearmament. That also involved us in an adventure—leaving it. It was a serious and risky adventure because one cannot without danger uproot a plant from the soil that has been nourishing it for so long. But we were being called along diverging paths: The movement was turning to an interest in politics, and I to medicine. One does not have two adventures at the same time. A decisive choice is the prerequisite of every adventure.

My own since then has evolved through my experiences in the consulting room, in travels, in meetings, in medical conferences, and in writing. And now my publisher has long been pressing me to write another book. But the thing I am always afraid of is that in writing more I shall cease to be an amateur, that writing will become a trade. I am afraid that people will expect me to know those tricks of the trade that will please the public, whereas what I want is to retain all my simplicity, to describe simply what I experience, what I think, without any artifice.

The risk today is no longer the same as with my first book, but I feel it quite as strongly. It is the risk of disappointing some reader. One will not find in this book what he has valued in the others; another will think that I always say the same thing, and that it is pointless to say it all again; a third will accuse me of talking too much about myself. In fact I do talk more and more about myself, because my life's work has taught me that living experiences attract and help people more than theories. Of course there is a strain of vanity in this, but would I be any less vain if I refrained for fear of such accusations?

What matters most, then, is to retain the spirit of adventure. A book written at the request of a publisher strikes me in itself as being more of a duty than an adventure. The truth is that no adventure can last long. It can only spring to life again, all new. For this to happen there must be a certain emotion, an indefinable inner vibration, which cannot be fabricated on demand. Several times now, over the last few years, I have made careful plans for this book. But they are too old now! I could follow them, but it would be more like a school exercise than an adventure.

The spirit of adventure is propagated only by contagion. And so in order to rediscover it I plunged first into what is for me a different adventure—that of reading books by other writers. Enthusiastically I read that fine book by Father de Lubac on the religious thought of Father Teilhard de Chardin,[1] whom he depicts so well as a great adventurer of science and faith, and a poet of the great adventure of the evolution of the universe

[1] Henri de Lubac, S.J., *La Pensée Religieuse du Père Teilhard de Chardin*, Aubier, Paris, 1962.

53

Then I set to work carefully to read Henri Frédéric Amiel's *Diary*.[2] An interesting point is that it was an American colleague, Dr. Bonnett, of Champaign, Illinois, who made me want to take up that book—one at which I had never done more than idly glance. True, in order to understand an author's adventure as also to understand an individual's personal adventure in the consulting room, one has to be prepared to spend time studying it with care. My American friend's pronunciation was such that I did not realize who the author was whom he found so like me in spirit. "But he came from Geneva!" he exclaimed, and I was quite embarrassed at not recognizing my illustrious fellow citizen.

I see now why it was that Dr. Bonnett compared me with him. Amiel was an amateur all his life! All his life he asked himself what his true vocation was and never found the answer. He reproached himself for not doing anything creative, for lack of choosing, of committing himself. And all the time, in the privacy of his own room, he was writing thousands of pages about what he was experiencing, what he was feeling, about the thoughts these things gave rise to, without realizing that *that* was his creative work, and that in it he was revealing himself as a true precursor of the psychological analysts, even inventing—half a century before Freud—the idea of repression into the unconscious.

But one of the most curious things about Amiel is something of which Dr. Bonnett in far-off America had probably never heard, namely, that refined, tender, and hesitant as he was, Amiel gave Switzerland one of its most fiery war songs:

> *Roulez, tambours, pour couvrir la frontière,*
> *Au bord du Rhin, guidez-nous au combat!*
> *Battez gaîment une marche guerrière:*
> *Dans nos Cantons, chaque enfant naît soldat!*

("Roll, drums, to cover the frontier,
On the bank of the Rhine, lead us to battle!
Joyously beat a warlike march:
In our Cantons, every child is born a soldier!")

[2] Henri Frédéric Amiel, *Fragments d'un Journal Intime*, Georg, Geneva, and Crès, Paris, 1922.

The king of Prussia, who a few years later was to assert his power by crushing the France of Napoleon III, had tried to pick a quarrel with my country. The Swiss had stood together courageously as one man under the threat, ready for anything.

Their military preparedness doubtless left much to be desired. I was once told that my great-grandfather went through the whole Rhine campaign with a rifle that would not fire. But his heart was in it, and if that does not suffice to win a war, it is at least the first requisite for waging it. Then Amiel, gentle Amiel, in a sudden burst of enthusiasm, wrote in a single evening the fulminating stanzas of his "Roll, drums," which is still so popular with us, exalting our military virtues.

For a long time this seemed to me one of the enigmas of history; but I understand it now. Under the stress of emotion, that perpetual hesitator, Amiel, had been bitten by the bug of adventure. All at once his divided heart had found its inner unity, and in explosive zeal he surpassed his most determined compatriots and impelled them to action. The words flowed from his pen, and his lines took on a Homeric accent.

I have already alluded to epic poetry, which, in human history, was the cradle of culture because it expressed afresh and vividly men's experience of adventure. There is a close link between poetry and adventure because the roots of both are deep in the emotions. All real poetry is an adventure, and all true adventure has its poetry. The world frequently fails to see this; it is said of a man unsuited to action, "What do you expect! He lives in the clouds—he's a poet!"

No greater mistake can be made. History was made by poets. It is not by intellectual reasoning but by communicating emotion that individuals and nations are aroused. Only a spark is needed, the release of a trigger, some adventure which, as with Amiel, suddenly changes a dreamer into a man of action. Then the adventure develops its own power, carrying the man who commits himself to it much farther than he expected. Moved, in my turn, by my encounter with these two authors —Father de Lubac, the learned Academician, and H. F. Amiel, the timid and secret writer who suddenly became an amateur warrior—I took up my pen once more. I began my book quite differently from the way I had planned it. After all, following a plan is hardly being adventurous. It is to set oneself up as a professional writer rather than as an amateur.

I realize the difficulty of demarcating the frontier between amateurs and professionals. There are plenty of arguments on the subject, with reference, for example, to the Olympic Games, from which professional sportsmen are excluded. I recognize also that my personal complexes play their part in the need I feel to remain an amateur in every sphere— particularly my feelings of inferiority and my lack of confidence in myself—like Amiel! The reason is that a professional is judged much more severely than an amateur. I can wander innocently about the domains of philosophy, theology, and psychology in spite of the terrible gaps in my knowledge of these disciplines. Such ignorance would be unpardonable in a professional.

But I think there is much more to it than that. I was once engaged in a discussion with Professor Hendrik Kraemer, then director of the Bossey Oecumenical Institute. In the heat of the argument I said to him, "You theologians. . . ." He cut me short. "No," he said, "I am not a theologian, I am an orientalist; I only do theology for love of it." That is the word: Amateur means lover. The attraction, the charm of being an amateur, even its value, lies in the love that goes into it, because it is work done not for gain but for love.

This is, for example, one of the lessons to be learned from the parable of the Good Samaritan (Luke 10:30-35). Before the Samaritan, two "professionals" of charity, of human succor, went down the road from Jerusalem to Jericho, intent on the duties of their profession, without stopping by the side of the injured man. But the good Samaritan, moved with compassion, stopped and became an amateur doctor, an amateur nurse, an amateur ambulance man. Put with this another saying of Jesus: "When you have done all that is commanded you, say, 'We are unworthy servants; we have only done what was our duty'" (Luke 17:10). Is it not this problem of professionalism that Jesus is alluding to here? I have seen plenty of clerics who once entered upon their ministry full of burning conviction, anxiously wondering whether they were not after all beginning to make it a business to talk about God, to pray, and to study theology. They sometimes come to envy the fervent devotion of a single evangelist, who is a sort of amateur pastor.

It is precisely this spirit of love and of total commitment that protects a minister of religion or a doctor against the danger of professional routine and constantly relights in him the flame of adventure. But there have always been plenty of amateur doctors against whom the corps of professional doctors has fought. Of course, some act as amateur doctors merely to make money, and it is for them that the name "charlatan" ought to be reserved. But others do it really for love; their life is a true adventure, and they have at times enriched medical knowledge with valuable discoveries. The public accords them its favor despite all the legal prohibitions.

I remember a young artist who was full of aggressive feelings toward his father as a result of psychological difficulties that had arisen in their relationship. We were talking about his work. I told him I thought one could become a great artist only through love, love for the people for whom one paints a canvas or composes a piece of music. "I know," he exclaimed, "and I know that because I hate my father I hate the whole world!"

You will certainly be able to judge the importance of Professor Kraemer's remark, for you will know that most people in our day do not love their work. It is not a wonderful daily adventure for them. I say "in our day" without claiming that it was any better in the past but because it is a problem that needs to be tackled urgently. To help a worker discover a fresh attraction in his daily work is to help him live a fuller and very often a healthier life. Many ordinary illnesses are nothing but the expression of a serious dissatisfaction with life. Extraneous pleasures—even when they are numerous—are rarely sufficient to make up for real love of one's work.

I find this dissatisfaction even among men and women whose profession is generally considered interesting, the sort of creative, varied, self-giving, and personal job that many people would like to have—among doctors and nurses, for instance, as well as teachers, artists, and even ministers of religion. It may be that their careers have moved through the very curve of which we have been speaking. They began full of enthusiasm, treating their work as a fascinating adventure. And then gradually, imperceptibly, as a result of disappointments, through the deadening effect of routine, even without their realizing why, it became a burden, just a duty to be performed, a habit, a prison rather than an adventure.

But for the vast majority of our contemporaries, their daily work has never looked like an adventure, and they feel it could never be so. The very way it is organized—rigid, fractionalized, impersonal—and the atmosphere of the office or the factory seem to make such a thing impossible. If on the spur of the moment any one of them were inspired to use his initiative and introduce some change into his method of working, even if it seemed to be in the interest of the job, his boss would object and promptly tell him to desist, on the grounds that "it has never been done like that before."

In several lectures, particularly in Finland, I have maintained this idea that the meaning of man's work is the satisfaction of the instinct for adventure that God has implanted in his heart. In the discussion that followed, objectors have taken me to task. "It is possibly true in your case," they say, "but how do you expect it to apply to the great mass of workers whose jobs are merely a mechanical routine?" This quite legitimate objection confirms rather than weakens my thesis. It is less a criticism of what I said than of our present-day society. Obviously men suffer when their work is so organized that it seems to them to lack the lure of adventure.

In such a case adventure, for them, begins in the evening when they leave work, or on Saturdays when the week end begins. This for millions of people is the welcome safety valve for their unsatisfied instinct. At work they keep a weary eye on the clock, which seems to move so slowly. They feel tired. And then, all at once, their lost strength returns because they can do what they want—not merely in the usual forms of relaxation, such as a show, a concert, a walk, reading, fishing, or skiing, but often in real and strenuous work such as attending evening classes, gardening, training intensively for some sport, or making something in the workshop.

Furthermore, the more absorbing the evening or week-end adventure is, the more boring the next day's work seems. The whole of society, a nation's life, its economic progress, its state of health—all suffer from this general dissociation of work and adventure when the latter is sought only on the fringes of life instead of being its mainspring. The need for a two-pronged attack is clearly urgent: on the organization of work and on the conception that people have of their daily work and the attitude they adopt toward it.

In the organization of work, fruitful reform might well take the idea of the importance of the person as a starting point. When a worker believes that he is looked upon merely as a tool of production, he feels he is becoming just a thing. When he feels that an interest is taken in him as a person, in his personal life, in the adventure of his life, that what is expected of him is not just a mechanical gesture but a personal understanding of his work, intelligence, initiative, and lively imagination, as well as a sense of being one of a team engaged in a common adventure, he takes cognizance of himself as a person, engaged in a personal adventure.

As a mere instrument of production, a man considers himself dispossessed: he feels his work belongs to his employer; he feels he is expropriated and enslaved. None can doubt that this decay in the nature of work is contrary to the will of God. In Exodus 20:2 God reminds his people before he gives them his law, "I am the Lord your God, who brought you out of the land of Egypt, out of the house of bondage." So the escape from Egypt, the extraordinary vicissitudes of which fill the Book of Exodus, and the memory of which is constantly recalled to the Israelites, is the symbol of God's intervention to liberate man from all servitude. Egypt is the eternal symbol of rich and luxurious civilization. By snatching his people from it and casting them into a terrible desert, God thrusts them afresh into an adventure, so that they shall rediscover themselves at the cost of countless hardships and dangers.

To its responsible leaders an industry most often seems like a grand adventure. But only rarely are they able to communicate this view of it to their subordinates, who have difficulty seeing it as an adventure because they lack an over-all view of it. They work at one section, trying honestly to do their best perhaps. But if no effort is made constantly to widen their outlook to take in the whole process of production in the factory, they soon lose the feeling that their work has any meaning and lapse into a routine. The large-scale problems which interest the leaders of the industry—market study, for example, or the risks attendant upon economic changes—can much more often than is generally thought be grasped quite well by modest workers and awake a sense of adventure in them.

But all questions of organization and all social reforms depend essentially upon the attitude of the public, upon the concept of work that obtains in society. The usual thing nowadays is to look upon it only as an economic necessity, a means of earning a living. This is to confine it to the instinct of self-preservation—that is to say, to the animal side of man. This is what lies behind such common expressions as "a dog's life," "a willing horse," and "donkey work."

Of course, bourgeois society has made an idol of work. I am the first to smile at the hackneyed epitaph "His work was his life." But it is quite possible to deify work and at the same time lose sight of its true significance. Man's true value will not be restored to him by denigrating work but by helping him to rediscover its true human significance. I hope that this book will contribute to that end.

To the young people of today who are calling our bourgeois society in question and asking why it is necessary to work, it is not enough to reply, as in the last century, "Because it is your duty." I do not hide my sympathy for these young people, who strike me as being much more human than their parents, precisely because they are no longer content to live without thinking, to do everything unintelligently like everyone else without knowing why, to live to work, and to work to live. Think, for example, of the film *Les Tricheurs* ("*The Cheats*").

After talking frankly and at length with many of these young people, I know how difficult it is to give a satisfactory answer.

They must in any case find the answer for themselves, since a life is never truly human unless it grows out of personal conviction. Actually as I write this chapter I am seeing again one of these young people who have helped me most to perceive the seriousness of this problem and the inhumanity of our age. He was always arrested, "blocked" in his efforts to get down to work, in spite of the sincerest of intentions. We were, of course, together able to discover by means of psychological analysis a number of inhibiting factors deriving from his childhood. We were able to talk openly to each other in friendship about our spiritual lives; but this was not sufficient to bring the liberation he needed.

The fact was that the powerful inhibition against work from which he suffered was not indicative only of psychological problems, or even of spiritual problems, but of a human problem: It was absolutely essential for him to discover the meaning of work. He suddenly comes back to see me. He is working! He is working, not, as so often in his past attempts, lashing himself with a whip, as it were, or even from mere economic necessity, but with verve and joy. "I have realized what work is meant to be," he tells me; "a creative adventure." The remark is opportune! It seems to me that he has guessed accurately at the thoughts that are running through my mind as I write this book. He has found an answer that goes much deeper and is much more convincing than that given by our fathers when they presented work simply as a necessity of life.

CHAPTER 6

Commitment

THE SIGNIFICANCE of human work is something much more than a mere biological necessity. We must find an answer to the problem of work that is at once more scientific and more spiritual. More scientific, because it will depend on the study of man and his distinctive characteristics. While, like the animals, he has an instinct of self-preservation, he has in addition an instinct of adventure, a need to express himself personally in creative work, to commit himself to new paths, to invent something original. It is here that he is something more than animal—he is a person. But this definition of work is also more spiritual, since man is seen to be a spiritual being in the very act of his desire to understand the meaning of things, the meaning of the world, of life, and to understand the meaning of his own work so as to be able to see the part played in the whole, in the destiny of the world, by his own personal creative contribution.

The word "creative" comes naturally to my pen. We do not use it of the work of animals, even when they construct things as wonderful as a beehive. But the Bible uses the word "creation" when it speaks of the work of God: "God rested from all his work which he had done in creation" (Genesis 2:3).

A creative work is always something personal; it is always an adventure. To fulfill one's need of adventure in one's work, and not outside it, is to restore work to its truly human status. I myself once attempted to separate them. In the enthusiasm aroused by my religious experiences, I seriously considered in the year 1937 abandoning medicine—my "trade"—to take up a more direct ministry in the Church. But God called me to put my two lives together into one—my life as a servant of God and my life as a doctor.

It was astonishing how my professional work at once took on the character of an adventure. I can see now that I threw myself into the work rather naïvely. But there is no doubt that my candid enthusiasm made it possible for me to cure people whom I can no longer cure now that I know much more about their diseases, scientifically speaking.

I am not advocating obscurantism—far from it. I am always interested in study, and I keenly regret not having the time to learn all I should still like to. Science is a marvelous adventure. But there is another side to it: The more learned one becomes, the greater is the risk that one will treat one's professional work merely as a way of earning a livelihood—thoroughly learned, well regulated, trouble-free, but also free of the tang of adventure.

The important thing, therefore, is the preservation or rather the reawakening in oneself of the spirit of adventure. One must grow in adventure at the same time as one grows in knowledge. In my consulting room I am constantly aware of the danger of my work's degenerating into a routine. My patients are as aware of this as I am and are as keen on avoiding it. If I treat them as just another job of work, they feel that they are just cases as far as I am concerned. If I retain the spirit of adventure, they feel they are persons. The more learned a doctor is, the more he must cultivate the spirit of adventure in himself.

Technical knowledge and science, repetition and routine, tend constantly to stifle the spirit of adventure. I must always be trying to retain it, to retain that indefinable freshness of outlook which makes me see at once in my patient not a case to be labeled but a unique being, an opportunity for a unique experience. It is not only his life which is at stake, but my own as well. Our consultation is an adventure for me as well as for him. Then he will feel that my interest in him is not merely professional but personal.

I often dream about a conversation that I have had with a patient. I am glad of this, because it is proof that the interest he has aroused in me has gone deep, has penetrated below the superficial conscious level of my mind into the intimacy of my unconscious psychic life. I often tell the patient himself about the dream. First because it generally expresses something that I should have liked to say to him but have held back and repressed for some reason or other, perhaps through fear of unduly influencing him. If I dream about it, I feel that some other part of myself is protesting against such excessive prudence, that in this particular case my reserve is sinful. As he listens to the account of my dream and its significance, the patient sees both my great anxiety to respect his moral autonomy and also the fact that I have something to say to him which I cannot withhold without betraying the trust he has reposed in me.

But above all, to tell one of my own dreams to a patient who is telling me his shows the reciprocity of our mutual relationship. Reciprocity is characteristic of all spiritual experience, as Nédoncelle has demonstrated in his book *La réciprocité des consciences.*[1] Not only, that is, do I have for the patient as much love as he has for me, but my own personal life is as committed as is his to the common adventure of his treatment; our dialogue arouses in me, as surely as it does in him, a fruitful inner debate; the evolution of my own life is going to be affected as much as his—my own self-knowledge, my own liberation from complexes, as well as his. This is what characterizes the medicine of the person, this commitment of the person of the doctor himself in his personal relationships with his patients.

Fine things are often said about disinterested love. But dis-

[1] Maurice Nédoncelle, *La réciprocité des consciences*, Aubier, Paris, 1942.

interested love is like the one-way charity of almsgiving, whereas all true love is reciprocal. I would not care for it at all if my wife's love for me were disinterested. I want her love for me to give her a personal—and so not a disinterested—joy. Our patients too are always afraid that we will be interested in their diseases but not in themselves as persons. They know very well that habit turns work into a mere routine. They know that through seeing one patient after another we are in danger of falling into a routine of no longer being sufficiently personally interested in them.

This is the explanation of certain frequently occurring dreams. A patient tells me that in his dream he came to see me, but my house and my consulting room were full of people. I was going about saying a word to everybody but paying no special attention to him. Of course, there is something infantile in this need, not only to be loved, but to be the object of a specially attentive love. All sick people show infantile characteristics—whether their disease is psychic or organic—because their sickness has made them weak like children, whose need for security is tremendous. If we understand and accept this need, this appeal, we will not mind having a sick person show an infantile type of behavior, since he is not capable of acting differently. By the very act of responding to his need we shall be helping him to evolve and overcome his infantile reactions. In any case the universal law is that one cannot help anyone at all to develop unless one first accepts him as he is.

Quite recently one of my women patients had a dream analogous to those I have just been speaking of: My room again was full of people. But now—still in her dream—she came up to me, and far from being jealous, she took a lively interest in what someone else was saying to me about his own difficulties. It is quite clear that this patient is beginning to be aware of a wider horizon, more adult and less egocentric, that she is finding in her own experience a pleasure in understanding others, and in her turn helping them. Another patient often asks me, when she first comes into my consulting room, to open the window wide for a moment. I realize that this symbolic action means that she wishes to clear the room of the memory of all the other consultations that I have had before. Indeed, she sometimes says, "You are very kind but don't you love all your patients in just the same way?"

Remarks like that always make me shudder. Suppose love did become a "job"! How horrible! Love can never be anything but an adventure, an adventure that is quite new every time. That is why I set so much store by always remaining an amateur. I do not like people to look upon me as a psychotherapist. I feel that it is a misunderstanding of the true meaning of the medicine of the person, because it is pinning a conventional label on me. The medicine of the person is an adventure! Psychotherapy is a technique that can be taught, and of course I make an effort to learn it. But even if I knew it all perfectly, I should not for that reason be a doctor of the person, whereas a surgeon, for example, though knowing little about psychotherapy, can be an excellent doctor of the person.

The medicine of the person implies taking an interest in the person of the patient, in the personal significance of his disease, whether one is a psychotherapist or a surgeon. There is, however, a primary requirement that is common to both psychotherapy and the medicine of the person, namely, honesty. The decisive factor in any psychotherapeutic cure, to whatever school of thought the doctor belongs, is this need for the patient to be utterly truthful. Often he feels this requirement even before the treatment begins, and thus hesitates, sometimes for years, to submit himself to it. But when confidence is established, hope grows: ". . . Perhaps, one day," a woman writes to me, "I shall have the courage to be utterly truthful" —and now she has been.

I have sent a man to see a psychotherapist, and he comes back to tell me about the success of the cure. "I see," he says, "that without suspecting it I was living a lie to myself." Now, a patient's honesty affects his doctor. His adventure in honesty requires the same adventure in honesty on our part. And our own honesty in our personal lives creates the climate in which he will be able to make his way toward a more complete honesty.

COMMITMENT

A patient confides his hesitancy to me. He has told me things that he has concealed from his wife. Talking to me about them was already a great step toward liberation. But now he wonders whether he ought to risk upsetting his wife by telling her. It is of course not my business to advise him. This must be a quite personal decision made without prompting from anyone else. He must weigh all sorts of factors of which I know nothing. But in order to help him I talk to him, I tell him how happy I am to be able to tell my wife everything, and talk about that complete mutual openness which everyone intuitively feels to be the ideal in marriage. He himself tells me how it hurts him not to be frank with his wife.

Then I suddenly remember that I have myself something to tell my wife that I have kept from her—something much easier to say than what this man is hesitating over confessing to his wife. Nevertheless I have put it off. Several times I have promised myself that I would do it, but each time I have postponed the confession. Oh! We are all alike, fainthearted! But now I must really make up my mind; I cannot see this man again before I have put everything right with my wife.

Marriage too is a great adventure in honesty, and that is what invests it with its prodigious human value. The marriage ceases to be an adventure the moment the partners begin to lie to each other, or merely to hide things from each other. It is sometimes done with the laudable intention of avoiding arguments! But the marriage is in danger of sinking into a gloomy twilight, into a mere routine of living together, and finally into boredom. On the other hand, as soon as husband and wife have the courage to be completely open with one another, whatever the cost, their marriage becomes once more a wonderful adventure. They begin to grow together again; they are able to face the problems of mutual adaptation that they have been tempted to avoid for the sake of peace; they must get rid of all sorts of prejudices; they must both grow beyond themselves.

That is why God said, "It is not good that the man should be alone" (Genesis 2:18). Alone, a man quickly loses his spirit of adventure. He fossilizes. It is not long before he is deluding himself and lying to himself. In the encounter with another person, in frank and open dialogue, he learns to know himself, whether it be in the psychologist's consulting room or in the intimacy of marriage. But a course of psychiatric treatment lasts only a short time, whereas marriage is for life. Marriage is therefore an excellent instrument for the constant renewal of adventure, at once both stimulating to the personal development of each of the partners and enriching to their union.

You have seen, in the incident I have just reported, how readily the adventure of work and the adventure of marriage affect each other. Life is a unity, and we cannot be different in our relationship with our patients from the way we are in our relationship with our wives. Either we play hide-and-seek with both, or we accept the great adventure of honesty. I am quite willing to tell a patient about experiences I have had in my personal life, thanks to him, following upon our conversations.

This may be a great help to him in realizing that I too have my battles and my defeats, my backslidings. But it is particularly a question of honesty toward him, since if he is exceptionally frank with me, it behooves me to be the same with him. I think what distinguishes me most clearly from the specialists in psychotherapy of all the varying schools is this commitment of my person in the dialogue with the patient, my readiness to talk to him about my own problems. This is what gives a spiritual tonality to our encounters, for all spiritual relationships are reciprocal.

A psychotherapeutic specialist, on the other hand, is bound by his "technique," by the rules or his art, to maintain an absolute reserve, to wait for his patient to open his heart, taking care not to open his own heart to the patient. It is understood that this rule is a proper one during a course of psychoanalytic treatment. But the moment will come, even for a psychoanalyst, as Dr. Flournoy wrote,[2] when he must "become human," that is to say, go beyond his role as a pure

[2] Henri Flournoy, "Un Cas de Psychopathologie," *Archives des Sciences Physiques et Naturelles*, May-June, 1944.

technician to commit himself in a relationship with his patient as man to man, in full reciprocity.

At that point the psychoanalyst, like every other kind of doctor, will reveal himself to be a doctor of the person. His consultations will become a personal adventure, not only for his patients, but also for himself. This is why the thing that characterizes the medicine of the person, the self-commitment of the doctor in the dialogue, seems to me to be impossible to teach. I am always embarrassed when asked what is the meaning of persons, what the medicine of the person consists of. I have felt this more especially in America, for Americans like a clearly formulated doctrine and a technique that can be taught. The answer is that I do not know, or at least that I do not know how to explain it; I can only try to help people to feel it. Many definitions of the medicine of the person have seemed to me in general to be excellent. But there always appears to be something missing, something that cannot be said but only experienced, something that is in fact an adventure of the person.

On the other hand, a thing that struck me in America was the spirit of adventure that animates the whole nation. It was when I was there that I saw how badly our old Europe needs a radical renewal. To the question "What is work?" the answer in Europe is "A duty." In America it is "An adventure." Americans readily change their jobs, or go from one task to another within the same profession. They move from Boston to Los Angeles or from Miami to Chicago, whereas Europeans cling to their parish pump and to their job, at the risk of losing all their spirit of adventure.

One of the results is that work is held in much greater esteem in the New World than in the Old. The shameful thing in America is *not* to work, even if one is rich enough not to need to earn one's living. There persists in the European mind, on the contrary, a certain prejudice against work. The honorable thing is to have inherited from one's forebears a fortune big enough to make possible a life of idleness. I remember a Frenchwoman of aristocratic family who came to confide in me her worries about her grown-up son, who was seriously ill adapted to life. "His father," she told me, "never worked all his life, nor did his grandfather. Working for their living they would have felt to be beneath their dignity."

Obviously I am speaking here of western Europe. In Communist Europe one finds once again a zealous attitude to work that is comparable with that of the Americans. It is doubtless no matter of chance that Russia and the United States have become the two great powers of our modern world. The reason why work is given a place of honor in Communist countries is surely that they have a spirit of adventure: they are intent on building the world of tomorrow, on living boldly the great adventure of technical and scientific progress.

Furthermore, in Europe we have a sense of history. Every new idea is at once classified and explained in terms of the slow historical process which has produced it. America is not interested in history; it is oriented toward the future. A new idea is grasped at and assessed in terms of what can be got out of it for the future. In every hospital I visited I was shown, with legitimate and rather solemn pride, the research unit, which embodies this passion for adventure so prevalent in America.

And yet, in that country, new as it is, I noted quite a number of signs of nostalgia for the heroic adventures of the early days. I remember the restaurants whose interior décor recalls the log cabins of the Far West, and around the outside of which are disposed large numbers of wagon wheels to remind one of the fantastic ventures of the race to the West. One feels that already the very perfection of the organization of the new continent, its success, its power and prosperity, the standardization of the "American way of life," are leaving behind a feeling of regret for the distant early days, when everything was still an adventure.

CHAPTER 7

The Adventure of God

THE QUESTION now arising in our minds is: What is the significance of this powerful instinct for adventure which animates us? What is the meaning of this indestructible instinct which when given free play impels us to action and when repressed goes on tormenting us inwardly? Well, I think the answer is contained in the famous biblical affirmation "God created man in his own image" (Genesis 1:27). If man is in the image of God, God must have implanted in him certain of his own dominant qualities; and one of those qualities is the spirit of adventure which subsists in God himself.

Man, therefore, as it were feels his divinity when he commits himself totally in an adventure. The fulfillment he experiences in it brings with it a feeling of exaltation. Whether he is a believer or not, he experiences in some measure his resemblance to God. This is the source of the religious tonality that every great adventure takes on for the person participating in it. He feels himself carried away by the afflatus of the Spirit. He feels himself raised above his ordinary humanity. Proof lies in the word we use to describe the state of mind of a person engaged in an adventure—"enthusiasm," which literally means "feeling God within oneself." This is still true even if the adventure is directed against God: The word "crusade"

—an eminently religious word—is readily used of an atheistic campaign against religion! To fight against God and to serve him are both ways of taking him seriously.

God is animated in the highest degree by the spirit of adventure. We might call him the great adventurer—without any of the bad significance that this word can have. This is precisely what we are saying of him when we call him the Creator. All of us feel that to create something is an adventure. How much more so the creation of the world! God committed himself to the work of creation freely, but also totally. What a commitment! It blazes out from the very first chapters of the Bible.

We recognize at once the law of adventure, developing and gathering speed and strength once it has started. One step leads on to another. After creating light—that is to say, energy and waves—God creates the physical world and the heavenly bodies; then the earth and the vegetable world; then the rhythms of time and the seasons; then the lower animals, reptiles, fish, and birds; then the higher animals, cattle, the mammals.

God abandons his majestic solitude and serenity to open the infinite page of physical reality. He burdens himself with cares, if I dare put it so, and multiplies them! He shoulders the risk that is always involved in passing from the abstract to the concrete, a risk which we ourselves run whenever we leave the realm of free speculation and face the material world with its stubborn resistance, and the limitations of finite time and space. In this adventure of reality we are always encountering unforeseen obstacles, unexpected difficulties, new problems to solve, things that continually renew the adventure and make it grow. As soon as we create something we hasten to compare it with what we hoped in theory that it would turn out to be: Is it pressing the analogy too far to imagine this same slightly anxious emotion in God himself? Like us, He did at each stage look over his work and reassure himself: "And God saw that it was good" (Genesis 1:25).

But the adventure proceeds! God immediately engages in an adventure that is much more risky still. He creates man "in his own image"—that is to say, a being himself endowed with a spirit of adventure, capable of allowing himself to be carried away by love of adventure to the point of resisting God and upsetting the perfect order of creation. At the Collége de Genève it was my good fortune to have as my professor of natural sciences Eugène Pittard, who was to become one of the most eminent authorities of our time in the field of anthropology. I remember the time when he suddenly asked if any of us had a Bible in his briefcase (we were at an age when religious instruction is normally given). He opened the book and made us read aloud the account of the Creation.

We were quite surprised and impressed, for our Collége, although founded by Calvin, was bound for the sake of religious peace by a regulation rigorously excluding all but secular instruction. This, however, was not religious propaganda. Eugène Pittard was concerned to make the quite objective point that the adventure of the world, as science allowed us more or less to reconstruct it, corresponded closely to the adventure of God as revealed in the Bible. Exactly the same theme was developed recently with great authority by another scholar, Father Teilhard de Chardin.

Unlike the Greek myths, which put the appearance of demigods before that of man, the Bible, like modern science, situates the appearance of man within the continuity and as the last stage of the whole saga of creation, following upon that of the higher animals. Furthermore, just as science finds that there is an inexplicable mutation from animal to man, so the Bible asserts that the creation of man is the result of a special creative initiative by God. Man is more than a perfected animal. God willed him to be quite distinct from the animals: Man alone he created "in his own image."

This means particularly that God endowed man with his spirit of creative adventure, as is expressly indicated in the biblical account, where God says to the first human couple, "Be fruitful and multiply, and fill the earth and subdue it" (Genesis 1:28). God thus gives man a share in his own sovereignty over nature, starting him off on the great adventure of technical advance, which is nothing other than the putting to use of the forces of nature. Later on he tells man to give a name to each species (Genesis 2:19), thus starting him on the great adventure of science, which in essence consists of giving a name to everything so as to be able to define, classify, and analyze it.

God surrounds man with all his solicitude, blesses him, and speaks to him with wonderful gentleness and consideration, as to a partner. He gives him a wife so that he may know the adventure of living in community. God calls upon man to collaborate with him: He lays out a magnificent and fertile garden for him and tells him to tend and cultivate it (Genesis 2:15), thus starting him on the great adventure of work.

Many people imagine that the biblical view of work is that it is a curse, a punishment imposed by God upon man after his proud disobedience. This idea is in accord with the pejorative interpretation of work and helps to maintain its currency; but it is quite false. As I have just pointed out, work is instituted by God before the Fall and is presented to man as an adventure, a sharing in the divine activity. As Pope Leo XIII said in the encyclical *Rerum Novarum*, "As regards bodily labor, even had man never fallen from the state of innocence, he would not have remained wholly unoccupied; but that which would then have been his free choice and his delight, became afterwards compulsory, and the painful expiation for his disobedience."

So work, which before the Fall was a pure and lovely adventure, is turned into wearisome toil—not as a result of the spirit of adventure itself but because of its wrong use: man wished to conduct his adventure on his own, in his own way, instead of entering into God's adventure. From then on the burden of toil weighs upon him, and takes on the form of slavery, and often is a crushing and fruitless effort. Man comes to curse his labor, forgetting its true meaning—that it is an adventure to which God in his goodness has called him.

In 1959, at the meeting in Bad Boll of the International Group for Medicine of the Person, we devoted a session to the question of man's attitude to his work and the repercussions it has on his health. Professor Lindeboom, of Amsterdam, showed us that a negative idea of work is very often a cause of illness. Professor Karlfried von Dürckheim spoke of the ambiguity of work, of its being at one and the same time an opportunity for adventure with God and a risk of adventure against him. Dr. Arnold Müggli, of Zurich, described the often inhuman conditions of work today in the age of technology and suggested means of restoring to it its true character as a human adventure. And Mlle. Suzanne Fouché, of Paris, stressed the incomparable therapeutic value of work and the human dignity which the invalid discovers when he is helped to rehabilitate himself in an interesting and useful career.

The fact is that despite the Fall, despite all men's disobediences, work still preserves, in part at least, and by God's grace, the significance he gave it. It is a gift from God, like life itself. It is "the expression of life," as Roland de Pury has called it. In a letter to Rodin, Rilke writes, "It was not only in order to do a piece of study that I came to see you . . . it was to ask you how we ought to live. And you replied: 'through work.' "[1]

The Bible, especially the Book of Proverbs, is full of the praise of labor and of warnings against idleness and laziness. The Bible speaks of the skill of goldsmiths and weavers, the patience of peasants and vinedressers, and the wisdom and intelligence of scholars as talents given by God. Yahweh says to Moses, speaking of Bezalel, "I have filled him with the Spirit of God, with ability and intelligence, with knowledge and all craftsmanship, to devise artistic designs, to work in gold, silver, and bronze, in cutting stones for setting, and in carving wood, for work in every craft" (Exodus 31:3-5). I could give many more quotations. I would point out that Jesus himself worked as a carpenter (Mark 6:3) and that St. Paul was careful to say that he was only an amateur theologian, that in the midst of his missionary activity he always continued to earn his living by the work of his hands (Acts 20:34).

But let us return to the tragedy of the Fall. This was the risk which God accepted in creating man in his own image. In spite of this terrible blow, however, he does not relinquish his adventure. We see him setting to work at once to meet the immediate consequences of the confusion into which Adam

[1] Rainer Maria Rilke, *Lettres à Rodin*, Paul, Paris, 1931.

and Eve have fallen: he makes them garments of skins! (Genesis 3:21). But it is on the vast scale of the whole of history that the adventure of creation was to be continued paralleled in the adventure of salvation. It is a thrilling adventure, in which God must intervene again and again. He wants to save man, who has gone astray, and with him to save the whole of creation (Romans 8:19). He attempts to hold back Cain from the path of murder, and even afterwards protects him against the vengeance of men (Genesis 4:15). He sees, "grieved to his heart" (Genesis 6:6), the increasing wickedness of mankind. He makes a great attempt with the flood to start man on a new adventure, and blesses him again, confirming his power over nature (Genesis 9:1-3).

There are many more instances, and I invite you to reread those astounding pages of the Bible, filled as they are with the dramatic vicissitudes of the supreme adventure of the love of God. He enters upon a new course of action. He chooses a man, Abraham, as the instrument of his adventure of salvation and impels him into the adventure of faith: "Go from your country and your kindred and your father's house" (Genesis 12:1). From the seed of Abraham he is to fashion for himself his people, through whom his purpose will be carried out. You know what follows—all the adventures of the patriarchs, and those of Joseph at Pharaoh's court (Genesis 41:14). Then God calls on Moses to deliver his people out of bondage (Exodus 3:10) and to dictate his Law to them (Exodus 20). Read again all the stories of the forty years in the desert; the dual adventure of God and man goes on in their dialogue, their conflicts, and their reconciliations.

The historical adventure is always made incarnate in personal adventures. There is the great and dolorous adventure of Moses, the picturesque adventure of Balaam and his ass (Numbers 22), the victorious adventure of Joshua, those of the Judges, then of Samuel, of the Kings, of their fidelities and their betrayals, and of their quarrels, which once again compromise everything. Then there are the prophets, Isaiah, Jeremiah, Ezekiel, the greater and the less, like Amos the humble shepherd, all of them, one after another. The adventure goes on because it is always starting again. A new adventure springs into being every time a man listens to God and faithfully obeys him. It is soon exhausted and has to be reborn. But Yahweh "does not faint or grow weary" (Isaiah 40:28).

The prophet is the man who can perceive the work and purpose of God in the apparently senseless process of history. But God does not speak to prophets only. He calls every man; he stubbornly maintains the dialogue. He speaks to the humblest, to Gideon; to the most sorely tried, to Job; he speaks to David at the time of his sin and to Solomon at the height of his glory. He remains faithful to his covenant with man; it is always through man that he pursues his creative work, calling him constantly to collaborate by his obedience, to enter into his adventure.

The God of the Bible is the God who acts. This is what distinguishes him from the God of the philosophers and from the gods of all the other religions. He is the God who commits himself. He commits himself in every man's life. He does not interest himself only in man's religious life but in his whole life, in his work, in his occupation—as potter, as shepherd, as official, as housewife—and he turns that occupation into a veritable adventure. He is a God who works. The Bible uses a powerful image when it speaks of the "hands" of God (Isaiah 45:12).

And then the adventure of God is worked out in that of his people, in history, in wars, in victories and defeats, in successes and failures, in prosperity and want. Israel is called the "vineyard of the Lord of hosts" (Isaiah 5:7), in which he toils, prunes, and harvests. He responds to the sufferings of men and comes everywhere to their aid, constantly committing himself in action. Read the prophets again; listen to the searing words he addresses to them and entrusts to them for his people. He hopes, he is moved, he calls, he travails, but each time, too, men's hearts are hardened again. The most clear-sighted prophet trembles before this threat of failure and cries out, "O that thou wouldst rend the heavens and come down . . . !" (Isaiah 64:1).

And God did come down in person. This was the supreme

adventure, with its supreme risk of disappointment and suffering. This was the earthly adventure of Jesus, of Christmas, of the Gospel. Jesus said, "My Father is working still, and I am working" (John 5:17). He does not work in words only; he acts: He heals the sick, he raises the dead, he helps fishermen to make a good catch (Luke 5:3-11), he cooks fish (John 21:9), he makes himself a whip of cords and wields it (John 2:15). He observes, he understands, he shares in the personal adventure of each person—the husband man who tries to save a fig tree that no longer bears fruit (Luke 13:6-9), the woman who has lost a coin (Luke 15:8-10), the sower who scatters the seed, some of which will be lost; he likens himself to this last, thus clearly indicating that he accepts the risk of the adventure, knowing his efforts will be partly in vain.

Again, every one of Jesus' adventures is at the same time also a decisive personal adventure for everyone who encounters him. There is that of Nicodemus (John 3:1-21), that of the woman of Samaria (John 4:5-42), that of Zacchaeus (Luke 19:1-10), that of the rich young man (Matthew 19:16-22), those of each one of his disciples, and all the rest. But it is his own adventure which unfolds inexorably. It begins in the miracles and triumphs of Galilee. Then the threatening clouds gather ever more darkly around it as his adversaries lay their plots.

To his contemporaries Jesus was a true adventurer. His disciples were filled with such enthusiasm that they left everything to follow him in his extraordinary adventure. Later on they were to become discouraged when they saw the adventure turning out quite differently from what they expected. The multitudes turned away, and Jesus felt that even his most faithful companions were doubtful. "Will you also go away?" he asked them (John 6:67). In the end, when the disappointment was complete, one of them, Judas, was to betray him out of chagrin—it is easier to destroy one's adventure oneself than to have to see it slowly falling apart.

While the common people admired in Jesus the adventurer who hits out at the injustices of society, for the same reason he drew down upon himself the hate of the cultured, the distinguished, and the religious people of his day. He was continually defying and scandalizing them. They had made a study of the Law and laid down exactly what was meant by obedience to God. And now here was Jesus, calling himself the Son of God and constantly flouting their code. He healed the sick on the Sabbath day. He frequented houses of doubtful reputation and sat at table with moneylenders and prostitutes. He took under his protection the adulterous woman, whom the Mosaic Law decreed should be stoned to death. And when they tried to discuss the matter with him, he hurled invective at them and described as hypocrisy the rigorous morality they imposed upon themselves to please God. Thus the adventure of the conflict unfolded relentlessly. Jesus accepted it and followed it to the end, as it came to a head in the drama of the Passion. He was dragged before Pilate by the leaders of the Jews as a dangerous adventurer. The calm objectivity of the Roman procurator was not sufficient to save Jesus, and his crucifixion followed.

But God did not let go. He raised Jesus Christ and fortified his disciples, sending to them his Holy Spirit. Once more he chose a people—his Church. Entrusting his sacraments to it, he started it out on the great adventure of preaching the Gospel "to the end of the earth" (Acts 1:8). There follows the absorbing adventure of the book of the Acts of the Apostles, the wonderful adventure of St. Paul. The apostles proclaim to the Jews, and then to the Greeks, the decisive intervention of God in the world. Henceforward a meaning, a direction, and goal are given to the whole of history as well as to the life of each individual person. "Forgetting what lies behind and straining forward to what lies ahead, I press on toward the goal," wrote St. Paul (Philippians 3:13-14). That is indeed adventure!

The Christian churches today are seeking to recover the missionary outlook of the early pioneers. Until just a few years ago, missions meant only the sending of Gospel witnesses out to distant and pagan peoples. Now we realize that it involves a much more immediate and comprehensive adventure, affecting us all: the need to restore its soul to our so-called

Christian (but profoundly de-Christianized) civilization. This is the significance of the integration of the International Missionary Council into the World Council of Churches which took place at the Assembly of the World Council in New Delhi in 1961.

On the Roman Catholic side, a typical effort is that of Father A. M. Henry and his "Word and Mission" team. In his book *L'Annonce de l'Evangile Aujourd'hui*,[2] Father J. Daniélou points out the distinction that should be made between the *Kerygma* (the "very first announcement of the Christian event") and catechesis, homily, or theology (the instruction of the faithful), to which preaching had hitherto been confined in countries that were within the Christian tradition. "The *Kerygma*," he writes, "has as its object the announcement of an event. It is the proclamation of something that is happening. This makes the *Kerygma* essentially different from instruction bearing on a theoretical doctrine."

What is this but the same distinction as I have made here between the first, explosive phase of an adventure and its later, systematized and organized phase? The primitive missionary adventure which must be rediscovered now is the proclamation of the adventure of God in saving the world, whereas all the theology that has developed over the centuries is only systematic reflection of this fundamental event. What gave Pope John XXIII his universal spiritual authority was the fact that throughout his pontificate, and especially through the Second Ecumenical Vatican Council, he sought to restore to the Church the dynamism, the suppleness, and the youth that characterize an adventure in its developing phase, when it is not yet overorganized.

Throughout the history of the Church renewals such as this have taken place whenever new servants, at God's call, have rediscovered the spirit of adventure. The distinction now suggested to us between the *Kerygma* and instruction is reminiscent of that which has often been made between prophet and priest. The prophet always has a universal character, while the priest belongs to a particular church. All men feel themselves

---

[2] Published by Le Cerf, Paris, 1962.

personally affected by the words of a prophet, whatever confession or church they belong to.

The ecumenical character of the *Kerygma* is also clear. I have had experience of this in recent years. It is not for the doctor to play the role of the clergyman, to give religious instruction to his patients. On the other hand, called as he is to succor men and women in all their sufferings, all their infirmities, and all their despair, he cannot conceal from them that beyond all the technical succor he provides there is available succor from God. This assertion is the *Kerygma*. There is a religious need common to all men; all men have a common religious experience which forms a shared background to their lives, antecedent to any individual formulation in accordance with a particular religion or church. Professor Karlfried von Dürckheim calls it the religion beyond religions,[3] and it is of tremendous interest to the doctor.

Religious instruction pertains to the churches, but the *Kerygma* is universal, and it is the duty of every doctor to proclaim it. This is the common ground on which for the last fifteen years doctors belonging to all the branches of the Christian Church have come together in the annual meetings on the "Medicine of the Person." The meetings have never been marked by any theological controversy or sectarian polemic. And this has not meant that we were maintaining a politic silence about our personal convictions or our religious experiences. On the contrary, we discovered how much enrichment and strength we could derive from each other, to help us in the universal spiritual ministry we must exercise toward our patients, precisely because we belonged to different churches. That is why the meetings have been a real adventure for us all.

It is as a result, then, of being made in the image of God that man throws himself so eagerly into all the adventures God opens up before him—not only religious adventures such as those I have just referred to, but all the others: the adventures of science, of the exploration of earth and sky, of art, of

[3] K. von Dürckheim, "Religious Experience beyond Religions," in *Modern Trends in World Religions*, Open Court, LaSalle, Ill., 1959.

culture and philosophy. It is the adventure of God itself which is being worked out in every human adventure.

The Bible is the book of adventure and must be read as such. Not only the adventure of the world and of humanity, but the personal adventure of each man and woman whom God touches, calls, and sends into action. In it we find that coming together of adventure and poetry to which I referred in connection with myths and epics. Children feel this spontaneously, and hence in one sense we are to divest ourselves of our cold intellectualism and become children again. In the Bible we rediscover the deep emotion which rekindles in us the fire of adventure. The Bible also gives adventure its true meaning, for from end to end it reveals what is at stake in all our work, all our activity, all our choices, and all our self-commitment.

Part II

THE RISK

CHAPTER 8

The Characteristics
of Adventure

THE TIME HAS COME to try to define adventure more precisely. Once again it is in the light of the Bible and of what it tells us of God's adventure that I shall be able to describe its characteristics. There are five which seem to me to be the most important:

1. Adventure is a manifestation of oneself, a form of self-expression.
2. It innovates and invents; it is ingenious.
3. It is coherent, evolving in the pursuit of a single final goal.
4. This goal is love; it is love which suggests the goal, and love which directs and sustains the adventure.
5. Lastly, it involves necessarily the running of a risk.

Adventure, then, is first a form of self-manifestation. The Bible proclaims this supremely in respect of God: God manifested himself in the Creation, in all his acts, in all his interventions in favor of his people, of all men, of the whole universe. The majesty of God shines out of nature, in its grandeur and perfection. The Psalms, Job, and the Song of Songs are especially rich in poems on this theme, and all are infused with a vigorous spirit. The high acts of God, the adventures to which he committed himself to succor his chosen people—for example, in order to bring them out of Egypt (Exodus 20:2)—are constantly recalled. They manifest his power and his loving-kindness toward Israel; they are the foundation of the sovereign authority which he claims over that people. Turning to the New Testament, we find that from beginning to end the person and the ministry of Jesus Christ are recognized as the manifestation of God. He manifested the divine glory which shone through him in all his acts, from his first miracle at Cana onwards (John 2:11).

God manifests himself in his works, expresses himself in them, reveals himself in them. They are not independent of him like things one produces and then abandons when they are completed. They remain in him, and he in them; they are in his hand and continue showing forth his presence. In this sense one can say that the Bible is existentialist: Never once does it present God as a philosophic concept, an abstract essence, an unexpressed potential. God is what he has done, what he does. His power is his creative acts, his goodness is his acts of goodness, his justice is his acts of justice. God's adventure is God himself, God who manifests himself, who manifests his life. So the fruit ripening on the tree manifests its life.

This function of self-expression has also been given by God to every creature, in an ascending scale corresponding to the scale of differentiation in creation. Plant life is endowed more highly with the function of expression than the mineral, the animal more highly than the plant, and man much more highly than the animals. Zoologists, such as Professor Portmann of Basel,[1] have made a study of this function in animals. Portmann has shown that many of the anatomical and behavioral characteristics of animals can be understood only from the point of view of self-expression. But this is more a collective expression, each according to its species, than a personal self-expression. Each animal displays what it can—the elephant its tusks and the tiger its whiskers.

[1] Adolf Portmann, *Um eine basale Anthropologie*, Rentsch, Zurich and Stuttgart, 1955.

A man, however, can cut his whiskers off! He manifests and expresses himself precisely insofar as he rises above nature, choosing an original and personal form of self-expression. In man too, each individual displays what he can but in his case there is infinitely more variation. One man displays his intelligence, another his good looks, another his devotion; one his family tree, another his university degrees, or his zeal, his ingenuity, or his humor; one his skill at cooking, at sewing, or at playing the violin, another his wealth or his faith.

I could, of course, prolong the list endlessly. Each individual plays the card he holds, and that is his adventure. What I am concerned to point out is the vital need felt by every human being to express himself, to manifest his person to the outside world—and in the most personal manner possible. And what a joy this is to him! Consider the joy of the child when he succeeds in building with his blocks a tower higher than ever before, so that he receives the admiration and congratulations of his parents. Or later when he comes home and shows them an essay prize that may perhaps kindle such an enthusiasm for literature as to shape his whole future career. Oh, how important it is for a child, and for his development, that he feel himself appreciated by his parents for his successes in the realization of himself, that he feel they are proud of him!

Consider also the ingenuous joy of a woman who sees that she is beautiful, admired, and desired; the joy of a scientist who manifests his genius in his discoveries; the joy of the artist who reveals his vision of the world in a masterpiece; the joy of the industrialist who manifests his power to work in the extension of his undertaking. An old man is telling me about himself. He has just lost a friend who played a part in political life. There are long obituary notices in the papers. The man speaking to me had also once been urged to enter politics but had refused. Had he accepted, he thinks, people would all be talking about him too, when he died. Do not smile; this is profoundly human.

It is a necessity of nature. To express oneself in action, in a creative work, is to fulfill oneself as a man, to put to fruitful use the talents one has been endowed with. Everyone who evades this fulfillment inevitably feels a sense of guilt. In 1961 the International Group for the Medicine of the Person held its conference at the Gethsemane Foundation in Casate Corte Cerro, Italy. We devoted the conference to a discussion of the fundamental need of man to fulfill himself. Professor Arthur Jorès, of Hamburg, spoke to us about what he called the diseases of man, that is to say, those which are peculiar to man, whereas many others are common to both human beings and animals. The former, he said, are always connected with failure in self-fulfillment. The animal, impelled by instinct, cannot fail to fulfill itself. But in the case of man, the price of his liberty is that he can spoil his life and fail to fulfill himself. The frequent result is that he falls ill, not only psychically, but also organically.

The converse is also true, that self-fulfillment always has great therapeutic value. There was one patient over whom I had taken great trouble, but in vain. His life was dull and unadventurous, lacking any dominant interest. How could he be made to have confidence in himself? He came back to me one day, transformed and cured. He had been abroad and had gone to an evangelistic meeting. Although he was a stranger there he had, without notice, been asked to lead in prayer. Unable to get out of it, he had in fact done quite well, and the evangelist had told him he had a real gift for prayer. His life was no longer mediocre—he had a personal gift that he could use.

At the Gethsemane Foundation we also talked about man's vital need to express himself in speech, in gestures, in mimicry, in laughter, and in tears. Here again, it is possible for a man to fall ill because of solitude, for lack of someone to talk with. And the tragedy is that his illness in its turn acts as an obstacle in the way of his making contact and having a real dialogue with anyone else. It is a vicious circle. The blocking of self-expression arouses guilt feelings, which make matters worse. All unexpressed emotion poisons the mind.

The second specific characteristic of adventure is its inventiveness, its propensity for innovation. I have no need to point out how conspicuous this characteristic is in the case of the divine adventure of creation! God was truly innovating when he made the world. But what I must emphasize is the insistence of the Bible on the abundance, the prodigious diversity, the fantastic ingenuity of divine inventiveness in the nature God created. All the Psalms, to which I have referred, singing of the glory of God, stress the superabundance of the unimaginable inventions presented to our eyes in the spectacle of nature. What would the Psalmist have said had he known all the marvels of nature that science has revealed to us since his day!

Every new discovery of science brings to light an original invention by God, an ingenious solution found by him to each of the technical problems raised by the functioning of the world and of all its component parts, of all the heavenly bodies, of all the physical and chemical reactions of matter, and of every living organism. It is in this connection, perhaps, that we can sense most keenly the atmosphere of adventure which surrounds his creative enterprise. What ingenuity! He does not present us with only one solution to a technical difficulty but with ten, twenty, or thirty. He invents feathers so that birds may fly, but he makes bats fly without feathers, and insects with a countless variety of membranes. And look at all the other means of locomotion he has invented: the fish that swims, the quadruped that gallops, the flea that jumps, the snake that crawls, and man walking upright on his two feet. He can transform fingernails into claws or into hooves. Think of the various means by which the dissemination of seeds is assured, of the means by which weak plants avail themselves of external aids in order to hold themselves up. Consider all the examples of symbiosis, the nitrogen cycle which makes animals tributaries of plants, the carbon atom which permits the numberless combinations of organic chemistry, the successive essays in visual organs, the various methods of reproduction in living things and the wonderful invention of sex, with all the differentiations it makes possible.

Since the time of the Psalmist man has discovered, or at least come to suspect, the immensity of the universe. We know now that the earth is only a small part of the solar system, and that there are vast numbers of suns and of nebulas. All the radiations, electrons, protons, and neutrons that dance everywhere about us and in us, in the nucleus of every atom—it was God who invented it all. Incidentally, the idea of the atom appears in the Bible (Proverbs 8:26) in a poem on the creative wisdom of God.

Of particular interest to the doctor is the admiration of the Psalmist for the wonders of the human body. "I am fearfully and wonderfully made!" he cries, speaking of his body, the formation of which in the womb was directed by God (Psalm 139:13-14). Not until twenty centuries later, if I am not mistaken, did men begin to dissect the human body, and it would seem that the Psalmist foresaw the marvels of ingenuity revealed by anatomy and physiology, as well as those of embryology, which is several centuries younger still! Psalm 8 sums up all that I have just said: the greatness of God which is manifested in nature, and in face of which man feels himself to be so small; and at the same time the greatness of man, who is "little less than God" because his Creator has endowed him with a power over nature which makes him henceforth a partner in the divine adventure of creation.

God indeed gives us the most authoritative example of creative imagination. He never copies himself—there is always something new and unexpected. This is what happens to our lives too, if we submit them to him. Do not all those who have some experience of a God-directed life tell us that with him everything happens differently from what we should expect? He has also endowed man with imagination. But man uses it chiefly to dream, while God applies it to reality. For every inventor, how many hundreds of thousands of people are there who never break out of the routine of their lives? They are life's prisoners. It never occurs to them that it is possible to think differently, to feel differently, to act differently from the way they have always done. Even the churches are astonishingly conformist, wrapped up in their traditions, averse to all innovation. Without a certain inner liberty, adventure is not possible.

God is liberty. He is a terrific inventor; and he is interested in everything—not in religion only, but in technology as well.

He has solved all the technical problems involved in the working and the continuity of the universe. Moreover, it was he who invented inventors, who invent by virtue of the creative faculties which he has given them. He loves them. I can imagine that he is proud of them as a father is proud when his son shows himself to be ingenious. He even shows extraordinary indulgence toward Jacob when he uses his cunning shamefully to deceive his too simple-minded brother Esau (Genesis 25:29-34) and his old father Isaac in order to get his blessing (Genesis 27:1-29). There are many other tricks recounted in the Bible, which seems to accept them with a complacency that is shocking to our moral sense: that of the midwives in Egypt who make false declarations concerning births and pretend that they were not present at the deliveries (Exodus 1:15-21); Samson telling lie after lie to his mistress (Judges 16:4-21); Tamar disguising herself as a prostitute (Genesis 38); and many more.

The third of the specific characteristics of adventure that I noted is its coherence and purposiveness. This is clear in the adventure of the creation, continuing into the adventure of salvation and all its vicissitudes. All human adventure also passes continually from resurgence to resurgence, because of the obstacles it meets and the problems to which it gives rise and which it has to solve. Hence the dynamic quality of growth that we have already noticed. But the adventure retains the unity of its goal; once committed, a man must be continually committing himself further if he is not to betray and lose his adventure, in spite of every obstacle.

The one-way character of adventure must also be noted. Unlike certain Greek philosophers, who had a cyclic conception of the world—history being seen as an eternal revolution without beginning or end—the Bible depicts it as a one-way journey which had a beginning, decided by God, and will have an end, in accordance with God's purpose. This is in fact what makes the evolution of the universe a divine adventure, what makes every adventure unique: It has its point of departure, and it marches inexorably toward its end—the missed chance never comes back.

One of my colleagues told me about his conversion. He came to faith on realizing the way in which events move in an irreversible procession, necessarily involving the idea of a divine purpose, and imbuing the world and history with meaning. Conversion took place, he told me, when he read Arnold Toynbee's book *Civilization on Trial*.[2] Either everything is absurd, as Camus feared,[3] going round and round forever, meaninglessly, or else everything has meaning, a beginning and an end, because God is engaged in an adventure into which are fitted all the adventures of men.

The great revelation of the Bible, however, is that the meaning of the whole of God's adventure is love. This is the third characteristic quality of adventure. It was for love that God created the world. It was for love that God made man in his own image, thus making him a partner in love, a being to whom he speaks, whom he loves like a son, and who can answer him and love him like a father. It is for love that God respects man's liberty, thus taking upon himself the formidable risk of man's mistakes and disobediences, the price of which he himself accepts and pays in the sacrifice of the Cross.

Love is also, in my view, the meaning of all human adventure. The instinct of adventure which God gave man in creating him in his own image is in fact, I believe, an instinct of love, a need to give himself, to dedicate himself, to pursue a worthwhile goal, accepting every sacrifice in order to attain it. This is the source of the joy of adventure, the joy of doing something, and of doing it for someone—for God who has called him to do it, if he is a believer, and in any case for mankind, to procure for mankind the benefits he is striving for. One is reminded of St. Ignatius Loyola's beautiful words: "We must make no important decision without opening our hearts to love."

Oh! I know all the objections that can be raised. There is the problem of evil, which no philosopher has yet been able to solve, evil which slips in everywhere and has also twisted the

[2] Arnold J. Toynbee, *Civilization on Trial*, Meridian Books, Inc., New York.
[3] Albert Camus, *Le Mythe de Sisyphe*, Gallimard, Paris, 1942.

92

divine meaning of adventure. There are adventures that are proud, cruel, deceitful, destructive, and stupid. But when we read the Bible carefully we discover a great mystery: that God reigns over evil, nevertheless without ever being its author or resigning himself to it; God's purpose is worked out not only through man's obedience but also by his disobedience.

I have already dealt elsewhere with this point, and I am not going to elaborate it here. But I must underline the extreme importance of this biblical perspective. Men may be mistaken in the goals toward which they strive in their adventures; they may be motivated by hate or a desire for revenge; they may be mistaken in the means they employ; but the force that impels them into all kinds of adventure, bad as well as good, is a divine gift, a sign of love. One only begins really to understand men when one sees that even in their worst errors they are moved by a desire to give themselves to something greater than themselves. When we realize this divine quality in our instinct of adventure, we feel our responsibility toward God to direct it in accordance with his loving will.

Moreover, from the psychological standpoint, it may be observed that all human conflicts are in the last analysis lovers' quarrels. People fight as fiercely as they do because both sides are convinced that they are fighting for a cause worthy of their love—for country, justice, or truth. This is true even of their conflicts with God, when they shake their fists at heaven. It is because they are disappointed in their need to love and be loved that they hurl themselves into the worst kind of adventures—into war and revolution. That is why there is always something noble in any revolt: a thrust toward an ideal, an outburst of adventurous energy, in which men commit their highest capacity for love.

CHAPTER 9

Success and Failure

IT REMAINS for us to consider the fifth characteristic of adventure: the risk that is always involved. We shall spend longer on it because it raises an extremely complex and interesting problem—that of success and failure. Obviously we cannot take part in any adventure without running the risk of failing in it, but it is just this that gives it what we call the "spice of adventure." The attraction of risk lies in its subtle ambivalence; a man fears it, but he loves it at the same time. When he loves it very greatly he represses his fear into his unconscious, and the feeling he has of being exempt from fear, of having overcome fear, excites him. But if he is very much afraid, his fear can also act as a spur, so that he puts forth a bigger effort of will in his determination to succeed. Clearly, then, it is the risk of failure which lends adventure—and also the study of the problem of adventure—its fascination.

The joy of adventure is an anticipation of the joy of success. One pursues an adventure joyfully and effectively so long as one has not lost all hope of success. Military leaders are well aware of this and must constantly be trying to keep up the morale of their armies, and especially that of the country, by means of reassuring news, even if sometimes it is false news.

But the leaders deceive themselves more than they deceive the people, such is the effect of an adventure on those who are committed to it. It takes such a hold on them that they fly in the face of the facts and still believe in the possibility of success when success is no longer possible. Doctors also are aware of the anticipation of success when they attempt to keep up their patients' morale. Very few skiers go skiing merely for the pleasure of the outing. What they want is the pleasure of racing downhill as well! If a person does not like parlor games, it is because he is afraid of losing. And if a player perseveres, despite numerous failures, against a stronger opponent, it is because he hopes in this way to improve his game and so some day get his own back.

The joy of success! Think of the joy a person has when he passes a difficult examination—or even one that is not very difficult! What is an examination success, even a graduation, *sub specie aeternitatis?* Yet at the time it seems to eclipse everything else. For a moment the world, life, and all other problems fade away. The joy of success is everything. On the other hand, a person who is not enjoying success is ill. I often see such cases. A student is terrified of failing in an examination for which he is nevertheless well prepared. He realizes quite well that his panic is unhealthy. But it is on the morrow of his success that the sign of his illness is most clearly seen, in his incapacity to enjoy it. Of this he is much less conscious. His success he feels to be an unmerited quirk of fortune which does nothing to reassure him on the subject of his personal worth. Truth to tell, I get far more pleasure from his success than he does himself!

Consider also the pleasure we can derive from the tiniest compliment from some important personage or someone whom we love. Much of the way we behave, even our protestation when we are complimented and our affectation of modesty, is a veiled means of soliciting compliments. A wife sighs loudly while washing the dishes; it is not that she wants her husband to come and help her, but she would like him to compliment her on her devotion to duty. And think of the minor pleasures afforded by various kinds of worldly success, and all the effort and expense that men and women will go to in order to secure them, all the clever tricks they are capable of employing. A pretty dress, a new hair style in the latest fashion—here is quite an adventure for a woman, and for her husband if he understands her. And success in business! For a good businessman every enterprise is an adventure, and when he pulls it off he is as happy as a sandboy. And success in politics, in war, on the stage, in the university or the Church! If there had been no fear of failure, neither would there be any joy in success.

Such joy is legitimate. Jesus himself gave a sharp answer to the Pharisees who wanted to curb the enthusiasm of the crowds on his entry into Jerusalem (Luke 19:39-40). The Bible goes farther; it praises success. "Being wise, in the vocabulary of the Bible, is not so much knowing the last mystery of existence as knowing how to conduct oneself well in life: the wise man is a man who succeeds."[1] "David had success in all his undertakings; for the Lord was with him" (1 Samuel 18:14). I was recently in Lebanon and received a magnificent gift in the form of a large old Persian tray. Engraved in Arabic characters round the edge is the following maxim: "In the name of the merciful God: I cannot succeed without his help; no success is possible without his help; no victory without the help of God." It is an excellent souvenir of the fascinating country of Lebanon, unique in the world for the harmony and cooperation that have been established between Christian and Moslem Arabs.

It is a souvenir of the incomparable welcome we received in that country, in all kinds of places—the American University, the French University, the Order of American Missionary Doctors, the Cénacle Libanais, a meeting place for all intellectual currents, and many others. This idea of our entire dependence on the sovereignty of God is common to us all. The Bible is constantly speaking of success and prosperity as a sign of God's blessing. The Promised Land is the symbol of it, "a land flowing with milk and honey" (Exodus 3:8); and it is

[1] E. Jacob, "Sagesse," in *Vocabulaire Biblique*, Delachaux and Niestlé, Neuchâtel and Paris, 1954.

the meaning of Solomon's fabulous wealth (1 Kings 10:14-25).

But more striking still are the accounts of warfare, in which success is always considered as being proof of God's good will, even in the case of wars of conquest that are apparently quite unjust. In the perspective of faith every victory is attributable to divine intervention, especially an unexpected victory. "The Lord gave victory to David wherever he went" (2 Samuel 8:14). Defeat is a sign of the withdrawal of God's favor (Joshua 7:13). It calls for repentance, as in this national prayer after defeat: "O God, thou has rejected us, broken our defenses; thou hast been angry; oh, restore us" (Psalm 60:1). When their enemies inflict a defeat on God's people, the Israelites, these enemies are considered as being the instruments of the divine will: "The Chaldeans shall come back and fight against this city; they shall take it and burn it with fire" (Jeremiah 37:8). "Thus says the Lord of hosts, the God of Israel: Behold, I will send and take Nebuchadrezzar the king of Babylon, my servant" (Jeremiah 43:10).

The joy of victory and of success never lasts long, however. In the heat of the struggle the hoped-for victory is felt to be a decisive term beyond which all the future remains in the half-shadow. Whether it is a war to be won or merely an examination to be passed, our minds are so filled with this immediate object that we are incapable of seriously envisaging what may happen afterwards, which may be the more disappointing the more we have enjoyed our success.

But there is a much more profound reason for the prompt and inexorable extinction of the joy of success. It is part of our human nature itself, always torn between its insatiable desire for perfection and the impossibility of ever achieving it. Every success makes us feel more keenly, and more cruelly, how far we fall short of complete self-fulfillment. So for every book I read, there are a score of others that I regret not having read, and not being able to read. For every book I write, I think with regret of many others that I should like to write, and that I shall never write. For every patient I heal, I suffer at my powerlessness to heal others. Every friendship, every fruitful experience of human relationship makes me feel more sharply how far short we fall of the full fellowship to which we all aspire.

Every victory recalls the remark made by Napoleon Bonaparte's mother: "Provided it lasts!" "The insurmountable obstacle," writes Varillon,[2] "lies at the end of a road marked by obstacles that have been surmounted." Animals are necessarily successful in life. They eat, drink, sleep, warm themselves in the sun, and mate when they can; they suffer pain or pleasure or fear, devour their prey or are overcome by others stronger than themselves. All this takes place without any meaning other than the fulfillment of the laws and functions of their nature. Man, on the other hand, is capable of spoiling his life. "I've made a mess of my life!" How often have I heard this tragic phrase in the intimacy of my consulting room! And yet the lives of these people are not yet over. They may often seem to outsiders to be brilliant successes; sometimes they have even achieved the most enviable celebrity.

These are the most clear-sighted people, the most keenly sensitive to the great problem of humanity. They are conscious of an inability ever to escape, whatever they do, from the consequences of past errors, lost opportunities, an inability to shake off the feeling of total failure for which no partial success can compensate. They feel that they may well win many tactical victories, but still the strategic victory will elude them; that the balance sheet of their successes and failures, even if it seems to show a credit balance, will never be able to satisfy their longing to make a success of their lives.

We all feel that we have something tremendous at stake in our lives; that we have only one life to live; and that the stake is at risk in every minute of our existence (and every minute is unique), in every decision and option we make. Our decisions derive their importance and their savor from it, yet what we have at stake, we feel, is far more important than any single decision. All men are haunted to some extent by the fear of ruining their lives. Those who do not feel it have thrust it into their subconscious. Think how often we dream of failure,

[2] In *Chronique Sociale de France*, No. 5-6, October 15, 1955 (Groupe Lyonnais d'Etudes Médicales, Philosophiques et Biologiques).

SUCCESS AND FAILURE

dream of missing a train, a ship, or a plane, dream that some
important objective escapes us just as we are about to achieve
it, or that fearful monsters bar our way.

All parents are anxious about their children's future. They
look after their health and strength, instruct them, teach them
good manners, self-control, and ordinary prudence, all in order
to equip them for the struggle of life. If they compel their
children to follow courses of study that they detest, and are
perturbed when they are put down into the bottom grade
because their marks are not high enough in Greek or mathematics, this is not so much because they are worried about
their intellectual development; it is because diplomas and cer-
tificates are trump cards that will help them to win in the game
of life. The well-known educator Louis Raillon tells of a
young mother who asked him if there was a rapid method of
teaching her child to read.

"How old is he?" asked Raillon.

"He's four."

"Then there's plenty of time for him to learn to read!"

"But think—if he's going to succeed in life, he mustn't waste
any time! The whole of his time at school is going to be a
race against the clock!"

The whole of education, the teaching of good manners, and
character training are designed mainly with this in mind. Non-
Christian parents send their children to Sunday School because
"it may after all be of some use to them in their lives."

Life does resemble a huge game, and all the things we have,
know, and do are like so many pawns which we manipulate in
an effort to win. There are never enough pawns. Each individual chooses his pawns, or rather uses those he has available—his
body or his mind, his health or sickness, his family, titles,
reputation, wealth. In this way the ego is enlarged to include
all its pawns in order to increase its chances.

I sometimes shudder as I watch this universal comedy: All
these innumerable individuals, in every country and every walk
of life, in fashionable drawing rooms and disreputable saloons,
in universities, religious meetings, and night clubs—all are constantly motivated by the single aim of making themselves ap-

pear in the best possible light. They are all, and always, on the watch, anxious lest their weaknesses, their faults, their ignorance, their fads, or their failings be discovered, anxious to distinguish themselves, to be noticed, admired, or commiserated with. Some do it openly and naïvely, and are considered vain. Others hide it better, but are no less vain. They are all capable of cowardice, duplicity, and cruelty when the stakes are high enough. And yet there is a better side, a noble side: This whole enormous, costly, and constant effort to make some small mark on the great chessboard of life has its source in man's very human instinct of creative adventure.

It is not enough, of course, to have pawns. One must also know how to use them. And the more one has, the more difficult this is—and the more ignominious it would be to fail with so many pieces to play with! So it is that many people deny their talents, both to escape the responsibility that goes with them, and to insure against possible failure. The reason why so many people take pleasure in thinking and talking about their past misfortunes and the injustices they have suffered is partly to excuse themselves for not winning at every move as they would have liked, to make it clear that they have been laboring under a handicap. At times this attitude can verge on hypochondria.

We are all engaged in a rat race. No one is disinterested. The attempt to seem so is one more pawn brought into play in order to achieve one's end. "We are all seeking happiness." The remark is one I heard from Karl Barth, a theologian who certainly cannot be suspected of taking a view that confines human life within too human limits. Naturally there are religious people who criticize worldly careerists. They despise what the careerist is seeking—wealth, favors, pleasures, and honors. But they themselves are heavenly careerists, who hope through their contempt of even the lesser pleasures to achieve supreme bliss and are often looking for some compensation for the failures they have suffered in real life.

This is the source of the success of all those who promise success. In primitive societies it it the sorcerers who know the omens, who can interpret them and say what enterprise can be undertaken with a promise of success, as Lévy-Brühl has shown.[3] But who would dare to claim that any religion is quite purged of all traces of this magical outlook, that the search for God can ever be quite freed from all vestige of the hope of reward? "Commit your work to the Lord, and your plans will be established" (Proverbs 16:3).

Today the whole prestige of science, technology, and psychology has its roots in the promises they make of success—promises of the collective success of mankind, which, as discovery follows discovery, nurses its dream of indefinite progress in order to console itself for the stubborn ills that beset it still. What a success it will be to land on the moon and annex it, to conquer diseases that up till now have been incurable, to conquer hunger and poverty, tyranny and war, to increase the world's sum of well-being! Promises also of individual success: Science, technical skill, self-mastery, knowledge of the human mind, and an understanding of one's own temperament seem to each of us to be the means of increasing our chances of success.

Hence also the success of the institutes of applied psychology, efficiency clubs, schools of parenthood, and courses and books aiming to teach the art of succeeding. Indeed, they are often very good, offering true and pertinent insights, as, for example, when Mrs. Carnegie gives prudent advice to wives to show them how to help their husbands succeed.[4] It should, however, be noted that these courses and books are of most use to those who have already a strongly developed instinct of adventure. People who have constantly failed follow or read them without great profit and soon abandon them with a painful sense of having failed once more, and of feeling that the advice which works with others is of no use to them.

Medicine and the prestige it enjoys can also be interpreted from the point of view of the universal struggle against fail-

[3] Lévy-Brühl, *Primitive Mentality*, translated by L. A. Clare, G. Allen and Unwin, London, 1923.
[4] Mrs. Dale Carnegie, *How to Help Your Husband Get Ahead in His Business and Social Life*, The World's Work, Kingswood, 1954.

ure. Disease is a handicap in life, an obstacle to success, a
suspension of the adventure of life. This is why the Bible
frequently says of a man who has been healed that he "re-
vived." All healing is looked upon by the Bible as a victory of
God. God always wills the healing of any who are sick. He
accepts all our prayers for the healing of the sick. Glory be to
him when they are answered. But when they are not, many
sick people are troubled, and even more, perhaps, the healthy
people around them, who love them, tend them, and passionately intercede for them.

Nevertheless, it does happen sometimes that a sick person
overcomes his feeling of failure. "Those who remain ill are not
people who have been defeated," writes Mlle. Suzanne Fouché,[5]
a woman who was struck down in the prime of life by disease
and infirmity. From her own experiences she has learned what
new energies can spring to life in a human being when he
fights for his own social reintegration.

Many chronic invalids look forward with anxiety to the
future because of the threat that permanent disability will prevent their taking up their work again. But such a disability, far
from being an insurmountable obstacle, can be the starting
point of a great adventure, of fulfillment and success, provided
they are given practical assistance to make readaptation possible, and real fellowship to sustain their enthusiasm. It was
with this principle in view that Mlle. Fouché founded the
League which she directs, and which does so much good work.
She has organized twenty-one houses all over France where
the handicapped are offered the instruction and training they
need in order to enter upon a career that is more useful than
that which they have had to give up. The idea is that
eventually they may be able to say to themselves, "I should not
have lived such a successful life if I had not been disabled."

Sickness always means the interruption of work. In modern
medicine there is a tendency for the criterion of fitness for
work to take the place of that of healing. In the medical corps
during the war our instructions were to sort out the wounded

[5] S. Fouché, "La Participation Personnelle du Malade à Sa Guérison,"
Cahiers de Ladapt, Paris, July, 1961.

and give priority to those whose recovery was likely to be complete and rapid enough for them to be able to rejoin their combat units. But it can happen that a sick person undergoes experiences that are more valuable than all the successes of the healthy. Just because illness has brought a man up short in the rat race for worldly success, it can become an opportunity for withdrawal, for fruitful self-examination, for meeting God. "You know, my lord," Calvin wrote to an illustrious invalid, "how difficult it is amidst the honours, riches and influences of the world to lend an ear to God. . . . God has willed to take you aside, as it were, so as to be heard more clearly. . . . He has given you this opportunity to profit in his school, as if he wanted to speak to you privately, in your ear."

But at the first attack of disease, the first reaction of everyone is fear: fear of the revision of values it involves; fear of the privations and renunciations it is perhaps going to require. The most ordinary and everyday consultation is an appeal for help in removing an obstacle from the path to success. Every prescription and every piece of advice given by the doctor is, in the patient's eyes, a means of restoring his chances of success, threatened by disease or by some symptom. The brief question "Is it serious, doctor?" does not mean only "Am I in danger of serious suffering?" but also "Am I in danger of being stopped prematurely in my career, in my life's adventure, in the pursuit of all that I value?" Paul Ricoeur observes that "every illness from which we suffer is like a pawn advanced by death."

Death is the great failure. The menace of death hangs over every person's life. To hold back death is to delay the moment when the final balance sheet will be drawn up. The Great Book of Life will be finally closed, and no further credit entry will be possible. We forget that on the other page, the debit side, the fearful account will also be closed. Death is still the great enemy (1 Corinthians 15:26); but it is also a friend, the necessary transition toward a new life: "and death shall be no more, neither shall there be mourning nor crying nor pain any more, for the former things have passed away" (Revelation 21:4). There will be no more disease or infirmity, no more error or failure. In the perspective of resurrection, "death is no longer a failure . . . death is much rather that which delivers us from failure."[6]

A word must be said here about that slow approach of death we call old age. It is the doctor's duty to prolong life as far as possible. It is his duty to fight step by step against the attacks of old age and the infirmities it may bring. But this is not the whole of his duty. How does the aged person use the years of grace that the doctor's art has procured for him? Old age has a meaning; the progressive weakening, the deprivation and isolation it involves have a meaning. To spend one's time merely in flattering an old man in order to sustain his morale, in congratulating him on being able at his age to perform some physical feat, praising his "young heart" or his still acute hearing, is fundamentally to deceive him.

It is to divert him from the revision of values which he ought to be undertaking while he is still in possession of his faculties. The pursuit of success, the hard struggle to avoid failure, is appropriate enough in the prime of life. But whatever fruit this long effort has borne, it will seem of small account in the face of approaching death. What counts then is serenity. Serenity implies detachment on the part of the aged person from the legitimate values which he had to respect when he had the necessary strength, and an attachment to other values that lie beyond success and failure, beyond the attacks of age and death. "Old age is spoilt," writes Professor Adolf Portmann, "if one has not already sought to know the meaning of life."[7]

Rare is the death that is truly conscious, lucid, serene, and accepted. But how impressive such a death is! A young woman with whom I have worked for a long time falls seriously ill in the flower of life. From the start she feels intuitively that she will not recover. She makes out a list of the relatives and friends whom she wants to see once more before she goes, and invites them one by one to her bedside. She prays that she will

[6] Varillon, *op. cit.*

[7] Adolf Portmann, "Mensch und Natur," in *Die Bedrohung unserer Zeit*, Reinhardt, Basel.

be able to give to each the message she has in her heart for them, and dies the day after the last visit. I have myself been called for in this way by several of my best friends, when they knew their days to be numbered. At such times how profound the dialogue between us becomes! Oh yes! It is simpler than ever. Gone is the abstract discussion about the meaning of life: we live it together, in true communion. A few calm words, without affectation, springing from the heart. Memories, silences, mutual thanks. I shall always remember the last words of one of them, who had been my pastor: "Tournier," he said, "I bid you good-by, and assure you of my unfailing affection." Then follows prayer together, the supreme personal encounter, for I know no more authentic personal contact with a friend than when we are both in touch with God. And he who has met God personally is able to face with serenity all the detachments that are required of him. He can then make his own the words of that other old man, Simeon, when the child Jesus was presented to him: "Lord, now lettest thou thy servant depart in peace, according to thy word; for mine eyes have seen thy salvation" (Luke 2:29-30).

CHAPTER 10

The Psychology of Failure

LET US GO BACK now to the time when the battle of life is still on. The doctor is expected to use psychology in helping those who consult him. It is only just beginning to be taught in our medical faculties. But as soon as the doctor enters practice he finds many surprises in store for him, when his patients behave in ways that were never envisaged in the classical psychology courses he followed at the medical school. Some patients whom he has given up as lost make astonishing recoveries; others, attacked by minor ailments, sink down into death despite the best possible treatment. Extremely gifted people sometimes meet with nothing but failure, while others, less talented, go from success to success.

These facts, among many others, suggest the notion of an inner determinism of which neither anatomy nor physiology, neither physics nor chemistry, can take account. The doctor is quick to see that the greatest obstacle to success in life is not physical disease. Against this obstacle he is relatively well armed, with his lancet, his medicines, and his advice. There are other much more frequent obstacles which are due to psychic factors, and which are very difficult to eradicate.

Often the patient is conscious of these blockages. Observe the way men live: Constantly on the alert against the risk of failure that hangs over them, they can be compared to a country which must constantly see to its defenses against a possible aggressor. But panic will break out in such a country when, behind its external line of defense, a "fifth column" undermines the morale of the population, indulges in acts of sabotage, and prepares to hand over the fortress to the enemy. This is the situation of the person who is psychically sick. He feels within himself an inner enemy, an extremely powerful fifth column, clever and cunning—the negative forces of his subconscious, organizing failure and undermining all the efforts he makes to succeed.

In this light failure no longer appears as an accident, like honorable defeat in the face of unsurmountable external difficulties, but rather as the effect of a mysterious and secret impulse in the subject's own mind. This is what Sartre maintains[1] when he "accuses failure of being a free choice of failure."[2] We all protest in some degree against such views, which would make us responsible for our failures—guilty of them, rather than the victims of them. But psychological analysis is constantly confirming the validity of this interpretation.

Freud was the first to demonstrate it in his study of "bungled actions," which are a kind of failure in miniature in which the unconscious betrays its presence. A lapse of memory, a blank in an examination, a slip of the tongue reveal in us an unconscious impulse contrary to our sincerest and most ardent desires, sabotaging them in the shadowy secret places of the mind.

Here is an example: I was in the Marché aux Puces one day, thumbing through some old books. I picked one up, entitled *Etrennes Religieuses 1866*. It was an edifying religious annual, very much in the taste of its day. Glancing through the table of contents I saw "Louis Tournier: From the cure of souls to the sick-bed." What luck! Here was an article by my own

[1] J.-P. Sartre, *L'Etre et le Néant*, Gallimard, Paris, 1943.
[2] Jacques Sarano, *La Culpabilité*, Colin, Paris, 1957.

father, which, almost a century later, I could rewrite in my turn. Without haggling, I handed over the fifty cents and took the book away.

Delighted with my find, I told my family about it on my return home. Later that evening my wife asked to see the book. I could not find it anywhere! It was not until six months later that I found it on my shelves, in its proper place, where I had so often looked for it in vain. I had been conscious only of my pleasure at coming across a memento of my father, whom I had never known, and whose dominating interests I so strangely share. Within me, however, unconscious forces were striving in quite the opposite direction. They were trying to eliminate any reminder of my sufferings as an orphan. And more subtly still, by means of an Oedipean sense of guilt, these forces were trying to prevent me from competing posthumously with my father, not only in my work of soul healing among the sick, but also in writing books, as he did.

This mechanism, opposing our conscious aspirations with dark and contrary forces, may of course assume more serious proportions. It may go as far as failure neurosis, which causes the sufferer to act in the very way which will insure the failure of the enterprises he has most at heart—studies, career, marriage, for example. A thing that strikes one in the daily practice of psychology is the fact that the people who fail are those who try hardest to succeed. It is because they think themselves not to be gifted that they try so hard. But it is also because they try so hard and are so anxious that they fail!

One man is so shy and embarrassed that he makes me feel embarrassed as well, and I have the greatest difficulty in establishing personal contact with him. But I perceive that it is personal contact that he longs for most, that he needs most. The very intensity of his need prevents him from being natural, spontaneous, and straightforward. As a result he has had nothing but failure in his attempts to establish close relationships, particularly with those whose friendship he most desires to win. And these failures aggravate his emotional reactions, his shyness, and his anxiety—and the vicious circle is complete.

A certain spinster suffers terribly from the fear of being an old maid. She is obsessed by her longing for marriage. She hides her suffering as well as she can, but it is what makes her behave awkwardly in the presence of men. She does the wrong thing, makes stupid remarks, and finds herself paralyzed in the expression of her feelings. She is able to act a little more naturally when she is with a man whom she could not possibly marry—a priest, or a solidly married man whom she knows to be very much attached to his wife, or perhaps a fickle-minded man whom she would not want to marry anyway. But she is awkward and seemingly cold in the presence of the man she would like to marry, and who, no doubt, would be best able to appreciate her.

A patient blames himself for not making sufficient progress. He is always afraid I shall weary of him, and finally he does succeed in annoying me with his suspicions that I am getting tired of him. He attaches little value to what signs there are of real progress in his condition—and if there are but few such signs, it is precisely because he worries so much. His efforts to relax only make him more tense.

A student has always felt that his parents appreciated him less than his brother. He is so set on winning their esteem by means of success at the university that as the examinations approach he is a hundred times more anxious than his fellow students. He works without respite, to the point of break-down. But he also finds it hard to concentrate because his mind is constantly occupied by his anxiety not to fail. For his fellow students the examination is merely an interesting adventure. They enter it gaily and in a relaxed frame of mind. But for them there is nothing special at stake. They have not the additional worry of anxiety about losing their parents' affection. If they fail this time, they will try again next session.

Furthermore, these fellow students have many other interests in life besides their studies. Their successes on the sports field or with the opposite sex will provide a ready consolation for a reverse in the examination room. Our anxious student, however, permits himself no distractions. At bottom he is envious of the other students, but he dare not follow them for fear of failing in still other spheres, and especially because he is afraid that if he fails, his parents will accuse him—or he will accuse himself—of not having worked hard enough. Though he does not admit it, he hates his work because it is a prison, and his zeal for it is but a sham. He is dull, sullen, and lacking in the gaiety and verve that lead to success.

I do not intend to deal here with the very complex problem of the origin of anxiety states of this sort. Inborn temperament and heredity, psychological complexes and external circumstances all play their part. I have spoken elsewhere of the disasters of the negative upbringing given by those parents who are most anxious to insure their children's success. It is precisely because they are so anxious that they jump on their children's slightest mistakes of omission or commission. It is also from fear that they will make their children swollenheaded that they refrain from congratulating them on their good qualities—even when they themselves are quite proud of them. On the other hand, the entire literature of psychology points out the unconscious factors which determine the behavior of parents as well as that of their children, and which open to the latter the door of neurosis.

What I wish to underline is the commonplace but tragic vicious circle which inexorably accelerates the race toward failure once it is set up. Anxiety to succeed compromises success. The more the subject feels himself caught in this vicious circle, the greater will be his fear of failure, and the greater will be his anxiety. Anxiety engenders fear; fear paralyzes, breaks the spirit, takes away joy, deadens life, and engenders self-centeredness, absorbing the mind and turning it away from adventure. There is the vicious circle of impatience. The more a man longs to wipe out his past failures by means of a brilliant success, the less will he be prepared to put up with the delays and disappointments inherent in any undertaking. He rushes into it and loses his balance; or else he hesitates because he is afraid of making a false step, and always arrives too late to succeed.

There is the vicious circle of ambition for perfection. In his anxiety to rehabilitate himself, a man takes to loathing the mediocrity of his life, so that he derives no joy from such partial successes as do come his way, which in another man would be a spur to further progress. We find this in every sphere of life. Montaigne remarks that quite often people are made ill by their efforts to get well!

There is the vicious circle of emotion. The more failures accumulate, the greater is the stake involved in the next test, and the greater will be the emotion with which it is approached, so that a man is paralyzed by his own emotion, incapable even of using to the full his often considerable talents and knowledge. It is the best who are checked by emotion. And so they come to deplore their sensitivity, when in reality it is one of the highest human qualities.

Those around them also take a hand. There are always well-meaning people who are ready to say to the sensitive, emotional person, "Come now, calm down. Take a grip on yourself; if you worry like that you are sure to fail!" He is only too well aware of the fact, and this only increases his panic, so that such exhortations have precisely the opposite effect to that intended. It is worse still when his friends combine their remarks with moral judgements: "It is your pride that is holding you back," they say. "Don't think so much about yourself, and you will do better! Your fear of failure is due to your excessive self-conceit. Be more humble; be like us, and recognize your limitations." The result is that our emotional friend starts blaming himself for being emotional, as if it were a moral failing. I do not claim that he is not proud. But I am as proud as he is, probably more so; and it is the same pride that impels me to action and petrifies him! And if I am encouraged by my successes, it is simply because they flatter my pride.

The work done by Adler[3] has shown us the workings of the vicious circle of feelings of inferiority. The victim is constantly comparing himself with others. He overestimates their value, fails to recognize their troubles, difficulties, and failures, and further underestimates his own value, to the point of systematic self-denigration. Adler's fundamental idea is to help people to accept their limitations, their failings and failures, and their inferiority in this or that sphere. But what they find

[3] Alfred Adler, *Connaissance de l'Homme*, Payot, Paris, 1949.

most difficult to accept is the stultifying additional sense of inferiority derived from the vicious circle of emotion, which prevents them from showing what they are capable of in other spheres.

This is the tragic thing and we see it daily—the paralyzing emotion which grows, snowball-like, with life itself, condemning anyone who doubts his own abilities to ever-increasing doubt and to failure even where he might have been successful. The process can take on fantastic proportions: "I have never succeeded in anything in my life," remarks a young woman whom I admire for her courage and tenacity in overcoming a serious disability. Another woman tells me how much she longs to have another child, but her husband refuses. "Why are you so keen to have this child?" "Because I feel that bringing children into the world is the only thing I can do in life!" The truth is that she is an outstanding woman in every respect—beautiful, intelligent, and talented!

Very few people judge themselves fairly. Some are too sure of themselves, a rather disagreeable trait which marks them out as of mediocre personality. But others—more sensitive, more adult, and more agreeable—easily fall into a sort of prejudice against themselves. The striking thing is the complete hopelessness of any attempt to bring them to a more objective view. It is no use pointing out all their good qualities. They look upon it as cruel irony, so clear does it seem to them that we are speaking of the very qualities they lack! For our part, we feel that this systematic negation of their obvious qualities is like an insatiable quest for compliments which, however, never reassure them.

A pretty woman has doubts about her own beauty and thinks she sees scorn in the insistent glances of the men who are attracted by her good looks. A man of modest gifts, who is nevertheless self-confident, knows instinctively how to make the most of the few talents he has at his disposal. Another, richly endowed with talent, stakes everything on other qualities which he would like to, but does not, possess. Or if he does happen to discover some authentic capacity in himself, he is so afraid of not making anything of it that he makes a blunder and suffers all the more from his failure because it is unde-served. Failures in such circumstances can have incalculable consequences on a person's whole life.

One can but deplore the injustice of fate which gives a much greater reward to the audacity, the clever maneuver, even the bluff of some than to the real value of others. And society is very much the loser for it! Think of the countless people whose valuable talents remain forever hidden, sterilized, because they did not receive the necessary encouragement at the right moment. It is the best who are most unsure of them-selves! I am always taken aback by this. Just because they are more keenly aware of what is at stake in life, because they have higher ideals of perfection and service, they are obsessed by how far they always fall short of the realization of their dreams, as well as of ours.

But how difficult it is to encourage those who lack self-confidence! It requires unfailing perseverance. Psychology can indeed delve into the past, bringing to light the frustrations and injustices in which an inferiority complex has its origin. I believe that when the patient manages to overcome it—which he never does completely—it is less through having been made aware of these facts than an effect of the loyal friendship that attaches him more and more closely to his psychotherapist. It is because they are really engaging together in a creative ad-venture!

Under cover of psychology something much deeper is tak-ing place. The steady confidence of the doctor is but a reflec-tion of the confidence that God places in each of his children. The former can help the patient to discover the latter. Noth-ing can be of greater assistance to a person who feels that life is too much for him than the certainty that God is interested in him personally, and in all he does, that God loves him per-sonally and has confidence in him. There is an odd paradox in life: We take lots of trouble over all sorts of things without ever really achieving our object, whereas our most significant successes are obtained without our knowing clearly why or how, without our making any great effort or working them out beforehand.

THE *Adventure* OF *Living*

What happens, however, is that we sometimes lay more store by our efforts than by the success they are designed to achieve. A woman artist once told me she did not feel she was really working unless it was difficult, as if the value of a piece of work could be measured in terms of the sweat it costs. I often fall into this error myself. I was talking about it recently to a colleague of whom I am very fond. I confessed to him my unease at being congratulated on a lecture whose preparation has cost me little in the way of time or effort.

"Then it strikes me," he said, "that you who are always talking about grace set more store by your own merits than you do by grace. Do you not think you ought simply to be grateful to God for the natural ability he has given you?"

This same colleague, once when I was very worried about facing up to my responsibilities, left me a little note on which were written these words from Psalm 127:

> It is in vain that you rise up early and go late to rest,
> eating the bread of anxious toil;
> for he gives to his beloved sleep.

Thank God for the friends he gives us!

It is not much use saying to a person, "Have confidence in yourself." If he lacks self-confidence, it is just because he knows his own shortcomings and exaggerates them; it is also because he has experienced the paralyzing effects of the vicious circle of emotion; he has not forgotten all his past failures. The thing that will help him is the feeling that he is understood, which he will not get if all we do is exhort him to be confident, as if we did not know all the difficulties he faces. At this point my "Calvinist pessimism" comes to my aid. I know that if a man is sincere he is always disappointed in himself and is incapable of saving himself. But though I am a pessimist as far as man is concerned, in regard to God I am an optimist. I know that trusting God is more sure than trusting oneself; I know that trust in God can always carry us forward, impel us resolutely into adventure despite our mistrust of ourselves.

It is, however, scarcely part of my job as a doctor to say to a patient, "If you lack confidence in yourself, then you must put your trust in God." In actual fact I rarely use the remark, and then it is unnecessary. Like all my fellow doctors I point out that confidence of success is the first prerequisite of success. This is a scientific truth. But the most important thing is not what we say to a patient but what we are in our inmost hearts, what we secretly think and believe.

The sick are extraordinarily quick at spotting our intimate feelings. They know quite well whether our exhortations to confidence are only words or proceed from personal conviction, whether we are inviting them to have confidence in themselves without *our* having any real confidence that they will succeed. Worse still, they project on to us their mistrust of themselves—they share it with us; they doubt whether we can have any confidence in their future, knowing as we do about their past failures and the way they are handicapped by all their psychological mortgages from the past. In such a case our warmest encouragement will sound falsely in their ears. They may even think we are being ironical.

The real problem is not between my patient and me but between me and myself, deep in my own heart. The faith that is needed is not that which I might exhort my patient to have, but my own. It is my own personal experience of God's power that gives me the certainty that he can transform my patient's life just as he has transformed mine, and give him, as he has given me, victories over self-doubt despite all his past failures. So there are two kinds of confidence: natural confidence—the sort we place in a person because of the good qualities we know he possesses; and supernatural confidence—the sort we place in a person because of what God can do in him.

Note that the situation of the non-Christian psychoanalyst is exactly similar. He himself has undergone in the course of his own psychoanalytical training a far-reaching transformation, which gives him real confidence in the possibility of his patient's being transformed also. The patient senses this confidence and is helped by it, even if his psychoanalyst is a Freudian who maintains the silence required by his technique. In every successful psychotherapeutic cure one of the chief phenomena is a process of transference. If the doctor is an unbeliever, he will not attribute either his own transformation or that of his patient to God, but merely to his technique. But in my case, I know that all healing comes from God, whether doctor and patient are aware of it or not, and that all techniques are instruments of his grace. And I know that nothing can strengthen a weak person more effectively than the certainty that he is being upheld by God. Is this not what was meant by St. Paul, who openly admitted his weakness, when he said, "If God is for us, who is against us?" (Romans 8:31).

The adventurous life is not one exempt from fear, but on the contrary one that is lived in full knowledge of fears of all kinds, one in which we go forward in spite of our fears. Many people have the utopian idea that others are less afraid than they are, and they feel therefore that they are inferior. All men are afraid, even desperately afraid. If they think they are exempt from fear, that is because they have repressed their fears. Fear is part of human nature. In the case of animals it reigns supreme. One has only to observe them to realize that they are constantly on the watch, attentive to every possible danger.

In the animals, however, fear is always the servant of life, whereas in man it may turn insidiously against life and compromise it. This is the case, for example, with those perpetual students who keep extending their studies because they dare not face the examinations. They fail in their careers and their lives rather than run the risk of failing in an examination. It is always better to fail an examination than to run away from it. "Nothing venture, nothing have," says the proverb. But the mechanism I have described is much more frequently at work than we suppose. It enters subtly into innumerable instances in which we prudently hold back from some too adventurous course of action, with the result that without our being completely aware of it the momentum of adventure is lost and we relapse into mediocrity.

Many men and women come into my consulting room to draw up an honest balance sheet of their lives. Sometimes they admit to me that through having tried to avoid the possibility of failure in one direction they have run into much worse failure in another, and their lives have become meaningless and lacking in the tang of adventure. Thus, many marriages fail in boredom or in a dull coexistence, a sort of insipid truce, because the partners have never dared to face the inevitable conflicts of mutual adaptation. Life is a constant game of "double or nothing." We are always tempted to save what we have by refusing to put it at risk again. But this means the end of adventure.

A young woman takes up horseback riding. This is real adventure. One begins by jumping easy obstacles, and then one has constantly to take on more and more difficult ones. I am much interested in this young woman's progress in horsemanship because in her ordinary life she suffers from a serious lack of self-confidence. Nothing would be better for her than to succeed in this equestrian adventure she has entered upon. I have been to the stable to have a look at her first horse. We prescribe potions—why not also a therapeutic horse? And as a matter of fact she has now bought a new mount. "He's much more difficult to ride," she tells me. "The last one was too easy—you didn't have to do anything. With this one you can't relax for a second. But I'm far more likely to win competitions with this one than with the other." There you are! Her adventure continues because she has not allowed herself to be content with her first successes, because she is prepared to accept the challenge of greater difficulties. Every adventure becomes constantly more and more complicated; it is always coming up against unforeseen obstacles and thereby it is continually being renewed; it keeps calling for greater efforts in face of greater risks.

There are people who go on indefinitely preparing for life instead of living it. They never feel that they are sufficiently well prepared, or strong enough. They go on studying for one thing after another, adding diploma to diploma, taking endless precautions. They fondly imagine that in this way they are improving their chances of success, but in reality all their effort is merely a compensation for lack of self-confidence. The only result of so much preparation is that their self-doubt increases and their chance of success is less than ever. We often see the same thing in our patients' dreams: It is time to leave on a journey, and the dreamer wastes precious time looking for some superfluous item; he packs so much into his suitcases that they will not close; he runs all the way to the station, but his luggage is so heavy and cumbersome that he is late; he gets stuck with his luggage as he tries to pass through the barrier, and the train moves out before his eyes.

CHAPTER 11

Paradoxes

THE CHIEF OBSTACLE to our adventurous impulses is generally, then, in ourselves. Few people are willing to admit this. Most of us prefer to put the blame on external difficulties; we exaggerate their importance and take pride in our prudence in not allowing ourselves to become exposed to them. The Bible points to the phenomenon of rationalization, well known to modern psychologists: "The sluggard says, 'There is a lion outside! I shall be slain in the streets!' " (Proverbs 22:13). Pessimism is another very common cover mechanism. A person constantly prophesies the worst catastrophes in order both to be less painfully disappointed if they do come about and also to be more pleasantly surprised if things do not turn out so badly after all. I sometimes catch myself doing it in the most ingenuous manner possible: Playing a game of patience at cards, and seeing the game going against me, I say to myself, "I bet it won't come out." Then, if it does come out after all, I am doubly pleased, and if it does not, I have the consolation of having won my bet!

In the same way many people proclaim that they are sure to fail in some enterprise they have embarked upon, in order to guard against the criticism to which they might then be ex-

posed. They may even go so far as to say that they want to
fail, or actually to try to fail, since in that case it is not really
failure, because they have willed it themselves. This is the case,
for instance, with the child who, having been too audacious
with his building blocks, triumphantly throws to the floor the
already tottering structure and applauds his own success in
having accomplished such a spectacular act of destruction.
Grown-ups, of course, are better at hiding what they are up
to, but it is often very similar. If one does not beat the record
of successes, one can still win the distinction of a record in
failures.

Another possibility is to hide one's disappointment at failure
behind the affectation of "being realistic," or even cynical,
about it. A woman fought heroically to save her marriage.
She forgave her husband for having been unfaithful to her
and tried at least to re-establish some sort of dialogue with
him. But the husband cut her short with a peremptory "What's
spoiled is spoiled!"

I am often reminded, too, as I listen to my patients, of
Aesop's fable of the fox and the grapes. Like the fox, they
claim to have had no desire to succeed, and so they feel less
bitter about having failed. It would be wrong, however, to
accuse them of duplicity. They are deceived by their own
game, and quite honestly and humbly believe themselves to be
exempt from the ambition to succeed. No one talks more elo-
quently than they of the vanity and stupidity of life. "What's
the point?" they say. "What good will it do me? If I get that, I
shall want something else afterwards, always something more.
The wisest thing is not to try for anything at all." "If we
would live happy," said the poet, "let us live hidden."

And so we come to the great chapter of consolation mechanisms! They take some very worthy forms, such as the philo-
sophical consolation of Boethius, or Nietzsche's dream of
power. The latter blames Christianity for being "human, too
human," for being the refuge of the weak. But his consolation
is also a refuge, an unreal dream, precisely because it is super-
human. I have already spoken of the more naïve dream worlds
in which so many people take refuge from the disappointments

of their real lives. There are still other doctrines of consolation —quietism, fatalism, even the idea of reincarnation, which attracts people who are haunted by the desire to begin the adventure of life afresh with a slate wiped clean. Those who have failed in their own enterprises often find it wonderfully consoling, too, to hand out advice to all and sundry on how to succeed in life.

There are more modest consolations, too—all the things one may call "toys." Everyone has his toys, some more expensive than others and some more effective than others—minor pleasures, little fads, private self-indulgences of which the conscience does not approve, but for which his excuse is the need to console himself for some painful failure. And there are entertainments and shows that are not related to any real cultural need in our lives. I remember one day when worn out with my efforts to see clearly what I ought to do in a certain matter that affected the whole course of my work, weary of waiting in vain for God's answer to my prayers, and tired of fruitlessly discussing it with my wife, I said to her, "I'm going to the movies." On the way I kept muttering to myself, "I'll console myself with a movie, console myself with a movie. . . ." I chose a cinema at random, and the natural result was that I hit upon a stupid film that was no consolation at all.

There is a certain philosophy of luck which is very widespread, and which is used as a consolation. If you fail in your marriage, you can fall back on the thought that it was just bad luck that your husband or wife turned out to be impossible to live with. Nothing is more trite and more sterile than this throwing of the responsibility for failure onto someone else— one's parents, one's boss, an unscrupulous competitor, the political system, or the government of the day. The supreme denial of responsibility is to throw the blame onto God, or even onto the devil.

The reader will be aware of the extent to which cover mechanisms of this sort can go, in persecution mania, for instance, in which the patient blames his failures on the freemasons, or a sorcerer, or perhaps Hertzian waves, nuclear test explosions, or some national leader who has far more important things to do than weave plots against poor sick folk. But the fact is that the idea of such a powerful personage's paying so much attention to him gives the patient a feeling of prestige and success.

The importance of these cover mechanisms gives some measure of the immense fear lurking in men's hearts, a fear that is contagious, and is transmitted from generation to generation. One can say that large numbers of people have grown up in an atmosphere of fear. Timorous parents, too, always find accomplices to help them. A few days ago I saw a nurse who first came to consult me twenty years ago, when she was still a student. A doctor had told her at the time that her constitution was not strong enough for her to become a nurse. Doubtless the doctor had allowed himself to be convinced by the girl's parents, who were afraid the job would be too tiring for her, or perhaps they were simply wanted to keep her at home. I had been able to restore her confidence in herself. She has done extremely well in her profession and is in much better health than she was at the age of twenty.

The whole of a child's upbringing, as we have seen, is a series of precautions against the risks of failure in his life in the future. In the age of bourgeois morality and manners, he was taught how to behave in a drawing room; now he must know how to behave in a cellar. The aim remains the same: Society is a game, and it is vital to know how to play it. But it is hard to draw the line between useful precautions and harmful ones. Take self-control, for instance. A person who is deficient in it is destined to failure after failure. But in others it has been so well inculcated that they have become its prisoners. They have lost all spontaneity, and without spontaneity adventure is impossible.

Then there is the teaching of morality, which must of necessity be given to children. But if it is overstressed, children can be turned into people incapable of ever making a decision, inhibited by the constant fear of acting wrongly. As for the instincts, it is quite necessary to learn to control them; but such control can easily promote chronic anxiety, paralyzing action and leading to repression—including repression of the instinct of adventure! An exaggerated concern for a child's security often leads parents to frustrate his wishes in the choice of a career. They thus condemn him to a life of mediocrity and instability because it has lost its character of being an adventure.

Where, then, is the subtle division between useful and harmful precautions? Doubtless it is less a matter of the measures themselves than of the spirit in which they are taken. Any given precaution may be inspired by wisdom or by fear. Failure may be the result of the neglect of important factors needed to insure success. But it can also be the result of timidity, of failure to act at a decisive moment with sufficient boldness. We can never be 100 per cent secure, and if we refuse to accept this risk, we run an even greater one—that of capitulation. One can fail through not having gone after success with sufficient determination; but one can also fail through having tried too hard and worried too much. This is a frequent cause of failure in psychotherapy: the doctor himself succumbs to the patient's anxiety, instead of delivering him from it.

So we come to the fundamental and tragic problem of fear, and of its inexorable laws, namely, that fear creates what it fears. Fear of war impels a country to take the very measures which unleash war. The fear of losing the love of a loved one provokes us to just that lack of frankness which undermines love. The skier falls as soon as he begins to be afraid of falling. Fear of failing in an examination takes away the candidate's presence of mind and makes success more difficult. But the person who imagines himself to be free from fear is likely to neglect the necessary precautions. He is sometimes capable of acting with a blind folly that is fatal. If on other occasions his audacity comes to his aid and gives him a measure of success, he becomes inflexible and hard, lacking the finesse and the sensitive perception that are indispensable to really significant success.

As with medicines, it all depends on the dose; the right amount produces a cure, but too much can be poisonous. What is the right dose in the case of fear? This is the problem facing the surgeon who must advise for or against an operation, evaluating the risks run by the patient. It is also the problem involved in all the big decisions of life. But it is present too in every decision we make, at every moment of every day.

Our natural temperament plays a considerable role in this respect. Some people are bolder by nature than others. The "lucky" ones have an instinctive flair for judging the risks they can take. They take just enough to retain the flavor of adventure in their lives. But they know how to avoid taking too many. They are generally simple, uncomplicated types, somewhat insensitive, not given to deep thought but following their instincts like the animals. They do not even realize that their ability to act quite spontaneously is a gift from God, like all our instincts, and they attribute their success to their "lucky star." Belief in a "lucky star" is a guarantee that one will face all the circumstances of life with a candor that is conducive to success.

In others, however, who are of a more reflective type, the mechanism of hesitation comes into play, and once set in motion it inevitably gets worse. They are incapable of arresting it. The more they turn the matter over in their minds and analyze it, trying to arrive at a certainty that is impossible, the less clearly will they see what they must do. Their fear of making a false move increases, along with their fear of letting this fear hold them up. Their perplexity grows, and with it the anxiety that strangles their capacity to judge clearly. They find themselves in one dilemma after another. They are torn between logic and sentiment, between charity and justice, between their need for adventure and their need for security, between nature and morality. Every problem leads to an impasse.

In face of this tide of fear, there are only three possible attitudes: Some repress it under an assumed air of assurance of which they are themselves the dupes, but which they must be constantly consolidating by asserting their certainty that they are right. They refuse to listen to advice; they intransigently thrust aside any objection which might reopen the door to fear and doubt. Others give way to the fear. They capitulate, renouncing adventure and withdrawing into routine or daydreams. The third group put themselves in God's hands and leave their fears to him. They are then enabled to find, beyond all their perplexities, through confidence in his inspiration, the same assurance that the instinctive type enjoys.

This attitude of faith is in my view the only one that is truly and fully human. Only with it can we be quite lucid, conscious of our fears and doubts, of the difficulties and limitations of our powers of judgment, and even of the errors that we inevitably make in our search for divine inspiration. We deny neither reason nor feeling but ask God to direct both. We become capable of every audacity and every renunciation. We no longer seek either success or adventure for its own sake, but only in the measure to which it is willed, commanded, and prepared for us by God.

Where, after all, is the frontier between success and failure? It is not always easy to say. Suppose a psychotherapist had successfully undertaken to cure Jean Jacques Rousseau of his complexes. Could one really call it a success? What can we take as the criterion of success? We can have no idea, ourselves; or rather, unless we ask God to lay it down for us, we are condemned to choosing it ourselves, arbitrarily, as Sartre maintains.[1] Of course, the attainment of an end that we have ourselves chosen provides a certain selfish satisfaction, but it is still a relative success since it depends on our own judgment. Many of the successes scored by dictators are of this type.

And so our problem is turning out to be exceedingly complicated! Where is the frontier between success and failure? This was the question discussed in its 1955 conference by the Groupe Lyonnais d'Etudes Médicales, Philosophiques et Biologiques, founded more than thirty years ago by Dr. René Biot.[2] There we heard a philosopher, Professor Hahn, set out all the paradoxes of failure and success. That of technology, for instance: Man takes pride in his technological successes,

[1] J.-P. Sartre, *Existentialism and Humanism*, translated by Philip Mairet, Methuen, London, 1948.
[2] See *Chronique Sociale de France*, No. 5-6, October 15, 1955.

and the aim of technology is indeed to make success more certain, but the triumph of technology means the elimination of man—that is to say, his failure *par excellence*.

We heard a sociologist, Professor Joseph Folliet, speaking of civilizations' having perished because they were too successful. "There is a perfection," he said, "which is both success and failure." He reminded us also of how it is often difficult to say which side has really won in a war—sometimes not the one with the military victory, but in fact the vanquished, who have bequeathed to their vanquishers the fundamental principles of their civilization.

We heard an educator, Professor Louis Raillon, telling us that a complete success in education would be a failure because it would be the bringing of a man to perfect equilibrium—and perfect equilibrium is death.

I am often reminded of this when a patient says to me, with a rather anxious smile, "You must think I'm quite unbalanced." And I reflect that he is in good company, with the majority of those who have given our world its greatest treasures of thought, literature, art, and faith. Of course I must treat my patient, trying to free him from the painful symptoms from which he is suffering. But I am interested in his person, not only his malady. What matters most from this human point of view—is it not that he should live a fruitful life, even if he is ill?

In the same way, we say of a sick person that he is unadapted to his environment. But would not the greatest misfortune be for a man to become so perfectly adapted that he ceased to be a person, became a robot? Society is often more to blame than the individual who can find no room in it for himself. I have just received *Guideposts*,[3] Norman Vincent Peale's magazine, and read that Albert Einstein was expelled from Munich school at the age of fifteen, because he showed no interest in his studies; that he failed the entrance examination to Zurich Polytechnic; that he failed to secure a post as a mathematical assistant; that he was even dismissed from a post as a simple tutor in a private boarding school and had to con-

[3] *Guideposts*, New York, March, 1963.

tent himself with a job in the patents office at Berne! There is a story from which those who are in despair over their failures can well take comfort!

It is, then, extremely difficult to define failure and success, the line of demarcation between them is so elusive. Is the atomic bomb a success or a failure? Today's failure will turn out to be tomorrow's success. Today's sucess will be revealed tomorrow to have been a failure. I am often struck that so few rich people really enjoy the fortune they have amassed. They have succeeded in life, but they have not made a success of their lives, and it seems to be a fact that the cause is in their very success. Some successes are won only at the cost of a betrayal of oneself and of one's true vocation, which means they are really failures. Dr. Sarano speaks of certain doctors who "succeed," and he goes on, "in the way a priest may 'succeed' in his job without being a priest."[4]

I have given many lectures, and I do not deny that it gives me pleasure when the lecture goes well. One of my most vivid memories is of a lecture I gave many years ago, one of my worst failures. It was at a university. I felt right from the first word that I was not going to make contact with my audience. I clung to my notes and laboriously recited, with growing nervousness, what I had to say. As the audience left I could see my friends slipping hurriedly away, to spare themselves and me the embarrassment of a meeting. On the way home in my car with my wife, I burst into tears.

But the next day a professor of philosophy called me on the telephone. He told me he had listened in his life to a large number of remarkable lectures which had scarcely left any impression behind apart from their brilliance. He had never heard one as bad as mine, he added, and this was what intrigued him and made him want to see me. This incident was the beginning of a wonderful friendship between us. I was the witness of his conversion to the Christian faith, and that was the source of more lasting joy to me than could have been procured by success in delivering a lecture.

A few years earlier my ecclesiastical career had been termi-

[4] Jacques Sarano, *Médecine et Médecins*, Le Seuil, Paris, 1959.

nated by a serious failure. I had fought zealously for the furtherance of my ideas in the government of my church. When the time came for my re-election there was strong opposition, and though I myself was re-elected, none of my former colleagues who had fought with me was. Reduced in this way to a position of powerlessness, I had refused to serve—not without some bitterness. But a few months later I underwent the most important religious experiences of my life. I do not think I should have had them if I had been successful in church affairs. I should have played my role as an ecclesiastical personage. I should have engaged in controversies the importance of which I do not fail to recognize, but which are not conducive to self-examination.

As I have written elsewhere, we all live two lives at once—the apparent and external life of our personage, and the deep, hidden life of our person. The two lives are indissolubly linked yet distinct, susceptible of coinciding to a certain extent, and also of differing from each other. Our personage is bound up with society, our person with God. The successes and failures of our personage are recognized by society. The success or failure of our person depends on the harmony or disharmony of our relationship with God. Our personage can win success after success in society—genuine successes, in the artistic, cultural, moral, or spiritual fields—and at the same time our person may be experiencing, at bottom, a profound sense of failure in life.

We must be careful, however, not to push this distinction too far. The person can never be revealed in the pure state, shorn of all trace of the personage. The destiny of our personage and that of our person are always interwoven, despite everything. These two aspects of our life are constantly interacting one upon the other. The successful development of the person is manifested only in that of the personage, and the failures of the personage are always indicative of a deficiency in the person, so that there is a perpetual ambiguity in the notions of success and failure.

The criteria of society are always of the order of appearances: power, wealth, knowledge, prestige, reputation. The serious thing is that society looks upon success as a criterion of value and truth: If you succeed you are right; if you fail you are wrong. Of course we protest against this distortion of the notions of truth and value. We should like to judge our successes and failures, as well as those of others, in full independence of mind, taking no account of social conventions and prejudices. But we do not manage to do so because society is also ourselves. We are bound up with it and with its prejudices more closely than we imagine. And society is terribly cruel with those who fail, "hard on those who have not made a success of life," as Sartre puts it. It despises those it does not admire, and social contempt is singularly hard to bear. We see this clearly in a man who is the victim of it and comes to unburden himself to us. We can never hope to examine him in the abstract, as if he could be isolated from his environment in the way the chemist isolates a body in his test tube in order to observe its reactions.

Such a man takes upon himself the social contempt of which he is the object. He sees himself as responsible for it, guilty. His is a false guilt, indeed, but no less heavy to bear on that account. And for him society is no vague abstraction—it is his wife, parents, children, and anyone who respects or condemns him. Moreover, I am no more independent than he is. Where does this powerful hold that society has on me come from? It comes from my human anxiety, from my fear of failure, from the scars left on me by all my past failures, all my disappointments with myself. Like all other men and women I need constantly to have my self-assurance built up through the respect of society, or at least through the favorable opinion of those whom I most admire.

Few people can really get away from the arbitrament of society and depend only on the judgment of their consciences and of God; I imagine that no one does so completely. Jesus Christ alone was capable of it, and that is a mark of his divine nature. The authority of society lies precisely in this submission by all its members to its verdicts. This is the cement of social comformity, which reigns over all and hurts those who dare to run counter to it. Social pressure imposes the rules of the game on all, rewarding with success those who play it cleverly. It is also the source of the moralism which claims in God's stead to lay down for us what is evil and what is good, what is success and what is failure.

Nevertheless, although society is pitiless toward those who fail, it is scarcely less so toward those who succeed and thus arouse its jealousy. Society's attitude to them is ambivalent: it praises them and denigrates them. The reason is the same as we were discussing just now: All men are disappointed with themselves and with their own failures, and that is why they find the success of others hard to bear. In order to make themselves feel bigger they belittle others and deny their merits. I have come across a nice remark made by Marshal Joffre, the victor of the Marne, in answer to his detractors who were asking whether the victory was really due to him: "I do not know who won the battle of the Marne, but I know who would have lost it." We applaud those whose success redounds to our advantage, and our applause is calculated to put us in their camp so that we can have some share in their glory. But we find it more difficult to do justice to those whose success puts us in the shade. This is the source of the spirit of contentious criticism and rivalry, and of the jealousy so rife particularly among the noble professions—among scholars, artists, writers, politicians, ecclesiastics, and doctors.

CHAPTER 12

Celibacy and Marriage

WE SEE, then, that social suggestion always influences us in our evaluation of success and failure, as well of others as of ourselves. I must deal with a particular case here because of its frequency and the great pain it causes: the case of the spinster. Many spinsters come to see me. I have seen such women, who seem to the superficial eye of the public to have succeeded better than most in accepting and overcoming the disappointment of their spinsterhood, dissolve into tears in the secrecy of my consulting room.

I know that for every normal woman who as the years go by sees her hope of marriage evaporating, spinsterhood is a terrible trial, and one the acceptance of which can never be final; it is always likely to reappear in the most painful form. Other sorrows, such as the tragic death of a husband, wife, or child, are also ineffaceable. But they can at least be freely expressed, and they arouse ready sympathy. The spinster has to conceal her sorrow. If she allows it to show she may have to suffer mockery and the sort of pleasantry to which people are so inclined as soon as any allusion is made to matters of sex. Or else she brings upon herself facile and wounding advice, such as "You have just got to accept it!" Or perhaps the stinging reply of some married woman: "You should consider yourself lucky! You can do whatever you want—no children to worry about, no selfish husband to kow-tow to. You've got a good income and can do what you like with your money."

It is not only a matter of being deprived of the sex life. It is not only a matter of being deprived of motherhood, which is a much more painful deprivation for many women. It is a matter of the loneliness which is so contrary to the needs of a woman, having to live both sorrows and joys alone, unable to share them with a husband who makes them his own. Having to carry alone all the responsibilities of her life, all the decisions, when she would so love to have a firm shoulder on which to rest her head. Being obliged to keep her distance so far as men are concerned; never able to make friends with a man without running the risk of being suspected of being his mistress—or of wanting to be. And if she has a lover, she is condemned to a secrecy which weighs more heavily upon her than upon him. Of course there are women friends, sometimes lots of them. But regardless of their number, they can never take the place of the special bond a woman has with her husband. There is no real joy in going out without a husband, and staying alone at home is even worse.

It is easy to talk to the spinster about sublimation. We recommend that she take up an interesting and outward-looking career; we talk to her about self-dedication, service to others, and finding an outlet for the maternal instinct in teaching or social work. In fact, it was a devoted and active woman social worker who said to me, "Throughout the daytime, everything is all right. I'm too busy to think of anything else. But when I get home in the evening I suddenly feel terribly tired, and I just sit down and cry." I do not think one helps such people by moral advice or by minimizing their suffering. They are helped far more by being understood.

Nothing is more legitimate than every woman's ambition to marry and have children. She ought to be able to express it in all its ardor without being stigmatized on that account as a rebel. It is absurd not to recognize the power of the instincts. Clearly woman was created as the Bible says, in order to be man's "helper," and "fit" for him (Genesis 2:18). Woman has, more than man, the sense of the person, of the personal bond. Dedication to an idea, however noble, never gives her the same feeling of fulfillment as she experiences in devoting herself to her husband and children. The greatest satisfaction she can find apart from marriage is in a job which gives her the opportunity of close collaboration with a man of worth whom she can help to give of his best to his work. Thus we sometimes find that a businessman's private secretary or a nurse in an operating theater bears the celibate life better than a schoolteacher. Even so she suffers, because the chief to whom she devotes her life does not devote his to her. She must even take particular care not to give expression to the feelings with which her heart is filled.

If the natural and divine purpose of womanhood is fulfilled in marriage, a woman must necessarily suffer greatly if she is deprived of this fulfillment. She may accept her deprivation one day, in an access of stoic resolution or of religious faith and self-abandonment to God's will. But on the morrow, at the sight of a baby carriage, of a mother with her children, or of a couple embracing in the park, she will have to confess to herself that she has been deceiving herself just a little. She finds it impossible to understand that God, having created her for marriage, does not grant it to her but remains deaf to her prayers. Certain passages in the Bible about prayers in conformity with God's will trouble her profoundly. Is it that God loves her less than her boss's wife—a woman who wants for nothing, and whom her husband spoils terribly, whereas to his secretary he is so exacting, and even harsh?

Between the painful feeling of not fulfilling her natural destiny and that of having spoiled her life there is indeed a distinction, but it is a very tenuous one. It is from the lips of spinsters that I have most often heard the awful remark "I have spoiled my life." What is one to reply? I confess that I make no reply. But I see clearly that this feeling of failure makes such a woman's suffering far worse. Ordinary disappointment would be easier to bear, but she cannot rid herself of this added feeling of failure, which is so unjust.

Social suggestion plays a tremendous part in this matter. The unmarried woman, even if she occupies an eminent position in society, is treated with a certain contempt. It is painful to her to see the most insignificant married woman more highly honored just because she has a husband. Some of my readers are perhaps going to suspect me of exaggeration. We are no longer in the eighteenth century, they will say; woman has won her emancipation, and the right to be esteemed for her own personal worth and not in accordance with her marriage status. Alas, it is not true! Spinsters know it only too well. They can see it in a thousand little signs, even if it is only in the place assigned to them at the dinner table, or in the glances of married women or the prudent reserve of those gentlemen who are not nearly so reserved when there are no witnesses about.

I have heard too many confidences not to reflect their general tenor here. A spinster turns over the leaves of her old parents' photograph album. All her brothers and sisters are married. The album is full of photos of these couples and of their children, their grandparents' pride and joy. Of her there is one little out-of-date passport photograph tucked away in a corner. Even if her parents say nothing about it to her, even if she has a useful job in life, she feels that she does not give them as much pleasure as do her brothers and sisters, who have given them children to carry on the family name and traditions.

The world honors the nun, who has taken an oath of celibacy, but it always takes the view that the celibate lay-woman, who would have liked to marry, has to some extent spoiled her life. She is the one whom men have disdained. This, at any rate, is the case in Europe. In America it seemed to me that her personal worth was more readily acknowledged. But of course the same applies to the married woman: In Europe she is seldom esteemed in her own right, apart from the prestige enjoyed by her husband. She perhaps feels this the more acutely, the more eminent her husband is, as in the case of a certain woman who said to me, "I can tell you that when a woman has a husband like mine, she is never anything else but her husband's wife!"

In addition there is the popularization of notions of psychoanalysis. Psychoanalysis has tended to banish the idea of luck. Consequently the spinster feels that people suspect her of having failed to marry because of her complexes. This may indeed be the case, and she may realize it later, either spontaneously or as the result of a course of psychological treatment. It hurts her not only to see that her lost youth cannot be called back, but also to find that she herself has been the unwitting cause of her own spinsterhood. But many other women have remained celibate because they have quite freely refused some proposal of marriage which they could not have accepted without devaluing themselves in their own eyes. All honor to them—that is a sign of health, not of psychological sickness.

The social judgment which condemns spinsters and assimilates their celibacy to a failure in life is, therefore, profoundly unjust. We ought to be working for a radical change in public opinion. This was the object of Mlle. Suzanne Nouvion and her *"Recherches et Rencontres"* team in publishing their fine book on "lay female celibacy."[1] In her conclusion she asserts forcibly, and rightly, that a spinster's life can be a successful one. True, it is not easy. Most eloquent is the chapter written by a social worker, Mlle. Chevron-Villette, whose down-to-earth realism forms a contrast with other parts of the book which, while being on a high level, are rather too optimistic.

But what life is easy? None. The real problem is to make a success of one's marriage if one does marry, and to make a success of the celibate life if one does not. Each vocation is as difficult as the other. This has been well expressed by Mlle. Madeleine Rambert: "The most important thing, in the end of the day, is neither marriage nor celibacy; it is to achieve fulfillment."[2] It is wrong and mischievous to suggest to a girl that her object in life will be fulfilled if she marries, and that she will have failed in life if she remains a spinster. This is the best

---

[1] Suzanne Nouvion and collaborators, *Le Célibat Laïc Féminin*, Editions Ouvrières, Paris, 1962.
[2] Madeleine Rambert, *La Femme Seule et Ses Problèmes Affectifs*, Delachaux and Niestlé, Neuchâtel, 1961.

way of insuring failure in either case, for she will be ill prepared to face the difficulties of marriage. And if she does not marry, the feeling of failure that has been implanted in her in advance will prevent her putting her whole heart and mind into her life as a celibate. One does not make a success of one's life if one is constantly longing for another, unreal, existence.

What I have just been writing in connection with celibacy has a quite general application. I may feel I have spoiled my life because my idea of success has been too set and narrow. In this case no success satisfies me or gives me any pleasure. I even get annoyed if people try to comfort me by pointing out where I have been successful. Such consolation seems to me to be bitter irony, for if I have not succeeded in achieving the thing I set most store by, nothing else can take its place. But I can also fail through not having chosen with sufficient resolve what my goal in life must be, through having dissipated my energies on all sorts of minor adventures instead of concentrating my efforts on a precise and worthy objective! So, if you fail, there will never be any lack of good people ready to help you by explaining why you have failed, and how you ought to have acted—and their opinions will cancel each other out. One will tell you you have been over ambitious, another that you have not been ambitious enough.

The truth is that life is always difficult, whether one is married or not. We can see with our own eyes enough marriages on the rocks to comfort any spinster and disabuse her of the utopian idea that she would have had a more successful and satisfying life if she had been married. But such reasoning has little effect. The failures of others never console us for our own. We all envy the privileges enjoyed by others, but their servitudes we see less clearly. Their difficulties never lessen the impact of our own. It is a matter of common observation that those who already have on their own account a spirit of patience and endurance in their own trials are full of sympathy for others, whereas those who lack this spirit, who are made rebellious by their own difficulties, also lack understanding of the problems of others and can derive no comfort from them.

There is a certain kinship of mind among people who accept their lives, whatever they may be, just as there is a similar kinship among rebels, whatever the object of their rebellion. The biggest difference is not between those who are married and those who are not, but between those who live their real lives with conviction and those who live them unwillingly. It seems to me to be more just to make the distinction between convinced and reluctant lives rather than between acceptance and revolt, as is generally done. A frank revolt is much healthier than a reluctant acceptance. Revolt and acceptance strike me as being less contradictory than is often thought. A phase of ardent revolt is sometimes the necessary precondition for genuine acceptance. And premature acceptance is often only an apparent acceptance hiding a mute and unexpressed revolt which has not dared to show itself openly and so remains tenaciously in the depths to poison the mind. All frustration arouses a natural reaction of revolt which can be cleared out of the way only by being expressed, since nature instinctively defends itself against anything that threatens it. A person who makes a virtue of smothering this natural voice of revolt and strives to accept any trial runs a grave risk of accepting it only reluctantly.

The greatest obstacle in the way of acceptance is the appearance of acceptance. The greatest obstacle to virtue is the appearance of virtue. The greatest obstacle to humility is the appearance of humility. The greatest obstacle to faith is the appearance of faith. The greatest obstacle to love is the appearance of love. What I say here in regard to celibacy is true of every kind of trial, of infirmity, and of frustration. Whatever our life and its burdens—there is no life that does not have to carry some burden—we never find fulfillment except in living it with conviction. And to live one's life with conviction is to live it in a spirit of adventure, as an adventure. To make a success of one's marriage, one must treat it as an adventure, a daily adventure, with all the riches and all the difficulties that are involved in an adventure shared with another person. But I believe that the only solution for success in unmarried life is to treat it too as an adventure, a different adventure, with

137

all the risks, all the sufferings, and all the privileges of the
unmarried state.

What is meant by accepting an infirmity, a frustration, a
suffering? What is meant by acceptance of celibacy? Quite
often a spinster has told me that she believed God must love her
less because he had condemned her to spinsterhood. I am always profoundly disturbed to hear people say this sort of
thing. Is it really God who has "condemned" her to celibacy?
Does God not love all his children with a love that is total?
Can God ever desire that any man or woman should suffer? I
do not think so. I know in fact that he has a quite special
solicitude toward those who suffer most. I shall never say to a
woman, "You must accept spinsterhood because it is God's
will." I do not believe that to be true. In any case, to make
such an assertion is to be singularly pretentious—what do we
know of God's will for other people? And I do not believe
that such exhortations would help a woman to accept her
celibate state.

What helps us all, on the contrary, is the knowledge that
God loves us all, that he wants us all to find fulfillment in our
lives; that whatever our circumstances, our frustrations, and
our sufferings, he has a purpose for us, for our complete fulfillment in this life of ours, whatever it may be. To live this real
life—and not dream of a different one—and to seek to live it
under God is to fulfill our human destiny, a great adventure
directed by God. To accept spinsterhood—for a woman who
is celibate not as a result of a vow, but through not having
been asked in marriage by a man whom she could really accept
as a husband—is, therefore, neither to repress the legitimate
desire for marriage, nor to take pleasure in the suffering of
solitude, nor yet to pretend that the suffering is willed by
God. It means seeking to live the celibate life in a spirit of
adventure, as God wills. In truth, it is not often easy for a
married woman to live her married life in a spirit of adventure,
as God wills.

I could deal at equal length with the problems of marriage
and of failure in marriage. But, unlike those of celibacy, they
are the object of a voluminous and, in general, excellent litera-

ture. I shall therefore confine myself to a brief observation, namely, that social suggestion seems to me to play an enormous role here as well, and one which overspecialized psychology tends to overlook. Large numbers of books appear nowadays on the subject of marriage, full of wise counsel. Young people and those contemplating marriage are given instruction in sex and the psychology of the sexes. Courses are organized for engaged couples. Enlightened specialists run popular features in magazines and on the radio, answering correspondents' letters on affairs of the heart. Doctors and churches, in increasing numbers, set up centers where marriage guidance can be obtained. We must be glad of all this. Yet never has the flood of marital conflicts and divorces been more disturbing. One may well be astonished at it. It derives, I think, in considerable part from a phenomenon of social suggestion—a sort of contagion. What happens is that the more couples escape from their marriage difficulties by way of divorce, the more will married people turn to the idea of divorce in their own case, and threaten each other with it as soon as some crisis blows up at their own fireside. The idea that there is always the possibility of divorce in the background makes the contention worse between them and undermines any mutual effort at understanding and reconciliation.

For this reason I value highly the firm stand taken by the Roman Catholic Church against divorce. However one denounces the hypocrisy of couples who remain officially united simply because they cannot obtain a divorce in Catholic countries, this legislation is nevertheless a welcome bulwark against the spread of divorce and the temptation it presents to other couples. Above all it protects the children, and no one can deny that the increase in the number of children of divorced parents is a real scourge in many other countries.

Running away from the difficulties of marriage, using divorce as a way out instead of facing up to them, is always a kind of failure, whatever the grounds—often quite valid ones —the couple may put forward for it. This is why divorced persons always feel a sense of serious failure, even though they may not admit as much. This is also why, in the course of the conflict, each partner tries so hard to throw the blame onto the other, so as to be able to blame the other for the break when it comes. In several Protestant churches measures have been taken to render more difficult the remarriage of divorced persons. The one that seems to me to be most in conformity with the Gospel would be a ceremony of absolution. A person who had made a solemn promise of lifelong fidelity and had not been able to keep it would come and receive, through the ministration of the Church, the grace of God which washes away all sin, before once more making a similar promise.

All life is an adventure, and all adventure has its difficulties. The path of life is always strewn with failures. What complicates the problem still further is that life's successes are as dangerous as its failures. "I fear success more than anything," wrote Bernard Shaw. "To have succeeded means that one has finished one's work on this earth. . . . Life has meaning for me only if it remains a perpetual becoming, a definite goal in front of one and not behind." This is the paradoxical law of adventure as we saw it right at the beginning of this study, namely, that the thing that puts an end to it is its success. Success is perilous.

I remember a discussion I once had with some Danish colleagues. They had been telling me about the great adventure of setting up a more just social system in their country that had taken place at the beginning of this century. The whole nation had been fired with such enthusiasm that a whole new system of legislation had been tried and adopted. No one indeed would want to go back on that and lose the benefits gained. "And yet," my colleagues added, "the heart of our nation suffers from a certain apathy; it has stopped beating—the objective has been attained."

Traveling in Scandinavia one is struck by the contrast between poor countries, such as Finland and Norway, and rich ones, like Sweden and Denmark, despite their nearness to one another. One is struck at the same time by the difference in moral climate. But the same sort of contrast is apparent in individuals. Is there anything more unpleasant than the self-satisfied man who has "arrived"?

Even more pernicious is the claim that one has achieved his moral ideal. This is what the Bible calls being self-righteous. Remember the parable of Jesus about the Pharisee and the publican (Luke 18:9-14). It is with reason that the Pharisee boasts of his moral victories, of the success of his efforts to obey God. Moreover, he does not attribute the merit to himself but thanks God for having led him into the way of perfection. And yet, as Jesus said, it was precisely because he was so satisfied with himself that he was deprived of the justification which the sinner received.

I remember a good fellow, a likable southerner, who had been sent to me because of the little war he was waging against his adolescent daughter. She was beginning to go out at night, and stay out rather late, and he unjustly suspected her of the worst possible conduct. He was so obsessed by his mistrust that the atmosphere in the family had become intolerable. He explained to me right away that he himself had been able to resist every temptation and did not intend to allow the family honor to be sullied now by his daughter. "Perhaps," I said, "it is because you are so proud of never having done anything wrong that you are so quick to fear that your daughter is doing wrong?" And I can still hear his reply, as he exclaimed in his rich southern accent, "Oh, yes! You can say that. My life has been spotless!" That was it—it was his spotless conscience that was making him bring suffering to everyone around him.

Into my consulting room come men and women defeated by life or by disease, caught up in all kinds of difficulties, and lamenting their failings and their inferiority. But there are also some who are extremely gifted and who confess to me that that is their misfortune. They can afford to snap their fingers at everyone; every adventure is open to them; there is nothing they dare not do. And yet they feel their lives have been a failure. Their easy existence lacks all solidity. Listening to them I am reminded of Demosthenes and of the tremendous struggle he had to overcome his disability. I have just been speaking of women who suffer as a result of being unmarried. There was one who told me about all her many successes. She was ravishingly beautiful, vivacious, and charming. I was struck by one remark she made: "The trouble with me is that I have just squandered boys!"

Other people, after a lifetime of useful work, look back and wonder what the true motives of all their efforts have been. When they were still in the heat of action they questioned nothing. There were adverse circumstances to face, powerful forces of resistance, dangerous opponents. They fought and they won. But now they are tortured with questions about the value of all this whirl of adventures. The author of Ecclesiastes was one of these men on whom life had smiled and who had spent himself without stint. He had accumulated all possible wealth and knowledge. Bitterly he wrote, "Then I saw that all toil and all skill in work come from a man's envy of his neighbor. This also is vanity and a striving after wind" (Ecclesiastes 4:4).

Mme. Françoise Mallet-Joris has told in an interview what made her write the essay in self-examination *Lettre à Moi-même*.[3] With the proceeds of the Prix Femina which she won for her novel *L'empire Céleste* she bought a farm in Normandy. There she was, happy in her rustic life, with her family and her work, busy on another novel while her husband painted and her children played. Suddenly she was disturbed by the visit of a friend, Lucien, a somewhat sinister character. "In your house on the hilltop," he had remarked, "with your children, your cows, your novels, and your pictures, you are nicely settled in your life. . . ." She shuddered—"nicely settled. . . ."

Success can seem like a sort of prison. In his lecture, Professor Folliet[4] spoke of the "fundamental dissatisfaction" that may be felt by those who are at the pinnacle of fame which comes from their feeling of "acting a part." It was perhaps some such crisis which overtook Elijah after his resounding success against the priests of Baal. What success could be more exciting than to bring about the triumph of God's cause against idolatry, and to work miracles in his name? Neverthe-

[3] Françoise Mallet-Joris, *Lettre à Moi-même*, Julliard, Paris, 1963.
[4] See *Chronique Sociale de France*, No. 5-6, October 15, 1955.

less Elijah withdraws to the desert, a prey to serious depression, even wanting to die (I Kings 19).

But there, in a secluded grotto, the prophet experienced a personal encounter with God. No longer the triumphant God in whose name the people at Elijah's call had slain the prophets of Baal, but a God who came to him as a "still small voice." One brilliant adventure was over for Elijah, but a new one was beginning. It is in contact with God that adventure is reborn. At that point the too human, too childish dilemma of "success or failure" in which we have been caught is resolved. Then we can accept our failures and be freed from the gilded cage of success, for in his presence we can measure the vanity of our successes and see that the greatest calamity would be to claim that our lives have been a success. Dr. Sarano tells of a remark made by a friend of his: "Fortunately we have spoilt our lives, otherwise our case would be hopeless; unhappy is the man who thinks he has not spoilt his life."[5]

[5] Jacques Sarano, *Médecine et Médecins*, Le Seuil, Paris, 1959.

CHAPTER 13

The Lessons of Failure

I wonder what my readers' reactions to the last few pages have been. There are doubtless among them pious folk who nod in approval whenever I quote the Bible or tell the story of some religious experience, either my own or somebody else's. They have themselves had spiritual experiences and are glad to find in what I have to say religious affirmations that confirm their own. Like me they believe that the most difficult human problems can find in religious faith an unexpected and wonderful solution.

But there are others who are irritated by such things. They feel that they are a sort of sleight-of-hand which is not altogether honest. A problem is first presented; its fearful complexity is demonstrated—here, for example, that of failure and success—and then all of a sudden, with the help of an anecdote, the problem vanishes. "Only believe, and everything will be all right." I have just been describing the imperious desire to succeed which fills the heart of every man, and the serious injury inflicted by failure; I have been talking of making a success of one's life, whether married or single. And then all at once I exclaim, with Dr. Sarano's friend, that fortunately we fail! It is the same with the problem of sin. One is told first of the horror of it, and of how one ought for love of God to turn away from it; then it is pointed out how believers are still as sinful as unbelievers; and lastly they are told to rejoice at this, since without sin they would not have the benefits of grace: *felix culpa.* . . . Some readers will indeed think that paradoxes are too easy a way out.

My sympathy is with such readers, the ones who express their doubts and the objections that trouble their minds, far more than with the believers who proclaim their faith. My vocation is not to exhortation or persuasion. That is the job of the theologians. My vocation is to understand men and women, to understand their difficulties and all the obstacles they meet on the road of faith. I often have the impression that they take religious problems more seriously than many believers do. They refuse to use sleight-of-hand. I try less to argue with them than to listen to them.

They are right, it seems to me when they accuse us of being too prone to oversimplify problems by means of an anecdote, which, however authentic, does not exhaust the problem. We talk of the victories of faith. It does appear that we do not say enough about the cost in tears, about the difficulties and doubts still lingering after even the finest religious experiences. Remember the tears shed by Elijah in his cave. Remember the bloody sweat that Jesus himself felt running down his face in Gethsemane when, before God, he faced the tragic failure of his earthly ministry. And all the believers the story of whose liberation one tells went through tortures that one says less about. The most beautiful days of my life have been those which have been marked by my tears.

I know well that my only security is in God's mercy, but I am none the less put out to find sin in myself every day, and to see more and more of its power. I know well the vanity of our efforts and our success, but I am no less sensitive to criticism, and no less anxious to succeed. I am filled with remorse at not having been able to help some sick person as I should have liked. Another is late for his appointment: already I have pictures of him having committed suicide. At this moment I am making every effort to make a success of this book—as is only human! Of course, it is out of loyalty to my vocation, in order to be of some use to some unknown reader who is in trouble. But I am also prompted by conceit and pride, because I want to be appreciated and listened to. Our sins and our virtues, our good and bad qualities, our conscious and our unconscious motives are always inextricably mixed.

One never really solves any problem. One may have the impression that one is doing so, thanks to some passing state of grace, but such states never last. We think we have solved a problem one day only to find it still with us on the morrow. Faith does not make life easier. Believers have as many difficulties as skeptics. In fact they often find a failure harder to bear, just because they are not skeptical. Look, for example, at the biblical story of Ahithophel. He is not an unbeliever, yet he commits suicide because he has fallen out of favor with Absalom (2 Samuel 17:23). He cannot bear to have Absalom reject his advice, although in fact it is God who has misled Absalom in order to prevent him from defeating David.

We can neither solve any of our personal problems nor rid ourselves of our pressing need to solve them. Why then do I tell stories, either biblical stories or anecdotes about things that have happened to me or to others in our encounter with God? Is it not, I am asked, a way of avoiding the problems? No, I think not. I tell them because they are true, because they are things that have really happened—they are "real-life stories." Real life is much more important than all the problems that we turn over in our minds. Such problems will always remain as intellectual problems, whatever religious experiences we may have undergone. From this point of view, the problem of success and failure remains insoluble. It seems to me, therefore, that we should not be talking so much about the solutions brought by faith as about the answer given by God. There is a difference. Our problems may well remain without rational solutions, but God is speaking to us about them, and that is all that matters—God's answer. God's answer is often quite different from what we expected. He speaks to us in our successes; he speaks to us in our failures. He speaks to us when we confess our inability to solve our problems; they are always an occasion for listening to God.

So Job passionately puts to God the insoluble problem of undeserved suffering. At the end of the book he receives God's answer. It does not solve the problem at all. But Job has heard God's voice; he has met God; and he is quite changed as a result (Job 42). What does it mean, to meet God? I am often asked, and I confess I do not know what to reply. It is a thing experienced, not explained. Is not God always there, close by, as close to the unbeliever as to the believer? Do we not meet him already, without knowing it, when we rebel? Against whom do we rebel if not against him? Why do we cry out against injustice, ugliness, falsehood, and hate, if not because God speaks to us of justice, beauty, truth, and love?

But we can have a more exact awareness of meeting God when there bursts forth in our minds some thought that imposes itself upon us by its authority, by its unmistakable savor of truth, a thought that transforms us, changes our attitude toward our problems, even if they are not solved on the intellectual plane. It is not the problems that change, but we ourselves; we evolve, and then the problems present themselves to us differently. What formerly revolted us is now seen as one of the great secrets of life, as a mysterious law of life. And at the same time we realize that the truth we have discovered not only is true for us, and for believers, but has a universal value; it helps us to understand ourselves, to understand all men, to understand life.

Then we see that the hard road of failure and disappointment, even in our most pious ambitions, takes us farther than our successes—"that through many tribulations we must enter the kingdom of God" (Acts 14:22)—that the true hope, the really human hope, as Pluegge has shown,[1] goes beyond the mere desire for what one wants. It is the hope that begins only when one can no longer get one's desire, beyond total despair. We see that the value of a man is not to be measured so much

[1] H. Pluegge, *Uber die Hoffnung*, Spectrum, Utrecht and Antwerp, 1954.

by his successes as by the way he bears his undeserved failures, that nothing is more dangerous for a man than unlimited success.

We do not, however, have to look to these extreme cases in order to see the part played in our growth by failure. It can be seen in ordinary everyday life. It is through a series of experiences of failure that the child gradually discovers the world and its proper relationship with himself. Every baby stretches out his hands to the lamp on the ceiling and cries because he cannot reach it. By falling he learns to walk. Through many misunderstandings he learns to express himself better. Through awkwardness and maladroitness he learns new movements and new activities, and through understanding why he fails he learns new skills. After the sweeping enthusiasms of adolescence he will experience many failures, which will teach him to apportion his ambitions to his ability, so as to realize something concrete instead of keeping everything in the realm of dreams.

Throughout his life his laborious progress along a failure-strewn road will be his training for manhood. He will observe that the privileged ones to whom success comes easily suffer from a serious lack of human understanding. At first he will be humiliated and irritated at every failure, but afterwards he will realize its value. As a doctor, he will always remember the mistakes he has made in diagnosis and treatment, and they will make him a man of experience. Some day he will understand that our successes benefit others, but our failures benefit ourselves. The shock of unexpected defeat will give a nation the surge of energy it needs and open its eyes to its mistakes.

Thus the Israelites, after the disaster at Ai, come together to ask themselves and God the cause of the curse upon them, and to root it out (Joshua 7:13). True courage does not consist in flying from victory to victory, but in recognizing one's mistakes and one's responsibilities. Oh, it is not easy! I shall always remember my first journey into Germany after the war, in the spring of 1946. Some thirty young people were sitting in a circle round me, in a field under a tree. I was the first foreigner to whom they had been able to speak openly, and they questioned me eagerly: "Tell us now where it was that we Germans went wrong!" How difficult I found it to answer them! Mostly I pitied these poor lads whom Nazism had taken almost out of their cradles to be indoctrinated, and who now felt that the whole world hated them, and they could not understand why.

But sooner or later we have to go one stage further in understanding the meaning of life. Failure will then be seen as a school of depuration as well as a school of perfection, in which we must learn the harsh necessity of being stripped, not only of our errors and failings, but also of our treasures—our highest ambitions, this very aspiration toward an always elusive perfection, together with what we have learned from science and from life, and even the tasks we have been given by God.

Here the Christian Gospel provides an answer that no other religion can give us. We see the figure of Jesus Christ, speaking to us of success, indeed, and of the victories of faith, but also of persecution. Jesus does not tell us that happiness is to be found in the satisfaction of our desires, but in a spirit of renunciation and poverty. He speaks of a narrow door, and says to us, "Whoever does not bear his own cross and come after me, cannot be my disciple" (Luke 14:27). Then we follow him along the road he took when everything was stripped from him. In Gethsemane he met the horror of failure: his disciples deserting him, the triumph of his enemies—whom he had wished to save, and who were now to crucify him—the insults, the torture, the sensation of having been abandoned by God, and death.

Even for him, true God but also true man, this collapse is terrible. He says, "My soul is very sorrowful, even to death" (Matthew 26:38). Then he prays. He begs his Father to spare him. But, faced with God's awful silence, he adds, "My Father, if this cannot pass unless I drink it, thy will be done" (Matthew 26:42). The will of God: that is the key to our problem. God has a purpose, and it will be realized also through the failures we must face in obedience.

God has a purpose: the entire Bible proclaims this. What

matters is that his plan should be understood and fulfilled. So, in the light of the Bible, the problem is shifted onto new ground. The question is no longer whether one is succeeding or failing but whether one is fulfilling God's purpose or not, whether one is adventuring with him or against him. It is, of course, always a joyful thing to succeed. But the joy is very deceptive if it comes from the satisfaction of an ambition that is contrary to the will of God. And of course failure is still very painful; but the pain is fruitful if it is part of God's purpose. A failure, within God's purpose, is no longer really a failure. Thus the Cross, the supreme failure, is at the same time the supreme triumph of God, since it is the accomplishment of his purpose of salvation. This is the true answer to the painful discovery that it is not possible to establish a clear frontier between success and failure. What is success and what is failure? The answer of the Bible is "What is the will of God? Are you obeying him?"

This attitude is not in the least masochistic; it involves no pathological seeking of pain or failure for its own sake. As we have seen, there are in the Bible some wonderful expressions of the joy of success. But success is always as a sign of God's blesssing, as a sign that it is his will that is being fulfilled in the success, that the success comes from him. Quite early in the Bible, for example, comes the beautiful story of the journey of one of Abraham's servants in search of a wife for Isaac (Genesis 24). What matters is that he should find the woman whom the Lord has chosen for Isaac. And his success, and the astonishing way in which it happens, is for him the sign that he has found her. Again and again throughout the Bible we find the same interpretation of success as a sign from God. Jesus himself, in answer to John the Baptist's message asking whether he is indeed the Messiah, points to his acts of healing and his miracles in order to reassure him (Matthew 11:2-6).

But long before his Passion, Jesus was announcing to his disciples "that he must go to Jerusalem and suffer many things . . . and be killed, and on the third day be raised" (Matthew 16:21). "He must"—this is a reference to a purpose of God which includes both the failure of the Cross and the triumph of the Resurrection. And throughout the Bible we find, side by side, these two apparently contradictory ideas—that the hand of God can be seen in success and also in failure; in miracles, acts of healing, victories over suffering, and also in the acceptance of suffering and persecution.

Ah, I know full well that the problem is not an easy one! Where is God's purpose? The Bible is not rational. It gives us no objective criterion. It always requires the enlightenment of the Holy Spirit—and, let us admit it, too, the hesitant gropings of faith, the painful perplexities of faith, the trials of uncertainty, and the patient, humble search through many an error for the will of God. So we often see people going to one extreme or the other—theologians, philosophers, artists, men of action—thinking that they are right because they succeed, or on the contrary thinking that they are right because they are misunderstood, criticized, and persecuted.

This procedure may be right in one case but false in another. They may be reassured, therefore, but have cause for disquiet, too. And often behind their apparent assurance we doctors find a profound disquiet, betrayed by their dreams. On the other hand, we may find that behind their display of doubt their dreams bear witness to a deep confidence. One can never be sure; one can only believe. The biblical revelation gives us no guiding principle for our conduct beyond a few very simple laws such as that of honesty or love, which unbelievers accept as readily as we do, which are common to the Christian revelation and to the natural law.

This is in fact the meaning of the account of the Fall (Genesis 3): The fatal error of men is this very aspiration to be like God, "knowing good and evil," wanting to have a moral code, so as to be able to act on their own, without any further need of God to enlighten them step by step. This autonomy was the very thing which God refused to give to man, despite all the spiritual insight with which he endowed him. Autonomy is his undoing. When he claims to know of his own accord what is good and what is evil, he deludes himself and goes after success instead of seeking God. There is always some uncertainty about our road—even for us believers—an uncertainty which obliges us to remain in close dependence upon God, and to seek his guidance constantly.

We find uncertainty about what to do in every domain of life. In every conflict we are perplexed as to whether we ought to dig our heels in or give way. In every illness, infirmity, or threat of death the question arises: Ought we to fight it or to accept it? The contradiction is only apparent. We can fight to the end for healing, and if we achieve it we can see our success as a blessing from God. But if we fail, we can also see God's will in the acceptance of our failure. With Kierkegaard we can say, "In his failure the believer finds his triumph."

Even in nature we do not see only successes. As Bergson has pointed out, nature is not coherent in this respect. Its incredible successes are often emphasized, but there are also disturbing failures in nature. So Dr. Sarano raises the problem of pain and its meaning.[2] He points out, with reason, that there are contradictory views of pain. First, that it is a providential alarm signal which reveals the presence of a disease and calls us to take up arms against it. Unhappily the signal is often absent. Some diseases—and among them some of the most serious—develop in secret over a long period without giving any painful signal at all. When they are tracked down it is already too late to fight them effectively. Then, in our impotence, we interpret pain not as a call to arms but as a school of patience, abnegation, and renunciation, which is capable of bearing spiritual fruit. Of course there is no logic in this! But whereas logic is indispensable in mathematics, it is a great obstacle to the understanding of life. To understand life is to try to understand God, to understand what he intends, where he intends to lead us by means of events, by means of our successes and our failures.

The value, the infinite value, of the biblical perspective is that it radically changes our attitude in face of the events of life. It is no longer a matter of knowing whether they are fortunate or unfortunate, whether they are favorable or unfavorable to us, whether they constitute a success or a failure,

[2] Jacques Sarano, "A Quoi Sert la Douleur?" *Revue Présences*, Champrosay (S.-et-O.), No. 70, 1st Term, 1962.

but rather of what they signify in God's purpose. St. Paul, for example, in his turn, after having resounding success in his missionary work—tempered, of course, with many a failure and many a trial—is led by the Spirit back to Jerusalem (Acts 20:22-23). He is well aware that in all probability he is going to meet persecution, imprisonment, and martydom. And his arrest takes place. But in prison the Lord appears to him and says, "Take courage, for as you have testified about me at Jerusalem, so you must bear witness also at Rome" (Acts 23:11). Thus his imprisonment was to become, in God's plan, a new and unexpected missionary opportunity. Later, writing from captivity in Rome to the Philippians, he confirmed this: "I want you to know, brethren, that what has happened to me has really served to advance the gospel, . . . and most of the brethren have been made confident in the Lord because of my imprisonment, and are much more bold to speak the word of God without fear" (Philippians 1:12, 14).

Throughout the history of the Church it has been this reversal in attitude that has raised up martyrs and the heroes of the faith, has given them their indomitable strength, their complete independence as regards men and events, even at the times of greatest failure. "We know that in everything God works for good with those who love him," affirms St. Paul (Romans 8:28). "In everything"—in our successes as in our failures; in our failures as in our successes. He speaks to us through success; he speaks to us through failure. He speaks to us through healing and through disease. What matters is to listen to him, to let ourselves be guided, to face up to the adventure to which he calls us, with all its risks. Life is an adventure directed by God.

CHAPTER 14

The Instinct of Security

AT THIS POINT I must deal with one further important aspect of the problem of adventure which I have resolutely left on one side so far. Many of my readers will no doubt have thought of it and will have been raising objections in their minds. "Are you really sure that all men are imbued with an instinct of adventure?" they may have been asking. "Are there not many who prefer security, who seek above all things to guard against any risk, who prefer the known to the unknown, routine to adventure?"

Surely, there is also in man an instinct of repetition, which is opposed to the instinct of adventure. *Bis repetita placent*, the Romans used to say: We like things to be repeated. Some people take pleasure in travel; in going away their experience of renewal of life makes an agreeable contrast with their usual mode of living, which seems to stifle them. But there are also home-loving people who have no liking for travel. They are happy only in the familiar surroundings in which they have always lived. They are lost as soon as they leave the scene they are used to, whose every detail they know. The unexpected, which for the first group constitutes the whole attraction of travel, makes the second afraid. Even at home, anything that disturbs their regular program upsets and irritates them. They cannot bear to have their wives change the appearance of a room by moving the furniture around or hanging new curtains. Those who are bitten by the bug of change and travel find the home-lovers very hard to understand and call them stick-in-the-muds. But the latter have as much difficulty in understanding the former, and think of them as fidgets.

Furthermore, among those who like traveling some are always wanting to see something new, can never stay long in one place but keep moving blindly on, as if they were afraid of becoming fixed in one spot. Others get more pleasure from seeing places they know already, which bring back happy memories. They like to sit on that same rock facing the sea where they spent such delightful hours during their honeymoon, to renew old acquaintances—a headwaiter who recognizes them and remembers the date of their last visit, perhaps—or to stroll again down a street they have known in the past. My wife and I are among those who appreciate both. They are two different but complementary pleasures, that of discovering something new and that of seeing once again what one knows already, and each derives from the satisfaction of a different instinct. In any case the thing known today was unknown yesterday, and the joy experienced in seeing it again is a flashback to the joy of the first adventure. There are thus places which retain a quite special importance for us: for example, the place where we stayed on our first visit abroad, because it was the background of an experience of emancipation.

And there is the sudden strange emotion aroused by a familiar odor from our childhood, a tone of voice, a tune, or a story that we liked to hear. Reading also has two quite distinct pleasures for us—that of discovering a new author, of enlarging our minds with new feeling and thoughts as we read, and that of rereading a well-known book, in which we find ourselves, as it were, at home but keep noticing new details that had escaped us in our hasty first reading, when we were hurrying on in our eagerness to find out what came next. Thus one child soon tires of the toy he has been given. He always needs a new one to reawaken his pleasure and interest. But another child will lovingly keep some old toy and use his imagination constantly to give it new life.

There are clearly, then, two instincts, an instinct of movement and an instinct of repose, an instinct of discovery and an instinct of repetition and consolidation, an instinct of progress and an instinct of stability. Customs, usages, the whole of civilization, as well as art, rest in large measure on the instinct of fixity, which is but an aspect of the instinct of self-preservation. The modern social ideal of security and the tremendous increase in insurance express this urge to eliminate all kinds of risk. White-collar workers whose future is secure have fewer children than manual workers who are always under the threat of unemployment. A privileged country like Switzerland suffers from a "banker's complex," hoarding its funds or lending them out abroad but hesitating to invest them in projects for national improvements.

If I have more to say in this book about the instinct of adventure than about the instinct of repetition, that is because the first is peculiar to man whereas the second belongs to the whole of nature, responding in fact to a universal principle which has been formulated by the philosophers: the tendency of all things to continue in their mode of existence. There is the law of inertia in the physical world. There is the dominance of habit and reflexes in biology. I have described in my book *The Meaning of Persons* this characteristic of life, which escapes our observation even as it makes its appearance, and only manifests itself in automatisms, in the inexorable repetition of the same stereotyped phenomena.

As a living being man is also subject to this rigorous law of the automatisms. It dominates his physical life, and in large measure his psychical and even his spiritual life. But what distinguishes him from the animals is his faculty of escaping nevertheless, in some small measure, from its power, of experiencing at times the pleasure of discovering or inventing something new. The animal is the prisoner of its automatic reactions, as Portmann[1] clearly demonstrated when he pointed out, for example, the wonderful architectural sense evident in the construction of certain birds' nests. He notes, however, that from time immemorial these nests have always been the same, whereas human architects think up new forms which arouse indignant protests from the traditionalists.

In the animal all is reflex, habit, repetition, training. Take the case of my dog: When my surgery time is ended and I am going out to visit a patient, he is there at the door waiting for me. When I appear he jumps for joy—the joy of going in the car with me, not because it is a new experience but, on the contrary, because it is a habit. What is peculiar to man is his instinct for adventure, and this is why I see in it an expression of the resemblance to God of which the Bible speaks. It is also why man feels truly man only insofar as he follows his instinct of adventure and becomes something more than a robot or a collection of conditioned reflexes.

There is in man, however, a conflict between the instinct of adventure and the instinct of fixity. Man can follow his instinct of adventure only if he represses his instinct of fixity, and he can satisfy his instinct of fixity only if he represses his instinct of adventure. The behavior of the animal is quite simple, regulated as it is by a single instinct. That of man becomes complex, problematical, even anguished, since all repression is felt as anxiety, and since he is of necessity repressing one or the other of his instinctive tendencies, to novelty or to repetition. We have come here to something characteristic of human nature and often described in connection with other internal conflicts peculiar to man—the way man is eternally torn between two worlds to which he belongs equally, the world of nature and that of the Spirit.

It is true that Pavlov was able artificially to place his dogs in an analogous situation, setting up in them an experimental neurosis, when their psychic systems hesitated between two different responses to an ambiguous stimulus. But man is in a state of perpetual natural neurosis because he cannot be at one

[1] Adolf Portmann, *Um eine basale Anthropologie*, Rentsch, Zurich and Stuttgart, 1955.

and the same time an innovator and a conservator, an adventurer and a routinist. Observe that the two opposite poles between which man is placed, that of adventure and that of repetition, recall those described by Jung:[2] On one axis he situates the two poles of intellect and feeling; on another the two poles of intuition and the apprehension of reality. Man is torn. He can follow his reason only by repressing feeling, and *vice versa*; similarly, he can follow his intuition only by repressing his apprehension of reality.

With the problem of adventure we can add a third axis to Jung's system. This would justify what Strauss[3] said: Give me any psychological function, and I will build you a perfectly coherent system upon it. When I read that, many years ago, I thought it a little farfetched, and inspired perhaps by hostility toward the great masters of modern psychology. But there is more truth in it than at first appears. For man is a being torn in two, and this same split will of necessity be found in every domain of his mental life. With Freud, one can see him torn between his sex instinct and the exigencies of society. With Adler one can see him torn between his instinct of power and his sense of inferiority. With Jung one can see him torn between his libido and his spiritual archetypes. Or again one can see him torn between his instinct for adventure and his instinct for security, between his love of risk and his fear, between the animal in him and the divine.

I remember one of my patients, a likable and sincere man, shy and hesitant, full of guilt feelings, who blamed himself for everything he did, when he acted, and for his inactivity when he refrained from action. He had consulted an excellent psychiatrist, who apparently had said to him, "You have not yet learned to reconcile your instincts and your moral conscience, your ideals and reality." I confess that I smiled at this. Which of us can flatter himself that he knows how to reconcile these irreconcilable powers? My patient, however, felt guilty about

[2] C. G. Jung, *Modern Man in Search of a Soul*, translated by W. S. Dell and C. F. Baynes, Kegan Paul, London, 1933.
[3] E. B. Strauss, *Quo Vadimus?* Tyrolia-Verlag, Innsbruck and Vienna, 1948.

that, too. He blamed himself for not having made this impossible synthesis. He was quite astonished when I told him that I was no better at it than he was, and that I did not try to do it, since I should no longer be human if I could escape from this unavoidable difficulty.

In any case it is not a problem that can be solved by sitting down and coldly examining oneself. If it is possible, in some measure, not to reconcile our contradictory needs and aspirations but to choose in turn between them in a lively and complementary fashion, it will only be in the excitement of adventure, which rescues us from the sea of introspection that drowns many of those who hesitate. The more they examine themselves, the less they act. The less they act, the less clearly do they see what to do. In vain do they interrogate even God on what they ought to do; rarely do they receive any reply. God guides us when we are on the way, not when we are standing still, just as one cannot steer a car unless it is moving.

So our human condition can never escape from a tension between irreconcilable aspirations. We cannot give way to them both at once; we can only give free play first to one and then to the other—if possible at the right moment! Yes, at the right moment: That is why problems of conduct are not so much questions of principle, that can be settled once and for all, as practical questions the answers to which depend on the circumstances of the time. Voltaire said that there were four ways of wasting one's time: doing nothing, not doing what one ought, doing it badly, and doing it at the wrong moment. A musician cannot play a *do* without first silencing the *re*, the *mi*, and all the other notes; he cannot play other notes without silencing the *do*, on pain of producing, not a harmony, but a frightful cacophony. Making music means playing each note at the right moment.

We can never satisfy all our instinctive or moral impulses at the same time. There is no life without repression. We cannot be generous without repressing our egoism, or give way to egoism without represssing our generosity. We cannot give free rein to our fancy except by repressing our need for order, or give way to our need for order without clipping the wings of our fancy. A woman said to me the other day, "There is both a nun and a bohemian in me. I've tried in vain all my life to reconcile them." We cannot boldly commit ourselves without repressing our fears, or succumb to fear without experiencing a longing to be bold.

Only the animals are fully spontaneous, living unmixed the feelings of the fleeting moment. The child, too, surprises us with his capacity to go rapidly from disappointment to joy. But in the adult there is no laughter that does not hide secret tears, either unadmitted or unconscious, nor are there any tears behind which is not some repressed enjoyment. There is no self-giving without some reticence, no withholding without some longing to give.

This is the lot of every man, and also of society. Society, for instance, admires the adventures of the past—praising a Christopher Columbus or a Joan of Arc—but it persecutes the adventurers of today and calls them maladjusted. This severity is explained by the well-known mechanism of repression. I have mentioned the noticeably conservative character of society. The price of this is the repression of the instinct of adventure, but the nostalgia for it persists in the depths. The adventurer who then snaps his fingers at society and cares nothing for its all-powerful social conventions, but asserts openly his right to be free, disturbs it profoundly. Awakening the sleeping instinct of adventure, he arouses once more the anxiety of the inner conflict and so draws upon himself the reprobation of society.

Once again we can follow Jung, adopting his term "integration." It is evident that fulfillment for man cannot result either from giving a completely free rein to his instinct of adventure, at the cost of repressing his natural need for stability, or from giving absolute primacy to his instinct of fixity, at the cost of repressing his need for novelty and adventure. But as we have just seen, integration is never a final and stable state; it can only be a perpetual approach, an adventure that is always incomplete. Only insofar as we become more aware of this ceaseless conflict between our contradictory tendencies, and accept that we must live in tension like this, can we arrive at a more harmonious integration of the person. This is the view of the psychoanalysts themselves, whatever school they belong to. They never envisage a life exempt from complexes, which would be quite utopian, but see rather a becoming aware of complexes hitherto unconscious.

One of my patients told me about a dream he had had in which two personages appeared—Descartes and Magellan. Descartes was for him a symbol of security, the inventor of a method that completely banished any risk of error. We know how useful his method has been, yet it was incapable of comprehending life. Magellan, on the other hand, was the symbol of adventure: the man who in storms and catastrophes lost all his ships save one—save one, fortunately—and who by his daring succeeded in reaching his goal, the Pacific, with this last ship and his last chance.

Of course, a professor of philosophy may well protest that there was also an adventurer in Descartes—the courage to make a clean sweep of all that had been thought before him, the sheer audacity of the *Cogito*. And indeed we can see in Cartesianism a typical adventure with its characteristic curve, its phase of all-conquering development, followed by the phase of weakening due to its very success. A historian will also perhaps teach us to do justice to Magellan, recognizing in him not only the adventurer but also the scholar who had made the rigorous deductions which experience confirmed, and who had carefully taken every necessary precaution. I am not concerned here, however, with philosophy or history. I am concerned to look with a sick person at the human condition common to us both; with him I am listening for what the Spirit is saying to us in this symbolic language. And I observe that very often in our dreams appear contradictory symbols which bear witness to the opposing tendencies between which we are all constantly torn.

Everyone stands between Descartes and Magellan. When one follows Descartes he loses sight of Magellan, and when he follows Magellan he loses sight of Descartes. At the same time my patient told me that he had discovered what his problem

THE *Adventure* OF *Living*

was: it was his repugnance for all real commitment. No commitment is possible except in a certain integration between adventure and fidelity. Adventure may seem to be a commitment and yet not be one, if it is used as a means of flight farther and farther away, from adventure to adventure, without any roots being sent down anywhere. So we see perpetual students who go endlessly from one faculty to another rather than completing a course in any one of them. These are not adventurers, despite appearances, because they are not free. True adventure implies freedom to commit oneself. It is because they do not have this freedom that they run from faculty to faculty, taking refuge from the responsibilities of professional life in interminable studies. There are many people who, one might say, get into a routine of successive adventures which are not true adventures at all.

On the other hand, there are people who are still the prisoners of some adventure in the past. Ten or twenty years ago it was really an adventure, one so thrilling that now they dare not let go of it—though it is grown quite old—for fear of losing their treasure and falling back into the void of a mediocre existence. They cling to it and so deprive themselves of that constant resurgence of adventure which characterizes life. There is, then, a necessary rhythm between engagement and disengagement if the instinct of adventure is to be able to develop.

Life evolves ceaselessly. It is incarnated in successive adventures that differ for every age. Similarly the successive adventures into which a man throws himself show a certain evolution: they become increasingly personal. When he is young he takes part in a collective adventure. He has the impression of engaging in a personal adventure because he devotes himself to it eagerly and identifies himself with the group he is working with. But it is still an adventure in which he has not taken the initiative. His experiences mature him, and he gradually learns to distinguish the more precise and personal goals that are going to attract him. He will have to disengage himself from his first adventures in order to be-

162

come free to commit himself to new and more personal enterprises.

Moreover, the same alternation can be observed in history. Every nation experiences periods of adventure and periods of consolidation. Those who today look back nostalgically to the "good old days of the stagecoach" are the stick-in-the muds who have no stomach for adventure. They feel ill at ease in our modern world, in which the rapid changes taking place fill the more adventurously minded with enthusiasm.

Even in the field of morality, paradoxical though it may seem, a certain disengagement may be the precondition of a more genuine commitment. I remember an intelligent, perceptive, and scrupulous man whose parents had been ardent champions in the struggle against alcoholism. Under their influence he had signed a pledge of total abstinence for life while he was still little more than a child. Indeed, he had no desire to start drinking, but he felt that his abstinence, decided in the way it was at an age when the child still identifies himself with his parents, had scarcely any moral significance. He requested and obtained release from his pledge, so that thereafter he might abstain from alcholic drinks in a free and responsible manner.

In the same way a woman had made a certain solemn promise to her pastor. She too had no desire to break her promise. But it seemed to her that her moral stand in this domain was imposed on her by the promise she had given and was not free and personal. She now asked me to free her from it, equally solemnly, so that her good moral conduct might be genuine once more.

I myself once, in order to give expression to my desire to dedicate myself more profoundly to my work, gave up smoking, one of the little pleasures I enjoy. Not, of course, that I looked upon smoking as a sin, or because abstinence from tobacco had any ascetic merit in my case, or even any merit as a testimony, as is the case in the fundamentalist churches, but because I had learned that a concrete act is worth more than any amount of vague intentions, and also so that I might be able to talk to my patients about inner freedom without feeling too uneasy. Several years later, however, when I had been humiliated by my behavior in another direction, I suddenly caught myself using this little sacrifice to reassure myself that I was not so bad after all. This pretense of having a clear conscience is really Pharisaism. I started smoking again.

But let us return to the rhythm of alternate engagement and disengagement that ought to mark the development of our lives. Without self-engagement there is no adventure. But when the adventure grows old, only disengagement makes us available for fresh adventures and restores a sense of freedom to us. Fifteen years ago, with Dr. Maeder of Zurich and Dr. Jean de Rougemont of Lyons, I founded the annual conference on the medicine of the person. My wife and I devoted ourselves wholeheartedly to the project. It was a wonderful adventure for us, to call together in this way doctors of differing confessions, nationalities, and specialties, to take part in frank discussion and to join in seeking to make medicine more humane. We became so closely identified with the group that many of our colleagues started calling it the "Tournier Group."

In vain did we protest, as did our friends, against such a label. It stuck. You see, it did signify something—that because of our deep personal commitment in the enterprise, and because of the friendship and respect of the other members of the Group, none of them felt the same responsibility as we did in the running of it. Since they expected the initiative to come from us, this movement, which we had wanted to be a community effort, was becoming too personal, too dependent upon me.

At first I reacted in annoyance to the criticisms that were made accusing me of playing too great a part in the movement. I protested that I never acted high-handedly. But one of my colleagues helped me to look upon the criticism as a warning. At the age of fifteen, he pointed out, a child ought to be breaking free from his father and learning to stand on his own feet. So I am still a bit the father—and my wife the mother—

of the "Bossey Group"; but we are like the parents of an emancipated and responsible son. A certain disengagement on my part was necessary both to free me for fresh adventures and to allow the Group itself to renew its spirit of adventure. Dr. Jacques Sarano, of Valence, with the collaboration of several colleagues, has taken my place at the helm. After all, it was no longer a new adventure for me; but for him it is, and it is by going from adventure to adventure that a movement stays alive.

The remarkable thing is that this disengagement, which a year ago seemed like an impoverishment of my life, I can see now to have been an enrichment, with a stimulating sense of liberty. Perhaps that is why I am taking such pleasure now in writing this book on the spirit of adventure.

Perhaps, too, what I have just said may console some reader who has been downcast by the sudden interruption of some exciting adventure into which he has been putting all his energy. Or it may encourage another who feels that the time has come to give up an enterprise but hesitates to do so because he is so closely attached to it. Think of all the undertakings that have outlived their usefulness and yet are carried on because someone is afraid of "betraying the glorious past." Think of all the people who have founded or directed for years with zeal and efficiency some artistic or literary group, some industrial or commercial enterprise, some religious or professional society, and whose closest colleagues long secretly, but in vain, for them to resign.

Think even of the situation which my colleague took as an illustration in order to enlighten me, that of the parents who try to prevent their growing children from seeking their freedom. Precisely because their upbringing, preparing them as well as possible to face life, and watching them grow up, has been an exciting adventure for the parents, they have become incapable of detaching themselves from it. The child who claims his right hereafter to dispose freely of his own life is in this very act taking away from his parents a task which has been a wonderful joy to them. What *can* help them to face

165

their difficult abdication is for them to see in it the beginning of a new adventure.

This succession of adventures is the very image and meaning of life. It never stops. Birth is an adventure and death is an adventure. Youth is an adventure and old age is yet another adventure. In this light the successive abdications demanded by old age are seen quite differently: no longer as an impoverishment but as an enrichment in a new adventure.

So self-commitment is an adventure, and disengagement is an adventure. Fidelity and detachment are both adventures. The instinct of adventure without the instinct of fixity involves a risk of dissipation of one's energies. And the instinct of adventure involves the risk of the petrifaction of all energy. But how are we to achieve the integration of the two poles of the being, that of extension and that of consolidation? My father-in-law, who understood me very well, said to my wife before he died, "Your task with your husband is to stop him spreading himself too much." I have never managed it, and I am sure I never shall! But it seems to me that what has done most toward fulfilling my father-in-law's wish is the vocation I have received from God. In calling me to dedicate myself to the spiritual renovation of medicine he has thrust me into a great adventure, but he has also obliged me to give up many other adventures in which I should have dispersed my efforts.

God personifies creative adventure; but he also personifies fidelity. He never looks back when once he has set his hand to the plow. The example furnished by Jesus Christ is a striking one. He brings in a veritable revolution and strives in particular with the greatest intransigence against the legalism of the Jews of his time. At the same time he scrupulously observes the religious traditions, declaring that he has not come to abolish the Law of Moses. If we learn from him we shall go on always rediscovering the spirit of adventure, but we shall also rediscover how to deepen our understanding of the meaning of our actions, so that we shall be preserved from jumping like a grasshopper from one thing to another. He shows us step by step the risks we have to take. But he teaches us prudence and patience as well. God created the world, and in his widsom he set up in it the automatic laws of physics and biology which harmoniously preserve it. Only in God are invention and organization perfectly joined. And so we come again to the point we were at just now, to the necessity of listening to God, of coming back constantly to him, to be guided by him along the road of adventure.

Part III

THE CHOICE

CHAPTER 15

Which Adventure?

YES, OF COURSE, adventure—but which? We must tackle the question now. No man can be content to live like an animal, without bringing into his life, of his own free choice, something that does not come from nature. No man can be content merely to take the chance opportunities that happen to come his way and arouse his desire. Perhaps some of my readers have thought I have been wrong to speak of adventure as if it were peculiar to man. Is not the life of every animal a series of adventures—that of the monkey in the jungle, that of the hare in the fields, that of the antelope on the steppes, and that of the migratory birds? And the daily struggle for life which brings the animals into mutual conflict, making the weak defend themselves to the last gasp against the strong—is this not a dramatic adventure?

I have just got back from a walk with my wife. On the way we saw a little dog trotting happily along with his nose in the air. There's a dog on an adventure, I thought. But the fact is that for him it is a matter of chance. He is moved only by instinct. The animal plays a phonograph record—sometimes a very beautiful one—whereas man can improvise a piece, less beautiful, perhaps, but unique, personal to him. He is conscious of being something more than a body and a mind consisting only of automatic mechanisms. He is conscious of being a person, conscious that in him a non-material reality, the ego, is using that body and mind in order to attain a goal that he has freely chosen. In this he is a spiritual being, for every choice supposes a scale of values, and the world of values is the spiritual world.

A young colleague comes into my office. He explains to me that he has all at once come to a decisive turning point in his life. He has worked enthusiastically for some years on scientific research. Now he has been obliged by circumstances to leave his research team. It is not going to be easy for him to find as interesting a post as the one he has left. Perhaps he will waste precious years waiting for it to turn up. But if he turns to a different type of work, even temporarily, he is running the risk of finding it impossible ever to go back to the sort of adventure in research that he has just been engaged in. I question him: "What do you want to do most of all in the world?" There is a long silence. And then he replies: "I want to do something worthwhile."

Ah! We have talked for hours about that phrase "something worthwhile." A passionately interesting dialogue! What does it mean, "something worthwhile"? And is anything ever really worthwhile? One of the chief difficulties of the discussion is that it involves, at one and the same time, strangely and intimately mixed, both objective and subjective criteria. It is clear that "worthwhileness" ought to appear, to the person who accepts it, as an objective worth, a value in itself, independent of himself, indubitable, certain enough for him to justify his self-commitment to it, and not as an arbitrary goal invented by himself. Nevertheless, I cannot make judgments of what is worthwhile for somebody other than myself. What is worthwhile for me is not necessarily so for my young colleague, and *vice versa*. If I wanted to impose upon him, or even propose to him, my own values, I should be treating him as less than a responsible person. That is why we say that psychotherapy must necessarily be "non-directive."

But I cannot therefore say to him, "That's a matter for

you alone. I don't want to influence you." That would be to abandon him to his solitude in face of the most important problems of his life. He needs a dialogue, for no one learns to understand himself in isolation, but only when he encounters another person. There are, indeed, some values that are universally accepted, but I cannot help him in connection with them, simply because about them there is no argument. As regards the rest, argument—on the strictly human plane—is fruitless. Some cause, a revolution for instance, seems to me worthwhile enough for me to devote myself to it body and soul. But to another man what seems worthwhile and worthy of his devotion is to combat it.

So to the universal struggle for life, common to all the animals, there is added in the case of man the eternal struggle about values. No wars are more terrible than wars of religion. What I can do to help men and to bring them closer together instead of setting them up against one another is to try to understand why each adopts this or that value. But I can never decide on my own whether he is right or wrong. The "worthwhile" is never of the same universal order as "knowledge." It is of the personal order of "belief," *pace* the agnostics who claim to believe in nothing and who nevertheless always serve—sometimes very nobly—the values they believe in.

There seems to me to be more sincerity in the position of a Jean-Paul Sartre, who agrees that man is only man insofar as he devotes himself to values, but says that he is condemned to choose them arbitrarily himself. Indeed, values cannot be other than arbitrary if one does not believe in a God who reveals himself. Hence Sartre's distress: "My freedom," he writes, "is distressed at being the foundation without foundation of values."[1] Camus also, though he resolutely refuses to go along with Sartre—Camus who asserts that life is absurd—adds, "Living is in itself a value-judgment." Making an apologia for the revolt in which man's greatness is revealed, he asserts, "Every rebellion tacitly invokes a value."[2] Lastly, though

[1] J. P. Sartre, *Existentialism and Humanism*, translated by Philip Mairet, Methuen, London, 1948.
[2] *Existentialism and Humanism*, p. 20.

Freud denied values, seeing them merely as illusions due to psychological projections, his best disciples are far from remaining faithful to him on this point. It was, in fact, to facilitate the recognition of genuine values that Dr. Odier[8] suggested a differential diagnosis between them and the pseudo values denounced by his master.

We are, then, well armed to help men by means of psychology to see more clearly into their own minds, and to understand the unconscious factors which may warp their value judgments. But we remain totally powerless, apart from a religious revelation, to guide them, like my young colleague, in the ineluctable choice they have to make of what is, for them, worthwhile. Certainly it is not the job of the doctor to invoke revelation. Men are puzzled enough already by the stubborn differences of opinion that divide the theologians. There are no fiercer arguments than those between people who claim to speak in God's name.

The colleague of whom I have just spoken, who said he wanted "to do something worthwhile," was a Christian. He told me at great length about his conversion. But it is not easy to relate the general concepts about the world, about God, and about man that are implied in a religious creed (whichever it is) to the particular choices that we are having constantly to make in the course of our daily lives. A creed is rather like a letter of credit in a foreign currency—in my own country I cannot even buy a loaf of bread with it. I must find a foreign exchange office which will furnish me with the small change I need for my little daily purchases.

The problem is no different for the unbeliever, whatever values he adopts. It seems obvious to me that whenever a man asks himself in this way about what is worthwile he is engaging in a religious discussion with himself. The meaning of religion is being bound to that which is beyond and outside us. Every man who discusses within himself what is worthwhile in his eyes is by this very fact seeking a norm beyond and outside

[8] Charles Odier, *Les Deux Sources Consciente et Inconsciente de la Vie Morale*, La Baconnière, Neuchâtel, 1943.

himself, even if he does not attribute it to God. It is always the faith of unbelievers that interests me the most. That of the believers is well known. There are religious books full of it. Believers believe they know God and are always ready to tell us of the crimes we are committing against him. Unbelievers believe they do not know him, but they are seeking him, without always realizing it, every time they seriously consider the question of what is worthwhile.

Recently I saw once again a young woman who lived for a long time in the faith, but it was a childish and naïve faith. She has developed in her personal and professional life. She is no longer a child. But she has not found a more mature or adult faith. Meanwhile she feels she is traveling in a painful desert where she has the impression that she has lost her faith. So she calls God "X." This appellation enchanted me; it struck me as being more valid and more suggestively rich in meaning than many of the definitions of the philosophers and theologians. Basically, for this woman, he still has his place in the center of her mind. He has merely changed his pseudonym. The Jews also knew him under a pseudonym, Yahweh, so as not to have to pronounce the awful name itself. After all, "God" is also a pseudonym, *a nom de guerre,* under which we are told some little bit of the doings of that mysterious unknown adventurer "X," if I may put it so, the full story of which we never hear.

But this unknown adventurer is there in the background whenever we are engaged in a debate within ourselves about values. He is in the offing in the arguments of a Sartre, a Camus, or a Freud, as in those of my young colleague and in my own. What I find striking is how alone men are in this search for values, in which the whole direction and conduct of their lives is at stake. Not that they lack good advice; masses of people are always ready to tell you what the right thing is to do ("If I were you, this is what I should do. . . ."). We do not have to know them very well in order to know in advance what advice they will give. Similarly, we know in advance which creed each theologian will teach us. And similarly my faithful readers, the ones who know me best, will have a good idea in advance what they are going to find in a new book from me.

But in the real, sincere search, apart from all preconceived ideas and all pre-established systems, for a truly personal insight into what road to take, men are very lonely and painfully unsure. Kierkegaard was keenly aware of this: "What I really lack is to be clear in my mind *what I am to do.* . . . The thing is to understand myself, to see what God really wishes *me* to do, the thing is to find a truth which is true *for me*, to find *the idea for which I can live and die.*"[4] In order to elucidate this great problem we all need to find someone who will not give a slick answer for us either in the form of advice or by quoting some article of faith; someone who will listen to us carefully, will understand us and identify himself with us. This is precisely the role of the doctor. Do not tell me that in such a case he would be meddling in what does not concern him, going beyond his proper function, because a man's health depends at least as much on his accord with himself, on his right choice of values and on the fulfillment which is the result, as on the germs he may encounter or the vitamins he may absorb.

In every age the best doctors have understood that man did not need medicines only, but also to be helped to live, to become a person, to choose his adventure and commit himself to it. Thus Dr. Paul Plattner writes that the medicine of the person is reintroducing into medicine the world of values.[5] This search for values, this difficult debate, is for every man an inner adventure which precedes and determines the external adventure of his life. On these solemn times of hesitation or illumination, on these "privileged moments," as Georges Gusdorf calls them,[6] depends the whole orientation of a period of

---

[4] Søren Kierkegaard, *The Journals,* edited and translated by Alexander Dru, Oxford University Press, London, 1938, p. 15 (No. 22, August, 1835).

[5] Paul Plattner, "Médecine de la Personne," *Artsenblad,* April, 1950.

[6] Georges Gusdorf, *La Découverte de Soi,* P.U.F., Paris, 1948.

a person's life. There lies the greatness of the risk. And faced with such a risk the unbeliever equally with the believer, without realizing it properly, calls on advice that is higher than all the human advice he could easily obtain if he wanted to unload his personal responsibility onto someone else.

Hence man—every man—reveals himself as a religious being. He cannot bring himself to choose at random. His intuition tells him that he has links with an order outside and beyond him. When he conforms to it he makes a right choice. He bears within himself a need for adventure and invention, but he cannot bring himself to invent just anything, without reference to some universal value. Nor can he choose not to choose, since not to choose is to choose abdication, irresponsibility, and inhumanity. "The worst failure," writes Professor Hahn, "is it not to have failed to act?"[7]

Nor can man only half-choose, "go limping with two different opinions," as Elijah accused the Israelites of doing (I Kings 18:21). He realizes that a true adventure requires complete conviction, and that no one can put his full conviction in an adventure that has been chosen lightly, as one might choose a toy from a shop window for a moment's distraction. There can be no real dedication to any cause unless the person feels that it has taken hold of him, and not he of it—that it has impressed itself on him as being worthwhile. Camus speaks of men "paradoxically dying for the ideas or the illusions which give them a reason to live."[8]

Further, every choice of a "worthwhile" object implies the courageous renunciation of many "possible" objects. Dr. André Sarradon speaks of all the stillborn twins that we carry about in us, of all the other lives, all the other personages that we have had to give up. At the same time there arises a feeling of guilt: As soon as one has a goal, a value, one feels responsible for every falling short, every betrayal of the goal. And with guilt comes the need for salvation, for a reparation for

[7] *Chronique Sociale de France*, No. 5-6, October 15, 1955.
[8] *Op. cit.*

our wrongs which is no longer in our power, for forgiveness for wrong choices made and unfaithfulness to what we have chosen.

If it were sufficient evidence of the worthwhileness of an action that it leave some mark in history, we should soon be disabused. How many men have written their names in history by bringing down on humanity the most terrible catastrophes in order to satisfy their personal thirst for adventure! But a generous action is not necessarily worthwhile. Its intention may be so, its realization not. Lastly, every one of us feels that there is a hierarchy of choices, that a man can succeed in many things without believing his life worthwhile, because he has not succeeded in the thing he valued most. But which of us can boast that he has achieved his dearest ambitions? Are our lives really without value on that account?

You will see that this "something worthwhile" spoken of by my colleague raises a very troublesome problem.

I have already told the story of a certain young Frenchwoman, but I must refer to it again here because it seems to me to throw a great deal of light on our problem of the worthwhile adventure. The girl had been brought up in one of those French families that profess an anticlerical secularism going far beyond hostility to the Church and extending to the rejection of any religious conception of the world and of life. It is a belligerent attitude, a real adventure, imbued with the conviction that men must be liberated from the thralldom of the Church and of religion, which are looked upon as standing in the way of full human development. Thus our little girl had never heard God spoken of except negatively.

Nevertheless, while still a child, she was haunted by an odd question: What is the meaning of our actions? "What does it mean," she often used to wonder, "that I go to the left and not to the right, or to the right instead of the left, that I do this rather than that?" She told me that at the age, I think, of twelve she suddenly experienced an inner illumination. She recalled the exact spot where it happened, right in the middle of a bridge over the Rhone. All at once she felt filled with joy: she had found the answer to her persistent question. She had realized that any act, however trivial, could only have meaning if it fitted in with the meaning of the whole world, if it occupied its proper place as a tiny element in the whole history of the world.

So she had questioned her parents as to where one might find out what the meaning of the world was. They replied that the question was an absurd one, and that in any case she was too young to understand. She went on asking the same question of all sorts of people. Several years later someone answered, "In the Bible." She bought a Bible at once, but she did not understand what she read because the Bible is not easy to understand. Nevertheless she had been given the only sensible answer to her question. Neither science, nor philosophy, nor any human mind can teach us the meaning of things, for the good reason that it is a secret that belongs only to the author of all things, and we can know only what he chooses to reveal to us of his plan and his purposes.

Now, it is man's nature to ask questions about the meaning of things. He cannot passively suffer disappointment and pain without asking if it has any meaning. He cannot give himself up to joy and pleasure without asking if it has any meaning. The reason the parents of our little girl had told her that her question was absurd was that in their antireligious fervor they had pushed the question out of their conscious minds. The problem of the meaning of things is the religious problem *par excellence:* Either the world has been created and forms part of a coherent plan laid down by a Creator, its meaning being the realization of this plan, in which case, as our young friend saw, the meaning of each individual action is that it is a constituent element in that realization, or else the world is the result of chance, in which case nothing has any meaning.

It is possible, with Camus,[9] to argue that life is absurd and to see in it nothing more than a merry-go-round with no meaning other than that which simpletons arbitrarily attach to it. But in that case why did Camus throw himself with such conviction into all the adventures he thought worthwhile? It is quite clear that our question as to what is "worthwhile" is connected with

[9] *Ibid.*

the question about the meaning of things. Only that which has meaning can be worthwhile. The idea of worthwhileness does not resolve itself into the idea of good and evil. What is good is not necessarily what is worthwhile. It is possible to work out a morality by rational methods, to give definitions of good and evil, to accept, for example, as certain natural ethical systems do, the idea of the progress and well-being of humanity as a criterion. But who tells me that to contribute to the progress and well-being of humanity is worthwhile? It is impossible to say that anything is worthwhile without implying some belief in the meaning of the world.

It was in fact the problem of choosing the worthwhile adventure that our little girl was raising when she asked herself why go left rather than right, why do this rather than that. And what she discovered was that each little adventure is worthwhile only insofar as it has its place in the great adventure of the world. Thus, our question about the worthwhile adventure may be formulated in the following terms: "Is my little personal adventure in harmony with the great adventure of God? Am I experiencing, in my little adventure, a part of the great adventure of God?" The question arises, as we have said, at those decisive moments when a man is about to commit himself in some adventure that is important to him—a vocation, marriage, a revolution, social work. But really it can be asked in regard to all actions, and all thoughts, which are in fact a chain of little adventures. It would be impossible, after all, to decide where to draw a line between our actions and say that all on one side were unimportant and all on the other were burdened with responsibility.

The whole of Teilhard de Chardin's work is a modern answer to the problem of connecting our daily adventure as men to the great adventure of the world as far as we can apprehend it in the light both of faith and of science. The interest it has aroused shows how eager men are to know whether their adventures and all that happens to them have any meaning. The way science has developed, with its emphasis on the mechanism of phenomena rather than on their meaning, has tended to turn our thoughts the other way. This is the reason for much of the bitterness and anxiety that permeates present-day literature. But the doctor sees quite well that to explain to a sick person that his disease is due to a certain germ does not suffice to silence that very human little voice within him which asks whether the disease has a meaning.

CHAPTER 16

Guided by God?

OUR LITTLE GIRL grew up. She completed her studies and entered upon a professional life. Discretion forbids me to tell you what her work was. One day she realized that she was being asked to do something against her conscience. She was very upset and told her chief about it. "That's nothing to do with you," he replied. "Just do your job like everybody else; it is not up to you to make judgments about a customer's requests, but only to comply with them." She left her job and came to see me.

I have been the confidant of many analogous cases of conscience. If a man has an ever so slightly delicate moral conscience, there are not many situations he can stay in without some qualms. Even if he himself is not required to do things he considers wrong, he feels he is responsible for his comrades and for the whole organization for which he works. Ought he then to hand in his resignation? It is not usually an easy question to answer. He realizes that if he keeps himself right away from the world of business in order to preserve his own personal purity, he is also running the risk of falling down on the task which God has entrusted to him by placing him in the world as a witness. And again, is it not presumptuous on his part to set himself up as the judge of the orders and actions of his chiefs or his fellow workers, of whose motives he is not completely aware?

I am quite convinced of the truth of what our little girl discovered on that bridge over the Rhone. God governs the physical world rigorously. Water never omits to freeze at 0° C. No heavenly body ever departs from the trajectory imposed upon it by universal gravitation. A vegetable organism is entirely subject to biological laws and tropisms. And the behavior of the animal is determined by its physiology and its instincts. Whether it is gay or sad, an animal cannot be at any moment other than it is. When it tears its prey to pieces, we must admit that here too it is still completely subject to the order of nature.

Only man is free to act differently. This, at least, is what I believe, along with all those who believe in human liberty and the moral responsibility which flows from it. But let us suppose for a moment that those scientists are right who see only what is animal in man, his instinctive impulses and his conditioned reflexes. If they recognize a certain purposive quality in his actions, this too, as in the animal, is only the pursuit of pleasure prompted by the need to satisfy an instinctive urge. Let us also add to this naturalist view of man what one might call the psychoanalytical meaning of his actions, that is to say, the impulse to fulfill his unconscious urges.

It is obvious, however, that in man the "principle of pleasure" is a less reliable guide than in the animal. In him it can take on exaggerated proportions and perverted directions which, unlike the case of the animal, move him right outside the order of nature, since they compromise his life and wellbeing instead of promoting them. I once questioned a zoologist, Professor Adolf Portmann, on what was the most elementary difference in behavior between man and the animals. His answer was that man has the faculty of postponing his response to a given stimulus. Give a dog his soup, for instance: he rushes to eat it. A man, on the contrary, can delay the act, enhance and refine his pleasure in relishing the anticipation of it, choosing his own time. Here we have the first manifestation of human liberty.

To speak of choice is in fact to speak of liberty. A man can approve or disapprove of his own acts. He can decide the moment when they shall be performed. He can act as and when he wishes. As a result he always feels responsible for his behavior, even if it is dictated by an instinctive urge, since he could delay the action. Further, the "meaning" of his actions necessarily takes on a new dimension in his eyes. It is no longer only the satisfaction of an urge but also the realization of an aim judged to be worthwhile. Even if he admits, with the Freudians, that this judgment is only suggested to him by social constraint, he feels himself to be free to follow it or not, to act or to postpone his act.

Christians believe what the Bible reveals: that this liberty was accorded to man by his Creator, whom he may obey or disobey; but that his disobedience has brought upon himself, upon his descendants, and even upon the whole of nature permanent disturbance and continual suffering. But the majority of non-Christians also have some inkling of the truth of this, and many myths and legends, for example, express it in a form that comes very close to the biblical idea of the Fall. In the hearts of all men, believers and unbelievers alike, there is a nostalgia for Paradise Lost and a longing to be reintegrated (freely!) into the order of the world.

This is exactly what our young French girl realized in the middle of her bridge: that every individual act must conform to the general plan of the world. But there's the rub! How are we to know, as she put it, whether turning to the left rather than to the right, whether this act rather than that conforms to the general plan of the world? Can God himself guide and enlighten us? Can he reveal to us not only a general moral law, as he did on Sinai (Exodus 20), but also his particular, precise instructions telling us to go here or go there, to do this or do that? Can we hear his voice?

That God speaks directly to man, and often in an extremely concrete manner, is affirmed unequivocally by the Bible and confirmed by the experience of countless believers in every age. Yahweh says to Abraham, "Go from your country and your kindred and your father's house to the land that I will show you" (Genesis 12:1). To Moses he says, "Come, I will send you to Pharaoh that you may bring forth my people, the sons of Israel, out of Egypt" (Exodus 3:10). And at Joppa the Spirit says to the apostle Peter, "Behold, three men are looking for you. Rise and go down, and accompany them without hesitation; for I have sent them" (Acts 10:19-20). And so Abraham, Moses, and Peter were committed to adventures they would never have imagined. It can happen to us all, at any time—whenever it pleases God—to hear the "small voice," of which Gandhi also spoke.

Yes, it can happen. I have even known people who have told me they would at once recognize that voice if it were to speak again, they would be able to distinguish it from any other voice. Others have the same experience as befell the young Samuel (I Samuel 3:1-18), who heard the voice but did not know it was God who spoke. It must be said, however, that that is rare. Personally, I have never heard a voice. This is what I have to reply to those who say to me, "I tried to meditate, to have a quiet time, as you recommend, but I heard nothing." If people are prompted to say this by a superiority complex, they conclude triumphantly that it is impossible to hear the voice of God; but if they suffer from an inferiority complex they think they have been rejected by God, since he speaks to other people but not to them!

The truth is that "hearing the voice of God" is often only a metaphor. Dr. Frank Buchman, who taught many how to listen to God, actually employs a quite paradoxical term: he speaks of the "still small voice."[1] A thought may come into our minds, and in some cases we may attribute it to divine inspiration. But we must be careful—we are never safe from error. Being a doctor, I must point out here that no one is more certain that he is receiving divine guidance than those

[1] Frank N. D. Buchman, "Nations that refuse to think," speech of June 4, 1956. (*Translator's note:* American and English readers will recognize the quotation from the English version of I Kings 19:12).

mentally sick people who suffer from hallucinations, who hear voices. A paranoiac rushes into peculiar interpretations and adventures with no doubt in his mind that he is acting under the guidance of God himself. It is no use arguing with him on the point. It is a dangerous thing for a man to be powerful, and there is no doubt that spiritual power is the most perilous, more so than that exercised by the Roman emperors, who had a slave with the duty of whispering to them as they made their triumphal processions, "Remember that you must die."

The assurance of the mental patient who believes himself to be endowed with divine authority is in marked contrast with the hesitant humility of healthy people, the genuineness of whose spirituality we sense at once. Sometimes people have consulted me because they feared that their inspiration was no more than an unhealthy hallucination. As with all other differential diagnoses in medicine, the answer does not depend on a single criterion, but on all that we can learn about the individual case. Even apart from any question of mental disturbance, the doctor knows how an unconscious psychological complex can mislead a man of good faith on what he believes to be a command from God.

Clearly this is a delicate problem, and it is important not to try to solve it on one's own, without the help of the Bible, of the Church, of friends, and sometimes of medicine. I have seen, for example, a number of marriages come to a lamentable state of conflict, with all the tragic results that follow for the children, because the couples married not for love but in the belief that they were answering an inner call which they attributed to God. I am not saying that they were mistaken, and that their marriage was not God's will. I would never allow myself to formulate so categorical an opinion. It is hard enough for me to know what God expects of me without trying to act as a referee in other people's lives. But I do say that we can all go wrong, that we advance in fear and trembling. Is this, however, a sufficient ground for not persevering in the search for God's inspiration? I do not think so.

We always walk, therefore, on a knife-edge between skepticism and illuminism, between a systematic doubt about God's guidance and the presumptuous claim to know what his will is. Blessed indeed are those who hear God's voice or who can recognize his inspiration in some thought that comes into their minds, and who still retain the humble prudence dictated by our always uncertain human condition. My own frequent experience is that God may repeat his commands with importunate insistence when we are in doubt as to whether they come from him. I have sometimes written an order down twenty or thirty times in my notebook during my "quiet times" before recognizing its authenticity and making up my mind to obey it. Despite all the risk of making a mistake, sincerely to seek God's guidance remains the surest method of living the adventure of our lives in accordance with his purpose for us.

I have, however, seen many believers profoundly disturbed by God's silence when, faced with some important decision, they have been zealously seeking his advice and guidance. Why did God give no answer? They longed with all their hearts to do his will but could not find out what it was. They begged him to reveal it to them and put an end to their hesitation and uncertainty. No reply. I have myself had this painful experience, and I know from what my patients tell me that it is frequent.

Quite often God's silence is a trial that can be for our own good, making us examine ourselves to find what obstacle in us is separating us from God, or sometimes making us listen to quite different questions that he is putting to us, and that we must heed before he will give us his answer. But it would be false, hypocritical, and unjust to say to a person suffering from God's painful silence that his own sin or lack of faith is the cause. Was I not just as sinful as he is, in that luminous moment when I heard God calling me? Had I greater faith? Of course not. Sometimes a believer, faced with God's silence, comes to doubt his love. A man tells me he has just heard an evangelist talking with assurance about the inspiration of God, which he apparently received with ease. He is upset, thinking that God has less love for him than for the evangelist. I must reassure him, since this is more of a psychological problem than anything else: He is a hesitant nature, whereas his evangelist is one of those men who are always quite sure of themselves.

True, seeking God's guidance is neither simple nor easy. This supreme quality of life to which we aspire—that of an adventure directed by God in every detail—is never fullly attainable. We know it only in part, as St. Paul says. Only Jesus Christ was perfectly and constantly clear as to the Father's will. God speaks; nothing is more precious than his word, but it is rare. There is a charming remark in the Book of Samuel: "The word of the Lord was rare in those days" (I Samuel 3:1). Now, it is just in times when men scarcely trouble to listen for God's voice that suddenly one of them, like Gideon (Judges 6:12), may feel himself called in the most unexpected manner.

We all realize, however, that if it were necessary, before taking any action or making any decision, to have a precise, sure, and concrete command from God life would be impossible. To hope for constant illumination on God's will, therefore, is quite utopian. What, then, is the answer? Well, I think that it is only when we give up the idea that we *must* be clear, and let ourselves be led by God blindly, if I may put it so, rather than demanding that he show us clearly at each step what our road is, that we shall get out of the difficulty. The stars and the animals obey him without knowing it. They keep to God's ordered plan because they follow their orbits or their instincts, but without asking themselves questions. Even our own vegetative functions happily obey God, quite automatically; our heart does not have to wonder whether it ought to beat, or in what rhythm.

We all have a restless longing to be reintegrated into God's plan, but intellectual awareness of his will for us, however lucid and constant, is not sufficient to reintegrate us. Only his sovereign action can lead us back, even without our knowing it. Religion has become too intellectualized, as if what mattered was understanding at every point what his plan is for us. Religion means binding ourselves to God, abandoning ourselves to him, asking him to guide us, even if we do not understand his guidance.

I am well placed to measure the difficulty and complexity of human problems. Constantly, men and women of all ages, conditions, and religious outlooks come to lay their perplexity before me. Sometimes a frank talk with me helps them to see more plainly the course they must adopt. Sometimes I can help by telling them about some experience of my own. Sometimes psychological analysis reveals an inner obstacle which must be removed before they are in a position to make a proper and prudent choice. Sometimes I may fearfully put forward the advice that seems to me to be best. But a clear and certain solution is, strictly speaking, impossible to find in the majority of the most important problems—those, for instance, in which one has to choose between a duty imposed by justice and one imposed by charity, between the head and heart, between two courses of action about each of which one feels guilty.

One of my patients recently said to me, "I've chosen not to choose any more." I at once understood the significance of the remark, because I know his history. I have often remarked that to live is to choose, that man is truly man only insofar as he chooses his ends and courageously shoulders the responsibility for his choices. Too many people simply allow themselves to be carried along by their instincts, desires, and fears, to be tossed about by events like a cork in the sea. But there are others who have found themselves prematurely obliged to choose, when they were still children and their parents ought to have decided for them.

Such had been the case with my patient. The misunderstanding and neglect of his parents had been such that while still quite small he had had to calculate every detail of his behavior in order to avoid the storms that constantly threatened. The fact that he had never known the carefree life of the child who is sure of his parents' protection had so stimulated his perspicacity, his sensitivity to the great problems of man's destiny, his intellectual development, and his interest in philosophy that he had become obsessed with it all. The burden, however, was a heavy one for his young shoulders. His conversion to Christianity at a later stage, far from consoling him, had added an ever greater burden—that of continually distinguishing what was God's will, and of witnessing to his faith by the exemplary purity of his life.

You will understand why I was glad to hear him say, "I've chosen not to choose any more." I see this as a sign heralding his approaching cure, a sign that his mind is eased, that his anxiety is lessening, that he is ridding himself of the obsessive perspicacity which has been such a burden on him all his life. One can speak, then, of God's guidance being both explicit and implicit. There is no need to see any contradiction in this. The two kinds of guidance are complementary. I have had plenty of experience of his explicit guidance. Quite often, despite the uncertainty that always remains, I have obeyed with conviction what I have thought to be his command, and afterwards have felt that I have been really inspired. But such gleams of enlightenment are pretty rare. Time and again I have been left in my perplexity. The more I realize in this way the limitations of human intelligence, even in its most enlightened and inspired moments, the more do I prefer to depend on God, asking him to lead me even if I do not see clearly where he is leading me.

The Bible often employs a different image from that of the voice of God, the less intellectual image of the angel, of a mysterious, invisible presence which comes from God to guide us. I have already cited elsewhere in this connection the marvelous story of Balaam (Numbers 22). The prophet asked God how he ought to reply to the summons sent by the king of Moab. He spent whole nights in prayer. He thought at first that God was saying "No"; then that God was saying "Yes"! Then he set off on his ass, but not very sure of himself—in a state of "ambivalence," as the psychologists say.

Then God sent his angel to stand in the way. But the prophet could not see him; it was the ass who saw him and refused to go on. The prophet, furious, struck his recalcitrant mount. A donkey that will not go, an adventure that does not proceed as we should like, and there we are, in a temper! But it is perhaps an intervention by God. We are surrounded by angels that we do not see. To seek the adventure that is directed by God is to ask him to open our eyes to see his warnings in events; instead of losing our tempers, it is to allow ourselves to be guided by his angels, who now stop us, now push us onwards, or turn us to left or to right.

There are many other stories of angels in the Bible. One of the most beautiful is in the Book of Tobit. I recommend it to my fellow Calvinists who do not know it very well, the Book of Tobit not being in the Reformed canon of the Bible. Tobias is a child whom his blind father, the pious Tobit, sends to Media on a confidential mission. He does not know the way, and his mother is afraid some misfortune may befall him on the journey. He goes out to seek a guide and finds "Raphael that was an angel, but he knew not" (Tobit 5:4-5). The book tells of the wonderful adventures of Tobias, his marriage, the accomplishment of his mission, how he practiced medicine and healed his father—all without knowing that his guide and traveling companion was an angel.

This book seems to me like a true parable of human life as we seek to live it. We are all children in life, seeking our way, looking for a guide. We feel ourselves to be called to an adventure, to the fulfillment a mission which we do not know how to carry out. We suffer from our impotence to heal those we love. And God sets at our side his angels, whom we do not recognize, but who guide us without our realizing it. Angels also appeared to Abraham, to David, to Elijah, to the Christmas shepherds, to the Virgin Mary; to St. Joseph, in order that the Child Jesus might escape Herod's plot; to St. Paul, to tell him that he must carry the Gospel to Rome. All these angels symbolize the constant and secret intervention by God in the history of men, to guide them in the adventure to which he calls them.

CHAPTER 17

Surrender

THE DIRECT CALL, as we have seen, is not God's only method. He guides countless men and women, both unbelievers and believers, without their knowledge, without any clear realization of it on their part, so that his purpose may be fulfilled. Faith is reliance on this invisible sovereignty of God rather than on our own ability to decide what is "worthwhile." If Gutenberg had been asked, as a boy, what worthwhile thing he might do with his life, he would not have known what answer to give. God guided him to the invention of printing. The majority of our finest adventures are like that. We have no true conception of them in advance but are led into them without knowing exactly how. Faith is the recognition that this is the action of God.

God guides us, despite our uncertainties and our vagueness, even through our failings and mistakes. He often starts us off to the left, only to bring us up in the end to the right; or else he brings us back to the right, after a long detour, because we started off by mistake to the left in the belief that we were obeying him. He leads us step by step, from event to event. Only afterwards, as we look back over the way we have come and reconsider certain important moments in our lives in the light of all that has followed them, or when we survey the whole progress of our lives, do we experience the feeling of having been led without knowing it, the feeling that God has mysteriously guided us.

It was he who made us meet this man, made us hear that remark, read that book, with all the decisive consequences they have had on our lives. We did not perhaps know it at the time. Time has had to elapse to enable us to see it. Thus, the disciples on the Emmaus road talked with Jesus without recognizing him (Luke 24:13-35). It was he who brought us up short by means of a dream which at first we did not understand, a serious illness, a strange hesitation, or a painful failure. It was he also who guided us by means of a success, and so opened up a new and unexpected horizon to us. Ah, that is the true answer to our perplexing problem of success and failure!

Whence then come our most original and creative ideas? In general we have no notion. God guides us through our associations of ideas, and through the working of our unconscious. An artist may be in despair, seeking an inspiration, then suddenly execute a work which astonishes even himself a little, and which he receives as a gift from God. We spend a lot of time wondering what is worthwhile, we discuss it with our friends, we seek advice, we pray and meditate, we complain at finding it so hard to see clearly, and then we find ourselves involved in adventures we have never thought of, and we feel that the hand of God is in them! What is "worthwhile" is in fact those very adventures, directed by God, even if we have not understood at once their whole significance.

Is there anything we can do to have this quality of life? We can all do at least one quite simple thing: place the helm of our lives, as sincerely as possible, in God's hands, entrust the direction of our lives to him, confess to him our inability to direct them for ourselves, our inability to see clearly what he wants of us and so to ask him to direct them himself. Of course, this does not mean that we shall escape from the limitations and obscurities of our human nature. We know well that, consciously or not, we shall still put obstacles in the way of the

THE *Adventure* OF *Living*

action of God in our lives. But why not ask God to direct our lives, since we long for just that?

I took this step one day some thirty years ago. Since I had already been a Christian for a long time, this was not a conversion. But up to then my faith had been somewhat intellectual—a body of ideas about God, about Christ, about man and his spiritual and moral life. I was beginning to realize that there was another side to it, which I lacked—the surrender of my own will, the acceptance of the sovereignty of God over my real, concrete, everyday life. I asked my wife to be my witness, as I was hers; we went into a wood near Geneva, and I said a short prayer of surrender. When I consider what my life has been like since then, all the unexpected and exciting adventures I have had, I can well believe, in faith, that God heard me, took me at my word, and granted my prayer.

A thing that is easier to see now, at a distance, than it was at the time is that my act of surrender committed me to a much more personal attitude. My beliefs have scarcely changed since then, but my life has been quite different. The main thing about a creed is that it is a collective treasure. It is not for me to hammer out my own, but rather to accept what the Church teaches me. On the other hand, the personal thing in faith is my commitment, the pact I concluded that day with God, which has remained the charter of my life despite all my back-slidings. The idea of "worthwhileness" that we were discussing just now is another very abstract, intellectual notion, like that of a creed. We have seen, too, how hard it is to determine what is worthwhile. On the other hand, God is a person, which is something quite different: a living, moving, active person, engaged in an adventure and associating me with him in it.

So the "worthwhile" now looks much less like an idea and more like a person. One adopts a scale of values in cold blood, as a result of dispassionate thought. But a person one meets on the move, losing him and finding him again—finding him again in commom activity. A scale of values is finite and defined. A person is infinite, mobile, unpredictable. This last word reminds me of a very dear friend. I saw him rise from his knees

194

one day: "I understand now," he said. "What I have to do is to put my signature at the foot of a blank page on which I will accept whatever God wishes to write. I cannot predict what he will put on this blank contract as my life proceeds—but I give my signature today."

I was most moved to hear him speak like this. He was a man I had been to see several years previously. A keen sportsman, he was at that time president of the ski club. My idea was to arrange weekday services for skiers who went off to practice their sport on Sundays, and I wanted his signature on the appeal I was sending out, thinking it would add weight to it. He refused point-blank. "I am not a believer," he told me, "and so I cannot put my name to a religious appeal." And now, a few years later, he was committing himself by means of a quite different kind of signature! His life since then has been a prodigious adventure under God.

A blank contract with God, surrender to his sovereignty, abdication to his will—perhaps these ideas too will irritate some of my readers and seem pretentious to them. They will be the same readers of whom I spoke in connection with the problem of success and failure, who accuse me of making a subtle analysis of a very complex problem (now it is the difficult problem of how to know what God is guiding us to do) and then conjuring it away with some oversimple recipe. As if I were saying that all we have to do is to surrender ourselves to God in order to be surely guided by him and so avoid all uncertainty, all obscurity, and all anxiety in the search to know his will!

No, I am not saying that. Quite the contrary. The more one surrenders to God, the more trouble does one take to find out what he wants, studying the Scriptures so as to get to know him better, listening for his voice in prayer, and being more severe than ever with oneself in one's efforts to track down the sin that makes us impermeable to his inspiration. But the whole atmosphere in which one does these things is new. It is an atmosphere, in fact, of adventure. It is the adventure of faith, exciting, difficult, and exacting, but full of poetry, of new discoveries, of fresh turns and sudden surprises. It is adventure

195

with God, a daily adventure, which does not belong only to a few exceptional pious times but to every minute, affecting every thought, every feeling, and every act.

The personal problems of our lives are still there. We are more aware than ever of their complexity and difficulty because we have the courage to look them more squarely in the face. Uncertainty, doubts, and hesitations remain, but now we can take them all to God and ask him to reveal himself and his designs to us. Instead of looking on our personal problems as annoying vexations, we find that they provide a vital stimulus, a factor of new growth, transforming our personality and opening up new horizons and richer adventures for us.

It is our fundamental attitude to life that is radically changed. Our attitude to life is always a reflection of our attitude to God. Saying "Yes" to God is saying "Yes" to life, to all its problems and difficulties—"Yes" instead of "No," an attitude of adventure instead of one of going on strike. In such an adventure we commit our entire being. It is not an escape. It is not obscurantism. We do not have to give up our reason, our intelligence, our knowledge, our faculty to judge, nor our emotions, our likes, our desires, our instincts, our conscious and unconscious aspirations, but rather to place them all in God's hands, so that he may direct, stimulate, fertilize, develop, and use them.

You remember our analysis of the curve of adventure: after an explosive phase it inexorably dies away. Many people cannot reconcile themselves to seeing their finest adventures spent and declining. Well! The answer lies in the surrender of our lives to God, for he is the very source of life, a source that is always new. He brings one adventure to an end only to open another to us. He is tireless and inexhaustible. With him we must be ready for anything. At any moment an unsatisfying life may become once more a grand adventure if we will surrender it to him. Even a life that remains banal in appearance. What is different is the spirit in which it is lived; the person sees things in a different light—the glow of adventure. In the same way any marriage can be turned into an adventure again, even when it has become a mere institution, a habit, or even a bore.

You remember too our analysis of the difficult blending of the apparently opposite instincts of adventure and of stability. This also finds an answer in surrender to God's guidance, for God is the source of all our instincts. Surrender to him means asking him to control them as an engineer at the electronic control panel of some big automated factory directs the various processes by manipulating his switches.

Of course it is often very costly. It is always hard to surrender the treasures we have acquired from past adventures and carefully hoarded, even when we have become their prisoners. The surrender of the bitterness, the rebellions, the rancor and resentment accumulated in the course of past adventures is also involved. Every life can be changed, pulled out of its rut.

A certain man was always late for his appointments—a significant fact, as both he and I well knew. It was the sign of a grudge against life because it had hurt him, against time because it would not stop but inexorably swallowed up his unaccepted failures. Suddenly, one day, he arrived on time! Oh, I shall never forget the look on his face! It was a look that seemed to be saying, "There, I've done it! It is true, then, that a man can change!"

It is quite true: a man can change. Why, then, do so many people think and say the contrary? Perhaps it is an attempt to justify themselves and provide an excuse for not changing. Many doctors affect this cynical attitude of skepticism. They say, "Once a drunkard, always a drunkard." It is not true. There are drunkards who give up drinking. Bitterness can change to joy, resentment to forgiveness, and hate can vanish away. Really, if we are so keen on justifying ourselves, if we say, "What do you expect? I'm made that way; you won't change me," it is because we secretly long to change, and suffer because the change is slow in happening. We want to be made new, eager and ready for new adventures.

We must go down on our knees and be quiet before God;

we must accept the necessity of being stripped of our treasures. This was what Christ meant when he spoke of the branch being pruned so that it might bear more fruit (John 15:2). And our attachment to the vine, to Jesus, is this surrender, this grafting in him so that we may receive from him the sap of adventure. Before the surrender is made, it looks as if we were being asked to make an almost impossible and frightening leap in the dark. When the step is taken it seems the simplest and surest of adventures. One of my patients writes to me of all her revolts against God. She bears a grudge against him for "always having the last word." Then she has a dream: She is on the seventh story of a strange building; she has to go down, but there are no stairs! Suddenly in a corner she sees the elevator and so reaches the ground with no difficulty.

How many disillusioned souls there are who no longer believe that any success is possible in their lives! Success is always possible for a person who will look, not back, but forward, who will not persist in dwelling on old adventures that are finished, as if he could himself mend what has been spoiled; for the person who will wait on God for a new beginning. The whole story of man's fall and redemption can be found in our problem of adventure: The adventure is lost—to be found again in the Redeemer. Holiness proves to be the greatest adventure of all—not, as many think, an unattainable perfection, a faultless life, but so deep-rooted an attachment to Jesus Christ that he can take us with him wherever he wills.

The surrendered life is also an adventure because it is always on the alert, listening to God, to his voice and to his angels! It is an absorbing puzzle, an exciting search for signs of God. Every circumstance and every event takes on a new significance, the bad as well as the good, the pleasing as well as the annoying. Everything must be examined for God's messages to us: What does he mean me to understand by this? Where does he mean to lead me by that?

The idea of signs from God permeates the entire Bible. The Creation is a sign of his greatness and his love. An illness, a healing, a war, a famine, a heavy crop, drought, rain—all are signs. Jesus himself rebukes his contradictors for being able to

198

discern meteorological signs while not perceiving the signs of God. The rainbow is the "sign of the covenant" (Genesis 9:12). That does not stop its being a physical phenomenon susceptible of study by science. But all phenomena are at the same time signs. Phenomena, as phenomena, are blind and meaningless, whereas as signs they tell of God's adventure.

Everything that exists and all that happens has thus a double aspect: As facts they can be objectively studied; but we can also decipher in them God's adventure. This is what makes the Bible so concrete. It does not deal in general theories—it tells stories. The adventure of God, the tremendous adventure of God, is at work in every adventure of every man, and in every episode, even in the smallest. The striking thing about the Bible is that it not only puts forward as signs from God the big events—the Creation, the Flood, the escape from Egypt, the Resurrection of Jesus Christ—but sees God at work in the tiniest details. So we are attentive, in God's school; everything speaks to us of God.

Read the Bible again from this point of view. You will see all those men who in one way or another are on the watch for signs from God to guide them. Gideon, in his surprise, is not satisfied with one sign. He wants corroboration (Judges 6:11-23). Jeremiah watches the potter at work in his workshop (Jeremiah 18:1-12). Jesus observes a sower sowing his seed (Luke 8:5-8). David watches his sick child (2 Samuel 2-16). The shepherds come to the manger (Luke 2:12). St. Paul sees in a dream a European who begs him to come over to Macedonia (Acts 16:9). Every dream is a sign to decipher, every failure a sign to understand, every meeting a sign to discern. What an adventure!

Why then do the lives of so many Christians, members of all sorts of churches, seem so dull, so inward-looking, so void of any spirit of adventure? Why do they seem so monotonous and stuffy? Why do they seem so often to be lived in a world apart, abstract and distant? Punctilious attendance at church appears to do nothing to shake them out of their ceremony-ridden existence, out of their ingrained habits and automatic observances. The world calls them sanctimonious, or bigoted, and pities them as being people without life, strangers to life.

Talk to them about things that excite people—football, the latest novel, movie stars, pop singers, Wall Street, politics, abstract art, Broadway shows, food, or fashions—they remain indifferent. They show signs of life only if you talk to them about philosophy, psychology, and especially theology. They read only serious, religious books and display deep ignorance of all the most burning questions of the day. They would like to convert the whole world, but they make no contact with the world because they speak a different language and no longer understand the world's language. At their work they are conscientious, even finicky, but the atmosphere is heavy about them. They have no laughter, no jokes. One feels that they look upon their comrades' conversation as futile, and that at heart they are not interested in their work. It is only a duty for them, not an adventure.

CHAPTER 18

Heaven and Earth

How is it that the majority of believers lack the spirit of adventure? I think it is a result of the tendency of all of us, believers and unbelievers alike, to think of spiritual values as being opposed to material values. We oppose the spiritual life to "real life," heaven to earth. Believers, because of the very fact that they have asked themselves what is "worthwhile," because they have realized that God is the only possible source of all authentic value, have stopped taking any interest in anything that is not religion. They have turned their backs on the earth so as to look only at heaven.

It is possible sometimes to see this attitude as a sort of flight. Their religion seems to be a refuge into which they can escape from their unsuccessful lives, their piety a consolation for their failures in everyday affairs. They have given up the attempt to face and solve the problems of their real lives, indulging themselves instead in a world of abstractions. This dereliction of duty they mistake for Christian self-denial. The psychological phenomenon of super-compensation has often been described. It is not always involved, however, in such cases. We see intelligent and well-qualified men and women, capable of useful lives, turning their backs on reality in good faith because they believe that in doing so they are serving God more faithfully.

I am not referring here to a vocation to the monastic life, which is the result of a special divine call. The rigorous conditions and discipline of the cloister are no fantasy, but a solid reality. In any case the religious orders are always on the alert to guard against false vocations to the monastic life. What I am concerned about are the large numbers of people who are the victims of a tragic misunderstanding. They take no further interest in worldly matters because their interest has—quite properly—been awakened in regard to the spiritual verities, as if the latter could exist in themselves, in the abstract, outside of their incarnation in the world. They think they are engaged in the most worthwhile adventure, but their lives are no longer an adventure, since all true adventure must be incarnate.

Of course they can quote biblical texts in support of this radical opposition between heaven and earth: St. Paul tells us not to be "conformed to this world" (Romans 12:2), invites us to detach ourselves from the things of this world, "for the form of this world is passing away" (I Corinthians 7:31); St. Peter says we are "aliens and exiles" in the world (I Peter 2:11); and Jesus himself tells his parable of the pearl of great value, which was so precious that a merchant sacrificed all he possessed in order to be able to acquire it (Matthew 13:45-46).

I say, however, that there is frequently a great misunderstanding in the interpretation of these and many similar texts. The pearl of great value, of course, is faith, more precious than anything else in the world, but faith does not turn us away from the world! It calls us rather to interest ourselves in it, because God loves it and is interested in it, because God created it and is engaged in his adventure in this reality that is the world. Of course, God is the source of all value, and moreover he gives value to things, to living beings, to the world, and to the events that take place in it. The Bible opens with the words "In the beginning God created the heavens and the earth" (Genesis 1:1). He did not create only a spiritual world but also the earth, and therein lies his adventure, in which he associates us with himself through our instinct of adventure.

Many Christian sects sharply distinguish between the spiritual and the material. Although I think that the distinction is the result of a misunderstanding, I wish to make it clear that I have a high respect for their sincere and fervent faith. They are often very lively, outward-looking communities, full of missionary zeal and the spirit of adventure. They claim real, solid sacrifices from their followers for the sake of their beliefs. For them, not being conformed to the world means abstaining from the theater, the cinema, dancing, smoking, alcoholic drinks, jewelry, and elegant clothes. For some it means submission to all the prescriptions of the Mosaic Law, not eating pork, and not working on Saturday because it is the Sabbath. All this has real value, since it is for them the sign of their faith, their love and devotion to God. It bears witness to the fact that fellowship with God is more precious than all the little worldly pleasures to which so many others are enslaved.

The doctor, however, has on occasion to treat their children. The position of the children is quite different. What for the parents is a joyous sacrifice, freely entered into, in exchange for the pearl of great value, is for the children nothing but a taboo, a prohibition, a diabolical temptation, a sin the prospect of which is a source of nothing but anxiety. So what was for the parents a liberation from bondage may itself become a bondage for the children. Happily there are pious, austere, even puritanical parents who do understand this and allow their children more liberty, so that they can in their turn freely adopt their own rule of life, for love of God and not from anxiety because of a taboo.

The same argument developed with tragic results between Jesus and the Pharisees. They also were devoutly and scrupulously careful to distinguish themselves from other men by means of their exemplary behavior. Jesus scandalized them because he healed some sick people on the Sabbath day, or because he kept company with people of doubtful reputation and sat down at table with prostitutes and revenue agents, who—in his day—shamelessly defrauded the people! And when Jesus was present at a wedding, he actually changed water into wine, the best wine, too—oh, impious indulgence!—with which to regale the guests (John 2:1-10).

The message of the Bible as a whole is the very opposite of a contrast between heaven and earth. It is their unity. In the biblical perspective there are not two distinct worlds, the profane and the sacred. Everything is sacred. The hand of God is not to be seen in abstract ideas, but in nature, in history, in all the adventures of all men. God is interested in everything. We in our turn when we come into contact with him experience a renewal of interest in everything, even in those things that are apparently most trivial.

Jesus does indeed tell Simon Peter to leave his boat and his nets: "Henceforth you will be catching men" (Luke 5:10). But before that he had taken an interest in his secular work of fishing and had given him a piece of good advice on how to make a successful catch. And so, although he is now calling him to a different kind of fishing, it is not because catching fish is of no interest. The truth is that it was of interest as an adventure, that it prefigured as an adventure the whole spiritual and ecclesiastical ministry that Jesus was to entrust to the apostle. This is the meaning of the entire Bible: not two things, but one; not an absence, but a presence in the world; not contempt, but care for the world.

What we do, however, is constantly to put asunder what God has joined together. It is all right to go to Communion every morning, so long as what we do then permeates the activities of the whole day, the adventure of the whole day. We cut the hours devoted to God from those devoted to everyday life. In the same way, in general terms, men and women separate into two groups: those who are so interested in religion that they hold aloof from secular affairs and those who are so interested in the adventures of life that they pay no heed to God. Of course this is an oversimplification, but I am trying to make the point that any dialogue between the representatives of the two points of view is extremely difficult. Religious people would like to get the others interested in the religion they themselves are involved in. But it is for the religious people to begin by taking an interest in what concerns the others. That is love.

In some married couples each partner represents one of the two camps. The wife, for example, has had her interest aroused by a great preacher and has become converted. She is his zealous proselyte, spending herself unstintingly in the service of the community he leads. This is her adventure. She never misses going to hear him wherever he is speaking, she reads all he writes, thoroughly understands his thought and interprets it faithfully to everyone she meets. All this activity absorbs so much of her energies that she has time for scarcely anything else. She even neglects her housework a little, as well as her husband and children. She attends all the religious conferences, reads large numbers of books, becomes more expert in this field, and more and more interested in it.

She would like to convert her husband—would it not be wonderful if they could follow this spiritual adventure together? She tries in vain to coerce him, to get him to go with her to church and to meetings. She does not even know whether he is a believer. He says nothing, makes no reply when she starts an argument about religion. She admits to me that she leaves one of my books lying ostentatiously on the table. Has her husband ever opened it? He perhaps scents a trap; he suspects it is a tactical maneuver at least. He makes a point of reading only detective novels, on the grounds that he needs some light relief from the heavy cares of his daily work.

He is an industrialist. His life is a quite concrete and absorbing adventure. He spends his whole day dealing with urgent problems, in a post of special responsibility. He is still thinking about them in the evening, when his wife would like to get his mind working in a different direction, that of religious questions, about which he knows very little but in which she is at ease. He would not come off very well in such an unequal duel, would he? But neither does he talk to her about his own worries, since it is plain to him that she only listens to him with half an ear.

And so it goes on. They become more and more strangers to each other. Religion, which ought to unite them, separates them. The wife thinks it is her husband's fault, and that religion would unite them if only he were willing to follow her along that road, and pray with her, perhaps. As for the husband, he wonders what he can give her as a present—a religious book, to please her? It would scarcely ring true. A pretty nightdress? He doubts whether she would appreciate it. The fact is that he thinks she does not pay sufficient attention to her appearance. An industrialist's wife ought to dress more smartly. It irks him when he invites one of his business friends home to dinner. She will not have her hair done or make herself up as he would like. Is this love she talks so much about in church really such a complicated and abstract thing? Could she not express her love by trying to please her husband and giving herself to him more unreservedly?

They do not argue; they do not cross swords with each other, except perhaps over the children, with whom he thinks she is overindulgent. But she has read so many books on psychology, she invokes so many authoritative opinions, that he has given up arguing so as to avoid a conflict. He has tried sometimes to proffer advice; he has felt she was tiring herself with all her meetings, and she has been excessively worried by the disagreements on the Parochial Council of which she is a member. He does at least know something about conflicts, for he often has to face them on his board of directors and in the factory. But because he does not go to church his wife reckons that he cannot have anything useful to say about the problems that divide the church Council. In any case he does not ask her advice either, about the running of his factory.

They are living in two different adventures, with no communicating door between them. Each has his or her own friends and interests. What neither of them realizes is that they are really one and the same adventure, because it is the same God who has called that wife to know and serve him in his Church and who has awakened in the husband's heart the love of adventure which finds expression in his work as an industrialist. Is God not everywhere present, in the factory as well as in the church? Does he not take an equal interest in all men and in everything they do? Is not God's own adventure being worked out in every man's adventure, without distinction?

You see where our problem of adventure has led us—to the rediscovery of the greatness of God, whom we have tried to keep within the confines of the churches; to the breaking down of the barriers which men are always setting up between the various departments of life, and which, so to speak, prevent God from passing freely from one to another; to the fusing of faith and vocation, of religion and life. The wife of whom we have just been speaking accused her husband of dismissing God from his life because he refused to take an interest in religious matters. But she was not so different from him as she imagined, since by seeking God only in religious meetings she was also helping to dismiss him from real life.

Despite appearances, the barrier was not set up so much between these two as within the heart of each—in that of the religious wife quite as surely as in that of her husband. We can return once more to C. G. Jung's schemas. Man can develop one of his functions only at the price of repressing another. As a result he impoverishes, divides, and fossilizes himself. His journey toward an integrated life continues only insofar as he brings to light his buried talents, becoming conscious once more of the things that have been repressed into his unconscious. The same is true of the two worlds to which man belongs, the spiritual and the secular. Our industrialist was passionately interested in his work but had repressed his thoughts about religion. It must be observed that his wife's attitude was a contributory factor, for she on her side had pushed out of her conscious mind her secular interests, had impoverished her personality, in spite of all the spiritual riches she had received through her conversion.

So it is within ourselves that we must reconcile these two worlds in order to become fully men, as Professor Karlfried von Dürckheim has remarked. This harmonious human plenitude is the person, man, as God wills that he should be. The medicine of the person aims at helping him to attain plenitude, to become a person. It cannot therefore neglect the importance of his physical health, of his psychological health, of fitting him to take his place in the world, of his adventure in the world, of his family, social, and professional relationships, in order to put the accent on a so-called spiritual development, which is nothing if it does not include all the rest as well.

That means, for the man who has been blind to the realities of faith, a discovery of the other vitally important dimension of life, which gives a meaning to all the rest. But for religious people it means a sort of second conversion, as Blumhart used to say, a return to reality, a descent from the ineffable spheres of abstraction to the practical adventure of secular and work-aday life, a renewal of interest in everything that has been thought foreign to religious faith, such as science, technology, economy, art, and politics. What is required is synthesis instead of antithesis.

I am surprised, for example, at how many people oppose psychology to faith, how many believers distrust psychology, and how many psychologists distrust religion. I am always embarrassed when a patient tells me that he looks upon me as a Christian psychologist and expects me to apply "Christian psychotherapy." It is frequently the very patient who would profit most from the rigorously technical course of treatment he is trying to avoid. There are not two psychotherapies, one Christian and the other not. There is only one. There are not two medicines, one Christian and the other not, but only one. There are doctors who try to help the sick to live and to get better, and who in so doing are performing the merciful work of God, God's adventure. In a fine passage, Dr. Charles H. Nodet[1] writes of these two adventures which are but one: that of man's psychological development and that of the Gospel which leads him to his fulfillment.

It is the same in every discipline and every vocation. After all, whether I am a doctor treating a patient, an amateur author writing a book, or a baker making cookies, the same thing applies. God's purpose includes them all, and all the other activities of all men, and everything else as well. If we really

[1] C. Nodet, "Psychoanalyse et Culpabilité," in *Pastorale du Péché*, Desclée de Brouwer, Bruges, 1962.

see that it is God alone who gives value to things—to our jobs, for example—we shall give up our prejudices about them and stop looking upon some as being more worthwhile than others.

The valuable thing is to see our job as the task which God has entrusted to us, and to accomplish it in that spirit, allowing ourselves to be guided by him. The valuable thing is to see our job, as well as all our other activities, as an adventure directed by God. In religious circles people have gotten into the habit of restricting the idea of "vocation" to the call to the ministry of the Church, or at most to a medical or teaching career. This tendency clearly indicates the distinction we make in our minds between the things of the spirit and secular things.

For the fulfillment of his purpose God needs more than priests, bishops, pastors, and missionaries. He needs mechanics and chemists, gardeners and street sweepers, dressmakers and cooks, tradesmen, physicians, philosophers, judges, and short-hand-typists. "My brethren," writes St. James, "show no partiality as you hold the faith of our Lord Jesus Christ, the Lord of glory" (James 2:1). Having a vocation means approaching everything one does in a spirit of vocation, looking upon it as an adventure shared with God. "In all toil there is profit" (Proverbs 14:23), or, as Calvin put it, in his pungent style, "There can be no work, however vile or sordid, that does not glister before God, and is not right precious, provided that in it we serve our vocation. . . . Every man . . . in his place ought to deem that his estate is as it were a station assigned to him by God."

I do not serve God only in the brief moments during which I am taking part in a religious service, or reading the Bible, or saying my prayers, or talking about him in some book I am writing, or discussing the meaning of life with a patient or a friend. I serve him quite as much when I am giving a patient an injection, or lancing an abscess, or writing a prescription, or giving a piece of good advice. Or again, I serve him quite as much when I am reading the newspaper, traveling, laughing at a joke, or soldering a joint in an electric wire. I serve him by taking an interest in everything, because he is interested in everything, because he has created everything and has put me in his creation so that I may participate in it fully. "It is a great mistake," wrote Archbishop William Temple, "to suppose that God is interested only, or even primarily, in religion."

The Preacher of the Book of Ecclesiastes is a great scholar, and yet, in incomparable words, he tells us how vain are all things in themselves. But he also re-establishes their value when he relates them to God: "God has already approved what you do" (Ecclesiastes 9:7). Every job is fascinating if one puts one's heart and soul into it. I feel I could take up any career with enthusiasm, I am so interested in all my patients' occupations. I enjoy talking about electricity to an engineer, about dressmaking to a dressmaker, about education to a teacher, about law to a lawyer, or about cooking to a housewife. Every occupation is full of parables, as Jesus Christ taught us. I remember a pig breeder who talked so enthusiastically about his job that I was quite carried away by it myself, and I took it as a lesson for my own work. Dr. André Sarradon tells of how he had a similar experience while listening to a rag-and-bone man whom he was treating talk about his job. Dr. Alphonse Maeder, of Zurich, on reading Trubka the lion tamer's book,[2] also realized that the occupations of lion tamer and physiotherapist were very much alike, in that they both required the same virtue—love.

Loving God, loving men, and loving animals means loving the world, loving life, and loving one's work, whatever it may be. God is interested in everything and in every job. Look at the part played by workers in the Bible—fishermen, merchants, farmers, goldsmiths. Jesus worked with his hands in Joseph's workshop. According to Aron,[3] there were still to be seen, toward the end of the first century A.D., plows that he had made. God's purpose is not worked out only through kings, prophets, and apostles. A prostitute, Rahab, played her part (Joshua 6:17), as did Naaman's servant girl (2 Kings 5:2),

[2] Vojtech Trubka, *Mes Fauves*, Delachaux and Niestlé, Neuchâtel, 1947.

[3] Robert Aron, *Les Années Obscures de Jésus*, Grasset, Paris, 1960.

a tax collector (Luke 19:2), a seller of purple goods, Lydia, the first European won for the Gospel (Acts 16:14).

Look again at the poem in praise of the perfect wife, who "seeks wool and flax, and works with willing hands. . . . considers a field and buys it; with the fruit of her hands she plants a vineyard" (Proverbs 31:10-31). You remember St. Paul's words: "We are fellow workers for God; you are God's field, God's building" (1 Corinthians 3:9). I do not think that we have the right, in the light of all this, to restrict the application of the biblical message to our spiritual activity alone. Rather must we extend it to our whole life, for, as Jesus said, God's field "is the world" (Matthew 13:38), the whole world.

In this perspective we can see our whole life, all our activities, all our thoughts, all our feelings, all our experiences both happy and unhappy, as a worthwhile adventure. And then we can put our whole heart into all we do. This means never leaving God out of anything, but trying in everything to see things, people, and problems from his point of view, as he sees them, in order to act in regard to them as he wills. I do not say this is easy to do, but that is precisely what makes it a great adventure. I do not forget the risks we all run, of making mistakes, but these risks are what make it an adventure. The prophet Isaiah is always asking his hearers to open their eyes, to realize that it is God who intervenes in history and turns events to his purposes. But he also knows how difficult it is to discern what the will of God is: "For my thoughts are not your thoughts, neither are your ways my ways, says the Lord" (Isaiah 55:8).

CHAPTER 19

Meditation

How ARE WE to discover the way of God and his will for our daily lives? How are we to bring about the necessary amalgamation of spiritual truth and practical reality? How can we broaden our vision and correct our view of the things that make up our lives, trying to see them as God sees them? Of course we must pray God to help us, we must study the Bible, and pay heed to the teaching of the Church and of the theologians. But something more is needed, since if we concern ourselves with theology we run the risk of disregarding and losing interest in material life, like the religious wife in the preceding chapter, instead of turning toward it. There are very worthy and learned theologians, orthodox in dogma, zealous and pious, who never succeed in building this necessary bridge between the religious and the practical life, and who are capable of suffering acutely as a result.

In my experience, the practice of written meditation can be a great help in bridging the gap between our two worlds, the spiritual and the material. I do not wish to suggest that written meditation is an indispensable method, and universally applicable. To some people it is quite unsuited, people who would be inhibited in some way from meditating by the very fact of having to write. People differ greatly, and God can never be confined within a method. For example, after a meditation during which I have written a lot of commonplace, useless things in my notebook, there may come into my head unexpectedly—at the wheel of my car, or in the elevator, like our little French girl in the middle of her bridge—a much more useful idea, and I sense that it has come from God. Once again, I do not wish to make too great a contrast between sudden inspirations and those sought in meditation. The fact that we give up time to meditation is an earnest of our firm intention to listen to God and an indication of the value we set on his guidance, even if it is not given just at the moment we expect it, and even if he gives it in some quite different manner—for instance, without our realizing it, by means of events whose meaning we understand only afterwards.

For many Christians prayer is only a monologue, in which they do all the talking, laying before God their desires, their love, and their faith but not listening for his answer. Meditation consists first and foremost in being silent in his presence, as Habakkuk says: "Let all the earth keep silence before him" (Habakkuk 2:20). For those with a contemplative cast of mind, this silence is chiefly adoration and spiritual communion, the uplifting of the soul, identification. Written meditation does not take the place of either prayer or adoration, but it has its place as a practical aid to the integration of the riches of the spiritual life into our material lives.

It serves this purpose all the better for being practiced with ingenuous simplicity. There are those who would like to include in their notebooks only noble thoughts—to write a sort of supplement to the *Thoughts* of Pascal. Others are concerned to write down only the thoughts and commands which come indubitably from God. Such scruples paralyze meditation because they induce a critical rather than a spontaneous attitude. Of course, the thoughts that come to me, and which I note down, contain reflections of my most ordinary occupations, considerations suggested by reason or sentiment, by simple common sense, by my experience, or some reminiscence of a conversation, or of something I have read, perhaps in the Bible. Reason and common sense are in opposition to faith only when they claim to be autonomous and outside the sovereignty of God. Submitted to him in meditation, they are precious. Think, for instance, of Jesus' words, when he said that "the sons of this world are wiser in their own generation than the sons of light" (Luke 16:8), or when he speaks of sitting down to count the cost before starting "to build a tower" (Luke 14:28). Into my meditations there enter, naturally enough, all my moral concepts, my aspirations and ambitions, my ordinary regrets, as well as my unconscious complexes, and surely sometimes even the voice of the devil.

But it is just in this very way that the bridge is established. Having placed myself resolutely before God, I think all these things in his presence, asking him to guide as far as possible my thoughts and my mind. Writing something down also makes it more real. If I do not write, my meditation is likely to remain vague and nebulous. When I come to note down my thoughts, I am compelled to formulate them clearly and precisely, and I am more firmly committed to putting them into effect. What I write is not confined to religious matters; it concerns all the problems of my daily life. Often it is merely a matter of arranging my timetable for the day, but making a conscious effort to organize my day in accordance with God's will, distinguishing more plainly what in his eyes are the most important things to be done. Think how many people have an uneasy conscience about the way they organize their time, allowing themselves to be swept away and submerged in a flood of secondary tasks—even sometimes welcoming this because it is a means of postponing other more difficult duties; trying to do too much because they do not have the courage to refuse the things they ought to cut out.

One of the first times I practiced this sort of meditation was with a French friend who had more experience with it than I. I was astonished to see him make a note of the fact that he had forgotten to tighten the radiator cap on his car. I was still making the old distinction between sacred things and secular things which this type of meditation is designed to overcome. Since Freud has taught us that every "bungled action" has a deep significance, we can no longer look upon any act of forgetfulness as purely fortuitous and insignificant. Forgetfulness has become a useful aid to the discovery of self. It has very often happened that, thanks to meditation, I have been able to put right much more serious omissions than forgetting to screw up a radiator cap.

Meditation does in fact preserve us from escaping into an otherworldly religion; it keeps us firmly in this world. It is a realization of our vocation in the world, of what God expects us to do to carry forward his adventure in the world. Look around you; see how lonely and "forgotten" people feel —perhaps even your own wife, or one of your children. Our patients are under no illusions: if you forget their appointments, or their names, it means you have forgotten them, themselves. They have brought their troubles to you, and you have felt sincere sympathy for them. But they know that the toils of life are inexorable, and that they will engulf and carry away everything if we are not careful. God never forgets anyone, however, and often reminds us of specific people during meditation. Looked at in this light, meditation is a sort of school for fidelity in intercession.

Consider how many people are shut in upon themselves, immured in their prejudices and their automatic thought mechanisms. Meditation is an open attitude—open in two directions: toward God and toward material life. It is a trusting and attentive attitude of waiting. A single word received in meditation can transform a person's whole life, turning it into a great adventure. Others, on the contrary, allow themselves to drift uselessly, rudderless, on any current that flows. Meditation brings order into their lives, giving them an axis, a structure, a point of reference, and a goal toward which to steer, without which there can be no fruitful adventure.

A young woman had consulted me once when she was suffering from the effects of serious difficulties in her childhood. She had taken my advice and begun the practice of meditation. This had made it much easier for me to take the first necessary steps toward her liberation. However, she had soon given it up; she had been approaching it in too childish a manner. The trouble was that she was not so much listening to God as copying me, and noting down the thoughts she supposed I was expecting of her.

I have always kept in touch with her and have followed her slow growth toward real maturity. I have never urged her to take up the practice of meditation again, since it is of value only if it is quite spontaneous. And now, more than twenty years later, she writes to me out of the blue, from an address overseas, to tell me that she has enthusiastically started daily written meditations once more! She has found herself at once launched into adventure. Her mind is full of new ideas. She has taken the initiative in courses of action which I should never have dared to suggest to her, even if I had thought of them. She is asserting herself. She has grown up. The triggering-off of an adventure does not depend so much on external circumstances as upon our own state of mind, that readiness to follow God's purposes which is forged in meditation.

I am always reminded in this connection of Adam hiding among the trees in the garden of Eden. God called to him: "Where are you?" (Genesis 3:9). God is constantly calling us: Where are we? What is our true situation? Where are we hiding? How many of our activities and thoughts are really attempts to escape—from ourselves, from the world, and from God? Do we, like those invited to the banquet in the parable (Luke 14:16-20), plead our family and professional responsibilities as excuses to escape from God's call? Have we really given him everything, our whole life? What does God think of our work, our attitude to our families and to society, our relationships with our patients, our colleagues, our friends, our chiefs, or our competitors?

Of course God can speak to us at any time, even when we are hiding behind some flowery bush. But if we really want to listen to him, we must set aside some time specially. Present-day life, with its bustle and its overcrowding, is not very conducive to meditation. A young woman was saying to me only the other day, "I always feel that when a woman gets married she is like a work when the copyright has run out—she belongs to her family, to society, to anybody; she has no more privacy." She added that her own private refuge was her bathroom. And why not? For my part, I find I can meditate in the anonymity of a restaurant, where I am safe from the telephone but surrounded by the buzzing, busy world in which I want to be present. Sometimes, instead of spending one's holidays devouring distances or rushing from one museum to another, one can spend whole days meditating in the silence of meadow or wood, or in a monastery. The busier we are, the more do we become burdened with responsibilities, and the more do we stand in need of these times when we can renew our contact with God.

One thing I have discovered is the great psychological value of meditation. It is a school of sincerity, and thus has a certain kinship with psychotherapy. I have often seen a patient note down, in the course of a brief moment spent with me in meditation, some insight into his own life which I should have been proud to help him discover after many sessions devoted to psychotherapy. In the profound atmosphere of meditation we become conscious of the real and hidden motives of our feelings, our desires, our fears, and our emotions. Like the psychotherapist who from time to time puts questions to facilitate the descent into oneself, God questions us sometimes in the silence of meditation. I am not setting up these two activities in opposition to each other; on the contrary, they can be wonderfully complementary. A psychological technique can break through the "censorship" which is preventing a painful awakening to a true assessment of oneself. And then this awakening can open a new field to the dialogue with God.

Another psychological value to meditation is that it is a school of self-assertion—of proper self-assertion. There are people who assert themselves easily and too readily, imposing their views and their will on others unscrupulously and with a tyranny and selfishness of which they themselves are often unaware. They can come to see this trait in meditation, and learn how to give way to others. But there are some, on the other hand, who find it very difficult to assert themselves, even when they are in the right. They have good ideas but are afraid to put them into words. Dominated unjustly by other people, they nurse their grudges and say nothing. They allow others to ride roughshod over them. It is often this timidity which brings them to the psychotherapist. Telling them they must assert themselves does no good. If they tried, they would be more likely to make matters worse by doing it clumsily.

But in meditation they can see that in some situation they have capitulated when they ought to have stood firm. They will see the course of action they must follow, the person with whom they must have a frank and courageous discussion. If they delay, the thought will come back insistently to them day after day until they obey. Furthermore, in meditation they will be able to prepare themselves for the difficult course of action they must undertake. They can ask God to show them what it would be imprudent to say and what it would be wrong not to say. In this way they will be more easily able to overcome their timidity, to speak calmly and authoritatively, to gain respect, to listen and understand. Many of my patients prepare in this way for their consultations with me, and I have always found that the consultation is then far more valuable, since they are able to come at once to the things that really matter, which otherwise they would have been tempted to postpone.

Sometimes a patient will suggest that we remain silent for a while during the consultation, so that he may calm himself after some emotional crisis, order his thoughts, or listen to God. Then I meditate with him, and this act sets up a reciprocal relationship between us that is extremely fruitful. It sometimes happens, too, that silence supervenes spontaneously during the course of a consultation. The patient becomes lost in a train of thought that has been set going by our conversation. Such a silence must be respected. It marks a decisive moment: it means that now it is God who is speaking to the patient, and no longer I. For my part I meditate as well, in order to hear what he has to say to me.

We must be careful, however, not to over intellectualize meditation, as if it were a sort of hunt for important ideas. Silence has its own value, a much more effective one than most people imagine. This depends, of course, on its quality.

Some silences are painful, burdened with unease, reticence, and dissembled thoughts. Some are distant, cold, absent silences. But a prolonged silence can become the highest form of personal communication, real communion, especially if we both feel we are in God's presence. One might then really say there was such a thing as "silentiotherapy."

The more a patient meditates, the more does he come to depend on God, and the less does he depend on me. And so I can be strict in observing that non-directive attitude which obliges him to seek God's guidance for himself, instead of relying on my advice. God knows so much better than I do what he needs. Take, for instance, the case of a woman who cannot make up her mind to commit herself definitely to any particular job. All she does is to take temporary stand-in posts of various kinds. I might naturally think that this is a case of psychological blockage, of escape. Even if I did not express it, this thought at the back of my mind would set up a barrier between her and me. But really, do I know enough about her to be certain of it? How can I be sure that God's purpose for her is not in fact a free and rootless life, whereas so many other people bury themselves in one job and live in constant fear of losing it? It is not for me to take God's place; he will know how to speak to this woman himself. This is what I clearly see in my meditation, and it frees me from all my preconceived ideas.

The ideal of the Freudians, that one should become adult, assert oneself, and assume responsibility for oneself; that of the Jungians, of the integration and acceptance of the totality of oneself; and that of the school of Adler, that one should realistically accept one's limitations—meditation makes a powerful contribution to the attainment of them all. It works in well with psychological techniques. Thus, for example, when one of my patients tells me about a dream he has had, I may question him in the accepted manner about his associations of ideas, in order to throw some light on the meaning of the dream. My experience in the analysis of dreams makes it possible for me to help him in this. But if the patient makes a practice of meditation, and if he himself suggests it to me, we can be silent together and ask God to show us what he is saying to each of us through that dream. It is quite Biblical. We can similarly seek through meditation to know what God is saying to us by means of a graphological or typological analysis or in a Rorschach or Szondi test.

But meditation goes beyond psychology. It is a powerful aid toward the awakening and the maturing of the person. The psychoanalysts are disarmed when faced with cases in which they observe what they call an insufficiency in the formation of the ego. Meditation, on the other hand, can sometimes help to solve even this problem. But the person is more than the ego. It is the spiritual entity which must acquire personal convictions, and choose what attitude to adopt toward God, life, events, and other people, and finally discern his vocation, what he is being called to do in the world. I have quoted elsewhere the very apt remark of Professor Richard Siebeck: "It is the vocation that creates the person." The converse is also true, however: often, in order to discover what one's vocation is, it is necessary first to become a person through the intimate dialogue with God, which is what meditation is.

The problems attendant upon a change of occupation are important and extremely delicate. Many people ask my advice on this subject, and I always find it very difficult to answer. For instance, a man is thinking of leaving a job he does not like, and in which he feels neither happy nor really useful. Is this merely a temptation to run away from the difficulties and troubles that everyone who tries to do his duty faithfully must put up with? Or is it a divine call, in which God is telling him to have the courage to give up a career he has entered by mistake, at the behest of his parents, at a time when he was not mature enough to make a valid choice? He will be running certain risks in leaving his employment—is this the proper price that must be paid for his boldness in the faith? Or is he merely lacking in a proper sense of responsibility toward his dependents? How can I possibly know?

By means of psychological analysis I can help him to see more clearly into his own deep motivations. But the decision must come from his own conviction. I can offer him an environment of fellowship, of openness and sincerity, of meditation, which will help him in his search for inspiration from God.

I once saw, almost at the same time, two men. One of them was a theologian who had given up the pastoral ministry which he had originally entered upon only in order to please his parents. The other was a workingman who had given up his factory job, into which he had gone solely in order to earn a living, and had become a pastor.

Meditation, however, goes deeper even than the formation of the person. It is the road to an ever-closer intimacy with God. Prayer, worship, and the sacraments create this deep intimacy, but meditation extends it to the whole of life and feeds into it all the problems of practical living. It is a means of opening to God, not only our hearts and our spiritual lives, but also our daily work, all our activities, the whole adventure of our lives. It is a means of bringing God in constantly, of questioning him about everything, of seeking his inspiration in everything.

As soon as we realize that God takes an interest in all we do, we can bring it all to him. About our religious problems, of course, we can talk with him as with a God; about moral questions, as with the One who alone knows where good and evil lie; but about scientific questions as well, as with a scientist, about professional problems as with a colleague, about family problems as with a father, about technical matters as with an expert, about philosophy as with a professor, about law as with a jurist, about painting as with an artist, about city planning as with an architect, about finance as with an economist.

For me, this near and intimate God, this companion ready at any time to talk on any subject, is Jesus Christ. But what I have been saying here is valid for all men, since everyone has an instinct of adventure which can draw him into enterprises that are either worthwhile or worthless. God, moreover, can guide not only believers but unbelievers, as the whole of the Bible asserts. God's purpose is not realized just through the obedience of those who know and love him but also through those who do not know him—even through those who resist him. Jesus Christ came not only for Christians but for all men. Jesus Christ, to Christian eyes, is God himself, who was made flesh, and who entered into history, who took our humanity upon himself in order to be nearer to us, who knew all our sufferings, our fatigues, and our difficulties. But other people, who profess a different religion, or those who claim to have none, stand to benefit equally from his mediation. The reconciliation of humanity to God was accomplished by God himself. Our only privilege as Christians is that of knowing it and proclaiming it.

Every man can seek God's help in all the problems of his life. God does not always answer us, and we often go wrong as to what his will is. It can happen, nevertheless, that God gives us precise, concrete—one might even say technical—instructions. I have often experienced as much, as have many others also, unbelievers and believers. The Bible is full of stories on the subject, from Noah who built his ark under God's direction (Genesis 6:22), and Solomon the Temple (1 Kings 6), or Elijah, sent by the Lord to the house of a widow of Zarephath (1 Kings 17:9), and on another occasion to King Ahab, his persecutor (1 Kings 18:1), to Philip, who received a formal command to go to a certain desert place, there to meet the first African to be won over to the Gospel (Acts 8:26-40), or again, the Church in Antioch, which sent Barnabas and Saul on a mission at the express command of the Holy Spirit (Acts 13:2).

There is no question of our turning our backs on science and technical progress; they have been given us by God. But we all know full well that science and technology have their limitations, that there are many problems they cannot solve, and that they are neutral, capable of being used for evil as well as good, of bringing benefits as well as disaster. Everything that is good can do harm. It is not enough to be a scientist. What matters is the use to which we put science. Dr. W. Brunat of Lyons once said, "I used to look upon myself as the servant of science; now I realize that I am in God's service, and that science is my servant to that end."

God can show us how to use our science, our experience, our reason, and all the talents he has entrusted to us (Matthew 25:14-30). To surgeons, I point out the prayer in Psalm 90: "Establish thou the work of our hands" (v. 17). All scientists are aware that the progress of science depends not only on their rational intelligence but also on their intuition and their creative imagination, and we can ask God to guide them, to cause new and fertile ideas to spring to life in our minds.

•

CHAPTER 20

The Adventure of Work

WE SOMETIMES FEEL proud as we consider the advance of science, of technology, and of civilization. But if we think carefully about it, we realize that the human race is suffering rather from a dearth of creative imagination. Really new ideas are rare. As soon as any such idea makes its appearance in any sphere—mathematics, art, politics, or industry—it opens a fruitful period in human adventure, triumphing over conservative opposition thanks to the powerful dynamism that is characteristic of adventure. And after some social reform has been brought about, people wonder why no one had thought of it before! Why was it necessary to wait for Lincoln for slavery to be abolished, for Henry Dunant for the founding of the Red Cross, for Galileo for the observation that the earth rotates, for Newton before anyone asked himself why an apple fell to the ground, for Marx before it was seen that great masses of the working class lived in poverty and economic deprivation?

Most people live their whole lives within the limits of a narrow specialization, hardly ever even glimpsing its relationships with other spheres of life. They work honestly within their small fields, but without ever imagining anything they have not already been taught, without seeing anything they have not been trained to look at, without understanding anything that has not already been explained to them, without asking themselves any questions outside the range of those they have studied. They know their jobs well and work at them carefully and conscientiously. They may even excel at them, and, because of the very perfection of their technical skill, never feel in the slightest degree that what they are engaged in is still an adventure. Thus great and perplexing problems, like that of hunger in the world, for instance, are like a no-man's-land for which no one feels any responsibility.

Most people live in a society ordered by usages and traditions. They always read the same newspaper, associate with the same people, and talk to them about the same things.

In our daily work, whether as lawyer or doctor, cook or mechanic, technical competence alone is not sufficient. It must be complemented with a lively presence of mind and an ever-watchful ingenuity. Everyone knows the tremendous part played by the lapses of memory of which we have spoken. "I didn't think! I forgot!" is the excuse of all those who work badly, whatever their job. In medicine, mistakes in diagnosis are less often due to ignorance than to forgetfulness: to failure to think of a possible alternative diagnosis, or to the omission of a clinical or laboratory test which might have revealed some hidden lesion. And let us admit as well that we all have lapses of memory that are more or less conscious and voluntary. I recall a little German-Swiss domestic servant saying to me once, "Since I have been sweeping my floor with Jesus, I never forget to sweep under the mat." Oh, how great, then, is the need for meditation! What a pity that people practice it so little and that those who meditate most—religious people—use their meditations for thinking of hardly anything but religious and moral subjects!

The fact is that we all make this harmful distinction between our professional lives and our spiritual lives. To unite them once more is to restore to both the quality of an adventure, or rather to make of them one great adventure instead of two: the adventure of the incarnation of the Spirit in concrete reality. For centuries the tutelage of the Church held back the march of science. It had to break free if it was to develop. Now it has succeeded so well in breaking free that the partition between the two domains is completely watertight, to the detriment of both science and Church. We learn our profession at the university, and there religion has no place. God is relegated to the spheres of morality and religion, so that a Christian doctor and a non-Christian doctor practice exactly the same medicine, the medicine they learned together in the lecture theater.

I realized this one day when I was in England, after several weeks of meditation. I had spent the whole afternoon with a Dutch colleague, Dr. Diederick Doyer, physician to the Queen of the Netherlands. We had passed the time together delightfully in a small boat on a river. I suddenly saw the tragic contrast there was between my exciting spiritual adventure and my still very commonplace life as a doctor. Of course I was trying to apply the Christian virtues of charity, honesty, and professional integrity to my work. But these virtues are not the monopoly of Christians. Many of my unbelieving colleagues possess them in the highest degree. Apart from such moral virtues as I could cultivate, and in the strict medical field of the art of healing, I looked for inspiration not to God but to the scientific and technical training I had received at medical school.

However valuable science is, it is capable of dealing with only one side of objective reality. There is far more to be observed in a patient than what we are normally taught—all his personal problems, his conflicts with others, his rebellions, his remorse, his moral injuries, his fears, and his negative attitude to life. As soon as we listen carefully to what the patient has to say about these things—things the importance of which our science has not taught us—as soon as we open our eyes, more especially as soon as we meditate upon this subject, we see the tremendous part played by personal problems in the appearance and development of disease. The general public sometimes realizes this better than do doctors. On the day of a funeral someone whispers, "What do you expect? He had the best possible attention, but the poor fellow had let himself go, ever since his divorce."

The best doctors have always realized this and have tried to help their patients to solve the problems in their lives. But in our own day, when medicine relies exclusively on science, doctors almost have a bad conscience about entering into a personal dialogue with their patients and trying to understand them, not only on the level of objective intelligence, but also through self-commitment to a personal relationship.

I had myself already begun, some years before, to spend more time listening to my patients and taking an interest in their moral difficulties. But I did not like to do so during the actual consultation, since in doing so I was not acting as a scientist. "Come back and see me this evening, and we'll have a talk at the fireside, as man to man." In this way I was practicing what Dr. Balint[1] later called the "prolonged interview," in which the doctor stops asking questions so as to give the patient an opportunity of unburdening himself spontaneously. But I was thus living two quite distinct lives, the classical practice of scientific medicine in the daytime and a fireside medicine in the evening—a situation which clearly enough expressed the divison we were speaking of between the domain of science and that of morality.

Well, I felt myself called to unite these two lives, to follow my adventure of faith within my work and not outside it. For it was soon apparent that when a fireside chat helped a patient to solve his personal problems it also contributed as much as medicines, dieting, or the lancet to the healing of his condition.

Psychosomatic medicine, which originated in America, has taken a hold in Europe and has shown what an enormous part is played by the emotions in the genesis of disease—not merely psychical but also organic diseases. It is a first step, and a very important one, toward a medicine of the person. The latter goes even farther, recognizing the influence on his health of a man's spiritual attitude. But then new problems present themselves: If it is true that a change in the state of a person's soul

[1] Michael Balint, *Le Médecin, Son Malade et la Maladie*, P.U.F., Paris, 1960.

can bring physical healing in its train, what is the mutual relationship of these two phenomena, so different in kind? Such questions can be answered only by scientists who are determined to enlarge the frontiers of medicine beyond the narrow limits of the natural sciences, and to evolve a science of man which views him in the totality of his being. This evolution in medicine has already started. During the last few years I have been glad to listen to, or to read, many inaugural lectures in which new professors of medicine have firmly taken up a position on the side of the medicine of the person.

I have been talking about medicine because it is my domain, my adventure. But it is quite evident that in our scientific and technical civilization analogous problems arise in every discipline and every occupation. On all hands warning is given of the same danger—that of depersonalization, of the human side of things being pushed into the background, of a man being enslaved by the impersonal techniques he has invented. In every walk of life we are witnessing the triumph of technical demands which are not subject to moral judgment, and which threaten to strangle that which is most human in man.

Consider, for instance, all the problems of conscience faced by a businessman, and how lonely he feels as he attempts to solve them. He may be an active church member, and one who listens to sermons and religious talks. Almost all they will give him is general principles, of little help in throwing light on the concrete problems with which he is struggling. Read a book like that of M. Louis Armand, who has just been admitted to the French Academy, *Plaidoyer pour l'Avenir*.[2] It shows us how exciting are the times we live in, times "without precedent in history," and the flood of problems raised by the "second phase of the industrial revolution," which is presenting the world for the first time with "the possibility of abundance."

In the face of all these new and important questions, on which the future of our civilization depends, Armand invites us to "cudgel our brains." And that is just what meditation is:

[2] Louis Armand and Michel Drancourt, *Plaidoyer pour l'Avenir*, Calman-Lévy, Paris, 1961.

228

a cudgeling of the brains. It is not a matter merely of arguing. We must think, we must look for new and fruitful ideas, having first put ourselves in that position in which man becomes most fully man: in the sight of God.

One of my colleagues, Dr. Gros,[3] of Paris, has pointed out how the great leaders of the world, the men who carry the heaviest load of economic and industrial as well as of political and even ecclesiastical responsibilities, lack time for meditation. They are harassed and overworked; they are constantly being called upon to improvise hasty measures. Dr. Gros has made himself their "professor of reflection." One could well say "professor of meditation," since he himself spends much time in meditation. *There* is a worthwhile adventure: to find answers, divinely inspired answers, to the problems of our time.

We need only to open the Bible to see how God concerns himself with the material lives of men and women, with the pain of their toil and their economic difficulties. The Mosaic Law is full of precepts whose general intention is the protection of the weak against abuse by the strong, that of the poor against abuse by the rich. It lays down the weekly rest; even "in plowing time and in harvest you shall rest" (Exodus 34:21); it is even to apply to animals and to foreigners (Exodus 23:12). It forbids overproduction (Exodus 23:11; Deuteronomy 22:9) and the sale of land in perpetuity (Leviticus 25:23). It prescribes the redistribution of land in each year of jubilee (Leviticus 25:28), the freeing of slaves —with gifts!—in the seventh year (Deuteronomy 15:13), respect for the share of the crop reserved for the gleaners (Leviticus 19:9-10), and even the retirement of civil servants at the age of fifty (Numbers 8:25). It inveighs against over-presumptuous trusts (2 Chronicles 20:35-37), and against Babylon, in which city "the merchants of the earth have grown rich with the wealth of her wantonness" (Revelation 18:3). The work of men leads only to disaster when it is

[3] "Un Professeur de Réflexion pour Cadres Supérieurs," *Réalités*, No. 146, March, 1958.

directed in defiance against God (the Tower of Babel, Genesis 11:1-9), but it is blessed and fruitful when it is put under his guidance.

One of the basic ideas running through the Bible is that the earth and all its wealth belong to God. Thus man is not an owner but a steward, who must work in accordance with the directives of his master. In several of his parables (Mark 13:34; Matthew 25:14-30) Jesus uses the image of a proprietor absent on a journey, who will come back and ask each man to give an account of his stewardship. We are the stewards of the earth and all it contains, of the whole of creation: "The Lord God took the man and put him in the garden of Eden to till it and keep it" (Genesis 2:15). This stewardship is exercised in our occupational and our social life. All the Christian churches nowadays are awakening to the importance of this idea. It is the theme of lay movements such as Catholic Action and the Evangelical Academies, which group men together according to their jobs and study their occupational problems in the light of the faith. The Lutheran churches have held big international conferences on the subject of stewardship.

I have just received a visit from an American colleague, Dr. Anderson, a surgeon, from Salem, Oregon, and his wife. He has founded groups of "Yokefellows." Their keynote is the carrying of each other's burdens. Dr. and Mrs. Anderson told us of the lively fellowship they have experienced in their organization, the new quality of life that is springing up among the members, because they simply tell each other of their personal problems. No reply is looked for, and all theological argument is avoided. They all commit themselves to giving a tithe of their money, their time, and their energy. Many communities require their members to give a tithe of income, but this is the first time I have heard of a tithe of time and energy.

Our time and our energy are also a kind of wealth of which we are the stewards. Time is not a capital that dwindles inexorably and tragically in our hands, as so many people like to think. Time is a gift of God that is renewed every hour. Time belongs to God, and we are meant to administer it in accordance with his purpose. That is indeed no small matter, and it requires plenty of meditation. Since it is in fact a problem that is always being raised afresh, we must come back constantly to God to review our program under his guidance. Think how many people there are who are always complaining of lack of time but who never take the trouble to see what they ought to cut out, or what tasks they ought, like Moses, to entrust to their fellow workers (Exodus 18:13-27). And plenty of people waste their time in vain attempts to make up for lost time.

Someone once told me that he was afraid to meditate for fear he might make plans so vast that he would never be able to carry them out! It seems to me that, on the contrary, the effect of meditation is one of sifting, that it is the great remedy for overactivity. This is clear in the case of Jesus. Perfectly guided by God, he proceeds in tranquillity, relaxed and available. He has time for everybody. He knows how to escape the pressure of the crowd (John 6:15) and he even refuses to perform a miracle if it is not in God's purpose that he should perform it (Matthew 12:38-39).

The proper organization of their time is a major problem for most doctors. Their families know this well—they are so often the ones to be sacrificed. They soothe their consciences by telling themselves that it is all in a good cause. But they would all do well to ask God seriously about the organization of their lives. God never asks of us more than one thing at a time. The inquiry is much more fruitful if both husband and wife meditate together on the subject.

My wife and I have had many such experiences. Today, as I write these lines, it is Easter Monday. I had some qualms about whether I ought to be spending my few days of Easter holiday in my study, writing, when the rest of my time is so fully taken up with my consultations, and when I have also lectures to prepare for a visit to Lebanon and Greece. We meditated together, and it was in fact my wife who thought I ought to work at my book. Now it is no longer time stolen from her, but time offered by her to God for our common vocation. But I must be careful not to abuse her goodwill. There are people who are always ready to require sacrifices from other people in the name of Christian self-denial. The important thing is that we should listen to God, rather than one his kind heart and the other his selfish desires.

Dr. Henri Mentha once spoke of aging doctors who complain bitterly because their younger colleagues' practices grow at their expense. He suggested that they devote more time to the medicine of the person, spend longer with each patient so as to understand his personal life, and so find themselves on the road to adventure once more. Indeed, one of the secrets of having a worthwhile adventure is to meditate to find out how to put our time to best use. Dr. Théo Bovet devoted a charming little book to this subject, *The Art of Finding Time*.[4] In it he refers also to a biblical idea, that of the *kairos*, God's moment. We are not called upon only to do what God wills, but to do it at the moment he wills, to know how to bide God's time.

To seek in this way to enter into God's adventure through all we do, all we think, and all we feel is, I believe, the meaning of life. If he gave us life, it was for that—for it to be fitted into his plan and thus to contribute to its realization—so that through this constant collaboration we might enter into ever-closer intimacy with him. This involves not only the great decisions of our lives but also the tiniest details, for which from meditation to meditation we can seek and obtain from him concrete guidance. At the beginning of the war the Swiss Federal Government called on my friend Dr. Arnold Müggli, of Zurich, to take charge of the arrangements for food rationing in Switzerland. He was not a robust man, and I was afraid he would not have the strength necessary to cope with such a task. You can imagine what a heavy task it was when Switzerland became, shortly afterwards, like a little island in the center of Europe, entirely surrounded by the triumphant power of the Third Reich.

My friend and I meditated together. He put down in his notebook certain directives, which he carefully observed throughout the whole of the war. They were that he should leave his family in Zurich; that he should work in Berne only

[4] Théo Bovet, *L'Art de Trouver du Temps*, Oberlin, Strasbourg, 1955.

until the Friday of each week; that he should spend Saturday alone, at home in Zurich, quietly thinking over his important problems; and that he should reserve Sunday for his family. At the end of the war he was in much better health than he had been at the beginning. He had fought effectively against the open social sore of the black market and had been so successful in insuring that the Swiss people were properly fed that the University of Zurich conferred upon him the honorary degree of Doctor of Medicine.

He has told me one anecdote concerning his adventure. Toward the end of the war he noticed that people were not making full use of their ration cards. This moderation was not due to lack of appetite but to lack of sufficient money to buy all the foodstuffs permitted. He therefore asked his committee if it was possible to prepare a second card, of the same nutritive value but of lower-priced foods. The experts, however, were unable to come up with a workable plan. Thereupon he went off into the country with one other colleague, in order to meditate upon the problem. Three days later he came back with a project which the experts considered to be excellent, and within a month he was able to give the people a choice of two ration cards.

CHAPTER 21

The Meaning of Life

WE MUST BE CAREFUL not to look upon expert opinion and divine guidance as being opposed to each other. Obviously, the ideal is not that there should be, on the one hand, highly skilled experts and, on the other, people who meditate. On the contrary, the ideal is that the experts themselves should add to their expert knowledge the enlightenment that comes from meditation. In reality, the more knowledge one has, the more one needs to meditate, and the more profitable meditation is. The reverse is also true: The more we meditate, the more do we make ourselves aware of important problems, and this in turn makes us work harder to solve them by scientific study.

There is, then, no question of criticizing science. Think what we owe to formal medicine: The average length of human life has almost doubled since my childhood. More than half the people of my age would not have survived to that age fifty years ago. God is the source of life; he is also the source of the science which safeguards life. Think also what we owe to technology, to progress in industry, in chemistry, in physics, in the production of power, which makes possible—or would do so if it were better organized—the feeding, housing, and clothing of all this increase in population.

But what are we going to do with this extra ration of life, of wealth and leisure? This is the question which every true scientist must be asking himself. Can listening to God lead us to a better utilization of our science, to a more complete and effective medicine, to a still more profitable industry? Finally, can it at the same time safeguard the humanity of our civilization? Only the experience of each of us in his own sphere can provide an answer to these questions. I do not say that it is easy, but that it is a great adventure we can embark upon, with God's help.

As Bergson said as long ago as the beginning of this century, the tremendous scientific and technological progress we are witnessing calls for a corresponding "soul supplement." Many doctors and scientists are worried today about where our civilization is heading, realizing that the problems involved are so far-reaching that they will not be solved by science and technology alone, without a spiritual renewal. The American Medical Association has recently set up a "Medicine and Religion" section. Georges Gusdorf has just published an excellent book,[1] pointing out the importance of breaking away at this time from an overnarrow positivism which takes no account of one whole side of human reality. In this connection Dr. Girardet,[2] the secretary of the Federation of Swiss Doctors, claims that the medical profession is much more alive to human and spiritual problems than is generally thought. If many doctors regard the Christian churches with some reserve, is this not precisely because certain traditional religious attitudes seem to range religion against material life, scientific medicine, and technical progress? It is vital to persuade them that we are marching together and not against one another, that in their scientific work they too are playing a part in God's great adventure.

If I write a book on the spiritual meaning of medicine, and one of my colleagues carries out some piece of experimental research in the laboratory, we are both equally in God's hand,

---

[1] G. Gusdorf, *Dialogue avec le Médecin*, Labor et Fides, Geneva, 1962.
[2] In *Bulletin des Médecins Suisses*, November 16, 1962, p. 852.

both moved by the spirit of adventure he has put in our hearts, both instruments of his sovereign work. The work of all of us, whether it be scientific, technical, commercial, educational, artistic, industrial, agricultural, or manual, has its appointed place in the divine adventure of the world. We all play our part in the adventure. We all share in the divine joy of adventure; the joy of doing something useful, which has a meaning in the total purpose of the world; the joy of bringing forth fruit. That is the image which Jesus himself often used in order to express the meaning of human life (John 15:5). Life is the current, the sap that flows into us day by day from God. Our work, all we do, feel, think, and believe—these are the fruits which it ripens in us.

That is why faith, far from turning us away from the world, brings us back to it. That is why it awakens in us a new interest in the world, in the concrete reality of every day, hard, laborious, difficult, often painful as it is, but wonderful nevertheless. The joy of living, of making an effort, of having a goal to aim at; the joy of moving a finger, of smelling a perfume, of looking at something, of hearing a voice, of learning something and loving someone. The pleasure of research, of success, of study; the pleasure of discovery, or rather of the hope of discovery, of the excitement of wrestling with a difficult problem; the pleasure of understanding something one did not understand before, of knowing what one did not know; the pleasure of the puzzle and its solution.

The pleasure of that harsh confrontation with reality without which everything is but wishful thinking. The pleasure of taking a risk; the pleasure of suspense and of the supreme current of energy that it releases in us. The joy of procreation and of creation; the joy of bringing a new being into the world, haloed with the mystery of all his unknown future; the joy that springs from bringing forth a piece of creative work, the fruit either of a moment of grace or of long and patient toil. The joy of feeling that what I am doing each moment is absolutely unique, that no one else will ever be me, that no other moment of my life will ever be the same as this one. The joy of each experience, of each act, of each success, as soon as we realize that this is what is meant by being in God's image, that he allows us to cooperate in his work, that he is with us in everything we undertake. It is from him that we draw our courage to live.

Nevertheless every human adventure has its limitations. First, we cannot go beyond the limits of the created world. All we discover already exists. Even our most fantastic imaginings are made up of elements drawn from the known world. And then, the more we explore, the more do we realize the immensity of what remains unexplored. Every discovery sets up a forest of new question marks on our horizon. The more we study, the greater do we see our ignorance to be. We echo the words of Socrates: "I know nothing, unless it be that I know nothing." The whole of science is only a language, a system of conventional signs which the mind can manipulate like mathematical equations. It can speak only of the relationships between things. Concerning their essence it is silent. Philosophy is not silent—it says too much, and gives too many contradictory explanations of the essence of things!

And then there are disappointments, snags, failures. Even our successes are never either complete or final. Even if we were to be a hundred times more successful, if we did enough to fill a hundred lives, the outcome would be the same. The older one grows, the more does the tally of abandoned projects and hopes increase, the more does one realize that they will never be accomplished. And old age comes slowly on, with its diminishing capacity for work and its declining faculties. Does that mean the adventure is over? As we have seen, adventure goes one way only: always forward. An old age which is merely backward-looking—whether in pride or in sorrow—is an attempt to run against the current of life.

Every age has its own adventure. In childhood, it is the gradual discovery of the world and the preparation for life, the fascination of a future that is still mysterious and magical. When you meet a child you ask him, "What do you want to do when you are grown up?" The adventure of adolescence is that of choosing: choosing a favorite author or artist; choosing a friend, or a fiancé; choosing a career, a goal in life to which one will sacrifice many other ambitions. When years of maturity are reached, there is the building of a home and a career, bringing up the children, marital problems to resolve, stepping up the ladder of promotion, and social, cultural, and spiritual life, in which one fights for what one thinks beautiful, true, useful, and worthwhile. And then at the beginning of retirement there is often an opportunity for new adventures, time to do what one has never done before but has longed all one's life to do. Always the same forward movement toward a goal.

But sooner or later, suddenly or gradually, the ferment of action dies down: a little more or a little less? What difference will it make? Everything will end inevitably in death. Is the adventure really finished? Is there room for anything but emptiness, skepticism, or bitterness? Old people are irritated by the young, their successors, who lead their adventure according to different principles and by different methods, toward different goals, destroying what the old once built up, and rebuilding what the old once destroyed, and scorning the advice of the old, upsetting old customs and pursuing dangerous dreams. "We did things differently in my day," the old man is fond of saying; but he feels that no one listens to him any more. He is in a backwater. Is the adventure over?

Indeed, I believe that it is not! This progressive renunciation of our ambitions, imposed upon us by old age, this casting off, this ever-increasing purging away of activity, this passage from the order of *doing* to the order of *being*, which is the law of old age, is also an adventure—and what an adventure! It is still another revelation of something new, something exciting and wonderful. It is a transition from the multiple to the single, from the disseminated to the concentrated, from the accidental to the eternal. It is then that one realizes that success in life and making a success of one's life are two very different things. And it is good, because it re-establishes equality among men. We are all variously gifted for success in life, but we are all equal where making a success of our lives is concerned.

One realizes then that the whole is not the sum of its parts. It is not enough to accumulate elements, actions, individual adventures, the sum of which will always be too small. It is adventure itself, in the singular, that must be found; adventure, not adventures, the global meaning of life. This does not mean denying the past and its adventures but seeing it as an apprenticeship for the great adventure. The individual achievements of the past have not been piled up one on top of another like a Tower of Babel, doomed to failure, but still they have not been without their value. The past has been a training for adventure. A man's lifework is his life. So old age can still be turned toward the future; yes, toward death! Jesus Christ made a success of his life by being "obedient unto death" (Philippians 2:8).

The meaning of life, its total meaning, which imparts to it its unity despite the diversity of its various stages, is obedience to God. In growing up and developing, the child is obeying God, who gave him life and its wonderful power of growth. In making his choices, the adolescent is obeying God, who granted him the liberty to choose and the responsibility of choice. In throwing himself passionately into all his creative adventures, the adult is obeying God, who has made him in his own image. And in detaching himself from particular things and ephemeral actions, and attaching himself instead to transcendent values, in accepting his human condition, necessarily fragile, temporary, limited, and incomplete, the aged person is still obeying God, who made men "strangers and exiles on the earth" (Hebrews 11:13).

In reality, the adventure of old age has already begun, imperceptibly, long ago. From the cradle onward life is choice, and all choice is a shedding, an abandonment of a possible reality, a step from the multiple to the single. And all through the course of our lives, even amidst all the creative adventures, acts of renunciation will be forced upon us. Renunciation of quite legitimate ambitions, of marriage, of motherhood, of health, of the success of a project to which one has devoted oneself, of a university chair for which one has been working all one's life. All these are stages in that other adventure, which is the revision of values that must take place in the evening of life. Parallel with creation there will be taking place the "decreation" that Simone Weil described as being one of the conditions of love. The giving up of that spirit of possessive-ness which is always present to some extent in the adventure of action, of that adherence to things which is really slavery to things.

This is the adventure of inner freedom from the world, of that Christian liberty to which St. Paul so often referred. "Let those who have wives live as though they had none, and those who mourn as though they were not mourning, and those who rejoice as though they were not rejoicing, and those who buy as though they had no goods, and those who deal with the world as though they had no dealings with it. For the form of this world is passing away" (1 Corinthians 7:29-31). Then, having fought for one cause against another, for one project against another, for one church against another, one accedes to tolerance, which is neither indifference nor capitulation, but a new adventure of love.

Our Cartesian civilization has given primacy to the visible over the invisible, to what can be measured and weighed over what cannot be measured or weighed, to doing over being, to *homo faber* over *homo religiosus*. This is a climate that is not very favorable to the adventure of old age, so that the aged today feel themselves devaluated and ill at ease. It hurts them to feel useless—rejected, that is, from the adventure of life, because adventure is defined only as action. The greatest of adventures is not action, it is our own development. This does indeed take the form of action at the stage when action is appropriate; but it is also our inner evolution, our encounter with God, our increasing dependence upon him, insuring our progressive independence of men and of the world.

We hear the voice of Christ: "Whoever would save his life will lose it, and whoever loses his life for my sake will find it. For what will it profit a man, if he gains the whole world and forfeits his life? Or what shall a man give in return for his life?" (Matthew 16:25-26). Pastor Ochsenbein[3] has explained that in this text the same word "life" is used to translate two distinct Greek words: *psyche* and *zoe*. The *psyche* is what

[3] Henri Ochsenbein, "Le Problème de la Santé et la Vision Biblique de l'Homme," in *Santé et Vie Spirituelle*, Oberlin, Strasbourg, 1953.

animates us in the adventure of action, our individual life. *Zoe* is universal life, life in God, that which triumphs over death and blossoms into eternal life.

He who loses his life for Jesus Christ is not only the martyr thrown to the lions, or the modern martyr of the persecuted churches of our own times. He is the man who accepts this new adventure of the revision of values, who is prepared to let go all the treasures accumulated during the adventure of action in order to attach himself to Jesus Christ, as St. Paul says: "For his sake I have suffered the loss of all things, and count them as refuse, in order that I may gain Christ" (Philippians 3:8). To lose everything, and to accept—that is indeed adventure. But the paradox is only apparent: What gives life its unity is the knowledge of God. The true value of the adventure of action is not in what we do but in doing it with God, in entering into the creative adventure of God, in entering into intimate fellowship with him. And it is this intimate knowledge of God that becomes the supreme adventure. "What is the end of man?" asks Calvin at the beginning of his Catechism. "To know God. What is his happiness? The same."

The discovery of the world in childhood is an approach toward God through wonder at his works. The adventure of the adult is the experience of God in action inspired and guided by him. The necessary progressive detachment from the world means closer fellowship with God. All through our lives we are learning to know him, first through study, then through action, and then through adoration: three adventures which are but one. There is always a new God to discover and a familiar God to rediscover, always a forward march.

The other day I met an old friend, an industrialist who has been wise enough to lay down his too heavy burden before he is too old, and who now gets great pleasure from everything he undertakes.

"Good day! How are you?" I asked him.

"Fine! I have realized that life begins with birth (*naissance*), continues with knowledge (*connaissance*), and ends in gratitude (*reconnaissance*)."

Yes, gratitude—a wonderful and peaceful sentiment, and

one that is a little too rare nowadays. I am reminded of it reading the beautiful introduction written by C. F. Ramuz for the *Family Booklet* published by the Canton of Vaud:

"Come and sit beside me on the bench in front of the house, wife; it is indeed your right; we shall soon have been together for forty years.

"This evening, because it is so fine, and because it is also the evening of our life, you deserve a little moment of rest, you know.

"The children are married now, and have gone their ways into the world; and once again there are just the two of us, like when we began."

Then follows the evocation of the adventure of the life of this old peasant couple, of their joys, their sorrows, and the times when they started again. Finally the conclusion:

"Come close beside me. We shall not say anything. We no longer need to say anything.

"We only need to be together again, and to let the night come, in the contentment of a task completed."[4]

Rest does not mean that the adventure stops. It means that the adventure has attained its plenitude. This is "entering into God's rest" (Hebrews 3 and 4). Professor Crespy explained this clearly in his address to the Evian Congress on "Fatigue and Rest."[5] This is the rest which Jesus gives (Matthew 11:28), which brings reconciliation with God, with life, and with oneself, which puts an end to all inner strife. The adventure continues, but with another rhythm, and more than ever filled with God. There is still a risk, there is still an unknown, there is still death.

Afterwards, in the resurrection, as St. Paul says, will come perfect knowledge: "For now we see in a mirror dimly, but then face to face. Now I know in part; then I shall understand fully, even as I have been fully understood" (1 Corinthians 13:12). What will that eternal resurrection life be like? It is a mystery. But we know that it will still be an adventure, life

[4] C. F. Ramuz, Preface to the *Livret de Famille du Canton de Vaud*.
[5] Crespy, Nussbaum, and Vernes, *Surmenage et Repos*, Delachaux and Niestlé, Neuchâtel and Paris, 1963.

242

with God, God's creation. The resurrection that is promised us is quite different from the great impassible and immutable emptiness of Nirvana, quite different from a depersonalization of man in which he is engulfed in a great All. Different too from the immortality of the soul taught by Plato, a mere prolongation of its existence. The resurrection, on the contrary, is a new departure, a leap into a new adventure. And it is a personal resurrection, a personal adventure, a personal fellowship with God and with others, a personal life.

Such is the meaning of the New Jerusalem which the visionary on Patmos saw coming down from heaven, "prepared as a bride adorned for her husband" (Revelation 21:2). It is no world of pure spirits, unincarnate, impersonal. There are ramparts and gates, jewels and gold, a river of life, trees of life! But "there shall no more be anything accursed" (Revelation 22:3). "New" Jerusalem—the epithet well expresses the meaning of the event of which St. John was granted a glimpse: a new adventure begins! The adventure of God continues, it is renewed, it springs up afresh, and we shall have a full share in it.

INDEX

Abraham, 76, 185, 191
Absalom, 146
Acts of the Apostles, 79; *1:8*, 79;
    8:26-40, 222; *10:19-20*, 185; *13:2*,
    222; *14:22*, 147; *16:9*, 199; *16:14*,
    211; *20:22-23*, 153; *20:34*, 75; *23:11*,
    153
Adam, 216
Adler, A., 11, 158, 219
Adultery, 13-14
Adventure, as escape, 162; defini-
    tion of, 85; stories, 7, 15-16, 20;
    mainspring of life, 59; of author-
    ship, 47-50; reality of, 50, 202-3
Advice, 49, 136, 176
Agnosticism, 25
Ahithophel, 146
Alexander the Great, 6
Amateur status, 42-43, 53-54, 56-57,
    66, 75
America, 10-11, 69-70
American Medical Association, 235
Amiel, H. F., 54
Amos, 76
Anderson, Dr., 230
Armand, L., 228
Aron, R., 210
Art, 35, 47-48
Atomic bomb, 8
Aviation, 4

Baden-Powell, 21
Balaam, 76, 190-91
Balint, M., 227
Barnabas, 222
Barth, K., 100
Bergson, H., 22-23, 152, 235
Bezalel, 75

Bible, the, 73-82, 91, 179, 198; mis-
    interpretation of, 202-3; on unity
    of spiritual and material, 204; on
    work, 210-11, 227; perspective of,
    152-53, 211
Biot, R., 125
Blocks to adventure, 45-48
Boethius, 120
Bonnett, Dr., 54
Bovet, Pierre, 20
Bovet, Théo, 232
Bradford, Alex., 34
Brunat, W., 222
Buchman, F., 185
"Bungled actions," 107, 214-15
Businessmen, 9, 228

Cain, 76
Calvin, Calvinism, 42, 73, 103, 114,
    191, 209, 241
Camus, A., 35, 92, 173-75, 177, 179
Carnegie, Mrs. Dale, 101
Celibacy, 131-43
Cézanne, 35
Change, of occupation, 220-21; of
    orientation, 49; possibility of, 197,
    198
Chevron-Fillette, Mlle., 135
Childhood, fantasies of, 15-16, dis-
    covery of the world in, 18-19,
    189, 215, 237, 241; games of, 19;
    difficulties in, 189, 215
Choice, of adventure, 171-81; of
    goal, 45-46, 52, 177, 189
II Chronicles 20:35-37, 229
Church, the, 40-41, 63, 79-80, 222,
    225
Claparède, 20

245

INDEX